Lecture Notes of the Institute for Computer Sciences, Social Informatics and Telecommunications Engineering 558

The LNICST series publishes ICST's conferences, symposia and workshops.

LNICST reports state-of-the-art results in areas related to the scope of the Institute. The type of material published includes

- Proceedings (published in time for the respective event)
- Other edited monographs (such as project reports or invited volumes)

LNICST topics span the following areas:

- General Computer Science
- E-Economy
- E-Medicine
- Knowledge Management
- Multimedia
- Operations, Management and Policy
- Social Informatics
- Systems

Nguyen Thi Dieu Linh · Manh Kha Hoang ·
Trong Hop Dang
Editors

Ad Hoc Networks

14th EAI International Conference, AdHocNets 2023
Hanoi, Vietnam, November 10–11, 2023
Proceedings

 Springer

Editors
Nguyen Thi Dieu Linh 🄳
Hanoi University of Industry
Hanoi, Vietnam

Manh Kha Hoang 🄳
Hanoi University of Industry
Hanoi, Vietnam

Trong Hop Dang 🄳
Hanoi University of Industry
Hanoi, Vietnam

ISSN 1867-8211   ISSN 1867-822X (electronic)
Lecture Notes of the Institute for Computer Sciences, Social Informatics
and Telecommunications Engineering
ISBN 978-3-031-55992-1   ISBN 978-3-031-55993-8 (eBook)
https://doi.org/10.1007/978-3-031-55993-8

This Springer imprint is published by the registered company Springer Nature Switzerland AG
The registered company address is: Gewerbestrasse 11, 6330 Cham, Switzerland

Paper in this product is recyclable.

Preface

In the relentless pursuit of seamless connectivity, the amalgamation of Ad Hoc Networks with the burgeoning Artificial Intelligence (AI) era and the impending advent of 6G technology herald a paradigm shift that extends far beyond our current understanding. This compendium stands as a testament to the evolving tapestry of wireless communication, exploring the future trends that will sculpt the landscape of Ad Hoc Networks within the context of the AI era and the 6G revolution.

Ad hoc networking encompasses a diverse array of network paradigms, including mobile ad hoc networks (MANETs), wireless sensor networks (WSNs), vehicular ad hoc networks (VANETs), airborne networks, underwater networks, underground networks, personal area networks, and home networks. These paradigms promise a broad spectrum of applications across civilian, commercial, and military domains. However, the distributed and multi-hop nature of ad hoc networking, coupled with the highly dynamic topology resulting from node mobility, introduces significant challenges. These challenges include scalability, quality of service, reliability, security, and energy-constrained operations for the network. In addressing these formidable challenges, AdHocNets has firmly established itself as a prominent forum for exchanging knowledge and ideas within ad hoc networks.

The 2023 conference, themed "EAI AdHocNets 2023 – 14th EAI International Conference on Ad Hoc Networks", brought together researchers, academics, and industry professionals to explore and discuss the latest advancements, challenges, and opportunities in ad hoc networking. The role of the AdHocNets conference, therefore, is becoming even more important and topical. This conference is expected to become an in-depth forum where international experts converge to make the necessary advances for these technologies to reach their full potential, ensuring a technological future that is smarter, more connected, and more intuitive.

We extend our heartfelt gratitude to all the authors for their dedication to advancing the frontiers of knowledge in ad hoc networking. Their contributions played a crucial role in shaping the intellectual discourse during the conference. We commend their commitment to excellence and applaud the depth of expertise demonstrated in their work.

The success of AdHocNets 2023 would not have been possible without the efforts of the organizing committee, the Hanoi University of Industry (HaUI), Hanoi, Vietnam, the reviewers, session chairs, and volunteers. Their tireless dedication to ensuring the quality and smooth execution of the conference is truly commendable, and we express our sincere appreciation for their hard work. We also acknowledge and appreciate the support of our sponsors, partners, and all those who contributed to making the conference a resounding success. Your support is instrumental in fostering the growth and impact of AdHocNets 2023.

Nguyen Thi Dieu Linh
Manh Kha Hoang
Trong Hop Dang

Organization

Steering Committee

Kieu Xuan Thuc   Hanoi University of Industry, Hanoi, Vietnam

General Chair

Kieu Xuan Thuc   Hanoi University of Industry, Hanoi, Vietnam

General Co-chairs

Nguyen Van Thien   Hanoi University of Industry, Vietnam
Pham Van Dong   Hanoi University of Industry, Vietnam

Technical Program Committee Chairs

Hoang Manh Kha   Hanoi University of Industry, Vietnam
Dang Trong Hop   Hanoi University of Industry, Vietnam
Nguyen Thi Dieu Linh   Hanoi University of Industry, Vietnam
Vo Nguyen Quoc Bao   Posts and Telecommunications Institute of Technology (PTIT), Vietnam

Sponsorship and Exhibit Chair

Pham Van Ha   Hanoi University of Industry, Vietnam

Local Chair

Trinh Thi Thu Huong   Hanoi University of Industry, Vietnam

Workshops Chair

Bo Quoc Bao   Hanoi University of Industry, Vietnam

Publicity and Social Media Chair

Nguyen Tien Kiem   Hanoi University of Industry, Vietnam

Publications Chair

Nguyen Thi Dieu Linh   Hanoi University of Industry, Vietnam

Web Chair

Bui Tien Son   Hanoi University of Industry, Vietnam

Posters and PhD Track Chair

Tong Van Luyen   Hanoi University of Industry, Vietnam

Panels Chair

Phan Thi Thu Hang   Hanoi University of Industry, Hanoi, Vietnam

Demos Chair

Nguyen Thi My Binh   Hanoi University of Industry, Hanoi, Vietnam

Tutorials Chairs

Le Thi Trang   Hanoi University of Industry, Hanoi, Vietnam
Dang Van Binh   Hanoi University of Industry, Hanoi, Vietnam

Technical Program Committee

Dang The Ngoc	Posts and Telecommunications Institute of Technology, Vietnam
Tran Duc Tan	Phenikaa University, Vietnam
Vijender Kr Solanki	CMR Institute of Technology, Hyderabad, India
Vo Nguyen Quoc Bao	Posts and Telecommunications Institute of Technology, Vietnam
Pham Minh Nghia	Le Quy Don University, Vietnam
Rafidah Binti Md Noor	University of Malaya, Kuala Lumpur, Malaysia
Nguyen Canh Minh	University of Transport and Communications (UTC), Vietnam
Le Nhat Thang	Posts and Telecommunications Institute of Technology, Vietnam
Chutiporn Anutariya	Asian Institute of Technology (AIT), Thailand
Tong Van Luyen	Hanoi University of Industry, Vietnam
Tran Xuan Nam	Le Quy Don University, Vietnam
Pham Thanh Hiep	Le Quy Don University, Vietnam
Hoang Van Phuc	Le Quy Don University, Vietnam
Nguyen Quoc Dinh	Le Quy Don University, Vietnam
Nguyen Huu Thanh	Hanoi University of Science and Technology, Vietnam
Nguyen Linh Trung	Hanoi University of Engineering and Technology, Vietnam
Tu Minh Phuong	Posts and Telecommunications Institute of Technology, Vietnam
Le Hoang Son	Vietnam National University, Hanoi, Vietnam
Nguyen Thanh Thuy	University of Engineering and Technology, Vietnam National University, Hanoi, Vietnam
Seok-Joo Koh	Kyungpook National University, South Korea

Contents

Network Solutions

Intelligent Integrated Systems

Combining MUSIC Algorithm and Adaptive Beamforming to Improve Online Call Quality

Huy Hoang Nguyen[1], Xuan Thanh Pham[1], Van Sang Doan[2],
and Manh Kha Hoang[1(✉)]

[1] Hanoi University of Industry, Hanoi, Vietnam
khahoang@haui.edu.vn
[2] Vietnam Naval Academy, Nha Trang, Khanh Hoa, Vietnam

Abstract. In this paper, proposing a uniform circular microphone array (UCA) model that combines the multiple signal classification algorithm (MUSIC) and the adaptive beamforming technique to improve the quality of online calls. MUSIC algorithm is used to accurately detect the direction of arrival (DOA) of signal sources, while adaptive beamforming using the least mean square (LMS) algorithm can eliminate unacceptable sources and noise. As a result, the UCA system can actively select the desired signal source. Based on simulation results for three narrowband sinusoidal signal sources, the proposed system shows that it meets the requirements of direction detection, changing appropriate adaptive weight values, and limiting the influence of unwanted sources and noise. From there, the desired signal is accurately filtered with consistent filtered power.

Keywords: DOA Estimation · MUSIC Algorithm · Adaptive Beamforming · LMS Algorithm · UCA

1 Introduction

With the global growth of the Internet and communication technologies, online calling has become one of the most popular methods of communication. New innovations and applications need to be launched regularly to improve call quality and user experience, improving sound quality is an important issue. Although simple frequency filters can filter the wideband signals, using an adaptive filter with the adaptive beamforming technique is always preferable when sources with the same or nearly the same frequency need to be filtered. To use this technique, we must first determine the angle at which the signals are received by using the DOA estimation method, which is high-resolution and plays an important role in array signal processing research. Certain common approaches, including the MUSIC algorithm, the minimum variance distortionless response (MVDR) algorithm, and the conventional beamforming (CB) algorithm, can be used to adequately detect the direction of the received signals [1–12, 23, 25]. Under identical input conditions, the simulation shows that the MUSIC algorithm always has a minimum main beamwidth at −3 dB and has a higher peak to average power ratio (PAPR) than the

N. Thi Dieu Linh et al. (Eds.): ADHOCNETS 2023, LNICST 558, pp. 3–14, 2024.
https://doi.org/10.1007/978-3-031-55993-8_1

CB and MVDR algorithms [7–9]. Adaptive beamforming is one of the most important applications of the LMS algorithm [14–18], which, together with the Wiener filter and the recursive least square (RLS) algorithm, is a well-known optimal filtering technique used in many different fields [14]. Unlike the Wiener filter, which only works in an environment with a priori statistical information, the LMS algorithm is considered stable and effective even in the presence of unknown environmental factors, since it does not require statistical features in the system's operating environment [14]. While the RLS algorithm is based on the least squares method, the LMS algorithm is based on the stochastic gradient descent (SGD) method [14]. Moreover, the LMS algorithm is less complex than the RLS algorithm because it does not require inversion of the correlation matrix of the received signals [14, 19]. The model combining DOA estimation method and the adaptive beamforming technique is a popular model for uniform linear array (ULA) antenna, the performance of this model is demonstrated in [20–25]. However, ULA antenna provides only 180° of coverage in the azimuth plane, while the UCA antenna geometry provides up to 360° of coverage, which is the distinct advantage of UCA over ULA [10–13]. In this paper, we propose to combine the MUSIC algorithm and the adaptive beamforming technique with the LMS algorithm to reduce the influence of unwanted sources and noise on the UCA microphone. From there, optimizing the microphone array's response to the target signal to enhance audio quality for online conversations.

The goal of this research is to provide the basis for developing a compact, high-performance beamforming microphone that can be integrated into smart mobile devices. The simulation results show that the proposed combination of the MUSIC algorithm and the adaptive beamforming technique on a 6-element UCA microphone for three sinusoidal signals in a narrowband frequency does not take much time to determine the direction of the signal sources and then eliminate noise and unwanted signals. The target signal is determined quite accurately and reliably after filtering. In the following sections, the mathematical model of the UCA antenna, the theories of the algorithm, the implementation approach, and the simulation results of the proposal are explained.

2 Signal Model and UCA Configuration

Figure 1 shows the UCA antenna model, which consists of N_e isotropic and in-phase elements uniformly distributed around the circle. The UCA geometry provides a coverage of 360° in the azimuth plane. The radius R of the antenna array is calculated according to Eq. (1), where λ_{max} is the largest wavelength of the received signal:

$$R = \frac{0.5 \times N_e \times \lambda_{\max}}{2\pi} \tag{1}$$

In fact, it is necessary to reduce the dimensions of the microphone to save money while maintaining reliable performance. The number of antenna elements N_e must be greater than the number of received signal sources D. The received signals are narrowband signals and come from the angles θ_1, θ_2, ..., θ_D, each signal source has a center frequency $f_c = c/\lambda$, where λ is the wavelength of the signal and $c = 340$ m/s is the

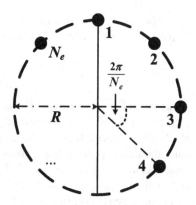

Fig. 1. Geometric structure of UCA antenna

propagation speed of sound in air. The angular coefficient of the signals k_D is calculated by $k_D = 2\pi/\lambda_D$.

If $s(t)$ is the amplitude of the received signals, $A(\theta)$ is the received signal's steering matrix at the array, and $n(t)$ is the white Gaussian noise in the received signals, the total received signals at the array is written as:

$$x(t) = A(\theta).s(t) + n(t) \tag{2}$$

where:

$$A(\theta) = [a(\theta_1), a(\theta_2), \ldots, a(\theta_D)]$$

$$= \begin{bmatrix} e^{jk_1 R \cos(\theta_1)} & e^{jk_2 R \cos(\theta_2)} & \cdots & e^{jk_D R \cos(\theta_D)} \\ e^{jk_1 R \cos(\theta_1 - 2\pi \frac{1}{N_e})} & e^{jk_2 R \cos(\theta_2 - 2\pi \frac{1}{N_e})} & \cdots & e^{jk_D R \cos(\theta_D - 2\pi \frac{1}{N_e})} \\ \vdots & \vdots & \ddots & \vdots \\ e^{jk_1 R \cos(\theta_1 - 2\pi \frac{N_e-1}{N_e})} & e^{jk_2 R \cos(\theta_2 - 2\pi \frac{N_e-1}{N_e})} & \cdots & e^{jk_D R \cos(\theta_D - 2\pi \frac{N_e-1}{N_e})} \end{bmatrix} \tag{3}$$

3   MUSIC Algorithm

The MUSIC algorithm is based on the decomposition of the covariance matrix of signals received from antenna array without scanning its beam along angles in space. Where X is the set of signals received by each element of the antenna array, the covariance matrix R_x is represented as:

$$R_x = E\left[X.X^H\right] \tag{4}$$

Since Eq. (2) and Eq. (4):

$$R_x = A.E\left[s.s^H\right].A^H + E\left[n.n^H\right] = A.R_s.A^H + R_n \tag{5}$$

where $R_s = E[s.s^H]$ and $R_n = E[n.n^H]$ are the corresponding covariance matrixes of signals s and noise n, and the matrix A^H is the conjugate transpose matrix of matrix A. The matrix R_n is described as:

$$R_n = \sigma^2.I \tag{6}$$

where I denotes the identity matrix and σ^2 represents the noise variance. Analyze the R_x matrix to obtain D large eigenvalues and $Ne - D$ extremely small eigenvalues for signals and noise, respectively. For each eigenvalue, the matrix space is divided into two subspaces: the signal space and the noise space, which respectively include the signal eigenvector $a(\theta_l)$ and the noise eigenvector E_n, with $l = 1, 2,..., D$. With $a(\theta)$ is the steering matrix of array, scan θ in the range from -180° to 180° according to Eq. (7) to obtain the spectrum P_{music} containing peaks corresponding to the angles of incidence $\theta_1, \theta_2, ..., \theta_D$ of the signal sources for the UCA:

$$P_{music}(\theta) = \frac{1}{a^H(\theta).E_n.E_n^H.a(\theta)} \tag{7}$$

4   Adaptive Beamforming

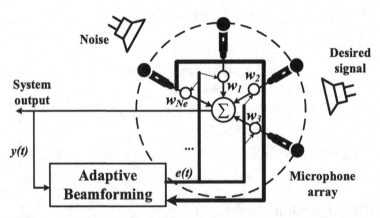

Fig. 2. Structure of Adaptive Beamforming system using LMS algorithm

Figure 2 shows the construction of an adaptive beamforming system on the UCA using the LMS algorithm. Re-express the total received signals by the antenna array using the following equation:

$$x(t) = A(\theta_0).s_0(t) + \sum_{i=1}^{D-1} A(\theta_i).s_i(t) + n(t) \tag{8}$$

where, $A(\theta_0)$, $s_0(t)$ are correspondingly the desired signal's steering vector and amplitude; $A(\theta_i)$, $s_i(t)$ are the ith noise's steering matrix and amplitude, respectively, with ($i = 1, 2, ..., D - 1$); and $n(t)$ is the white Gaussian noise included inside the received signals.

The output response of the UCA antenna is written as:

$$y(t) = w^H.x(t) \tag{9}$$

where w means the adaptive weight vector, and $x(t)$ denotes the total received signals by the UCA. If $d(t) = s_0(t)$ is the desired signal at time t, an error $e(t)$ occurs as:

$$e(t) = d(t) - y(t) = d(t) - w^H.x(t) \tag{10}$$

The mean square error (MSE) is minimized when the adaptive weight vector w has the optimal value, which is the error $e(t)$ used to calibrate w using the SGD method. The following equation is used to calculate the updated value of w at time $t + 1$:

$$w(t+1) = w(t) + \mu.x(t).e(t) \tag{11}$$

where μ is the learning rate, which governs the system's convergence speed and accuracy. Normally, it is a constant that is chosen within the given range of $0 < \mu < 2/\lambda_{max}$. However, choosing $\mu < \; < 0.01$ helps enhance the system's accuracy throughout processing. The following equation shows the response spectrum of the LMS algorithm on the UCA:

$$p_{LMS}(\theta) = \left| w^H.a(\theta) \right| \tag{12}$$

5   Evaluate the Effectiveness of the Proposal Through Simulation

5.1   Simulation Setups

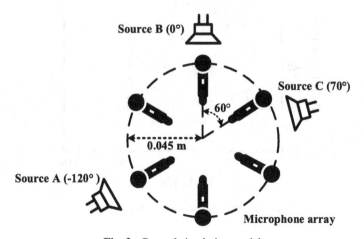

Fig. 3. General simulation model

Figure 3 shows the general simulation model of the system, using a UCA microphone with six elements equidistant from 60°. The signal sources for the simulation consist of three narrowband sinusoidal signals with the same amplitude of 1 mV, signal A at − 120°, signal B at 0°, and signal C at 70°. This configuration takes full advantage of the UCA in terms of coverage.

Choosing $SNR = 30$ dB; $R = 0.045$ m for the radius of the microphone array helps to satisfy the requirement of Eq. (1) and optimize the dimensions for the actual devices; $F_s = 48$ kHz – this is the standard sampling frequency, which is sufficient to regenerate the sound in near-original quality and widely used in research on digital signal processing and realism; and $\mu = 0.001$ to ensure stability and accuracy in processing. The center frequency of each signal is $f_c = c/\lambda$.

Matlab software is used for this processing and simulation. First, calculate the covariance matrix R_x using Eq. (4) to identify the direction of the signals using the MUSIC algorithm. Determine the eigenvalues and eigenvectors of the matrix R_x by applying $[u, v] = eig(R_x)$. Create a MUSIC directed spectrum plot using the eigenvalues and eigenvectors according to Eq. (7). After determining the direction of the signals, use the LMS algorithm to eliminate unacceptable sources and noise so that the desired signal is filtered. Adjust the weight vector w indefinitely until the optimal value of Eq. (11) is reached. According to Eq. (12), the spectrum plot represents the response of the LMS algorithm to the microphone array. Assess the effectiveness of the system in filtering audio signals by comparing the value of PAPR in the power spectrum of the filtered signal with SNR = [5:50] dB.

5.2 Simulation Results

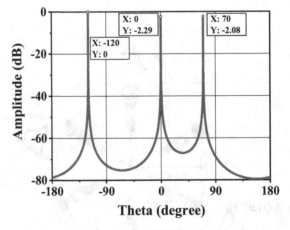

Fig. 4. Estimation the DOA of signal sources

Figure 4 shows the plot of the directional spectrum for the microphone array used by the MUSIC algorithm to detect the signal direction. The main beamwidth at -3 dB is less than 0.05°, so the directions of the three signal sources can be easily identified. As a result, with SNR = 30 dB, this estimated result shows the performance of the system. Use the MUSIC algorithm's above incidence angle estimation results to continue. Consider sources A and B as unwanted signals and source C as the desired signal. Then, sample the signals to change the weight vector w before examining the response spectrum of the LMS algorithm on the microphone array in Fig. 5.

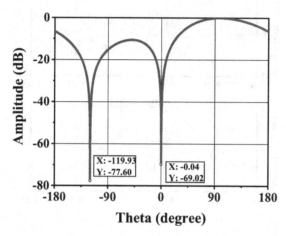

Fig. 5. LMS algorithm response spectrum

Figure 5 shows the response spectrum of the LMS algorithm for the microphone array, which contains two peaks in the negative direction with amplitudes of less than -65 dB, corresponding to two noises. There is also a large region behind 0°, showing that the two noises were reduced and only the desired signal was retained. Figure 6 shows the mixed signal $x(t)$, the desired signal $d(t)$, and the output signal $y(t)$ in the time range from 0.4 s to 0.45 s. The result is that after convergence, the system has virtually reduced the noise while retaining only the desired signal.

Figure 7 illustrates the value of adaptive weight w in the time domain for each element of the microphone array; it increases dramatically throughout the time the system is converging before optimization with the LMS algorithm. Figure 8 shows the comparable error $e(t)$ after the adaptive weights are updated. The system has a convergence time of less than 0.15 s, error values of less than 0.07 mV, and the value of w at each array element is saturated. After convergence, the weight w moves within a very small range and is considered stable for the duration of the operation.

10 H. H. Nguyen et al.

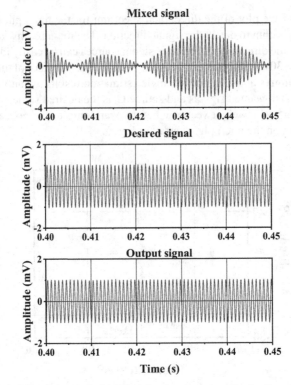

Fig. 6. Mixed signal, desired signal and output signal in the time domain

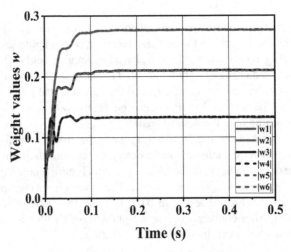

Fig. 7. Weight values in the time domain

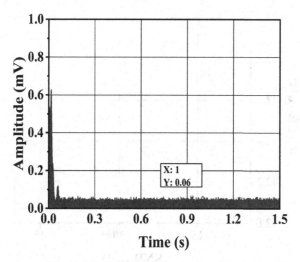

Fig. 8. Amplitude error in the time domain

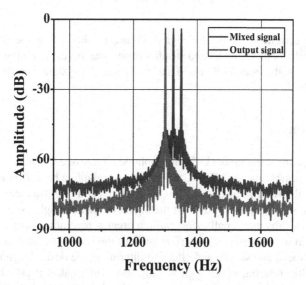

Fig. 9. Power of mixed signal and output signal in the frequency domain

The power spectrum in the frequency domain of the mixed signal $x(t)$ and the output signal $y(t)$ are shown in Fig. 9. It can be seen that the signals before filtering contains both desired signal and undesired signals and noise. The filtered signal has two principal components: The center frequency is about 1300 Hz with a maximum amplitude of about −7 dB, and the average noise power is less than -80 dB, which means that the noise is not overly significant in the important frequency range of the system and the performance of the system is excellent. Change the SNR from 5 dB to 50 dB to examine the performance of the system when filtering the audio signal through the PAPR ratio

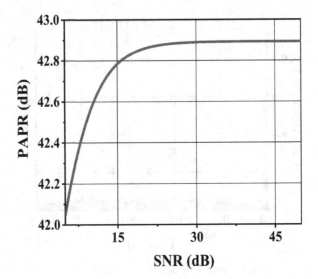

Fig. 10. PAPR versus SNR

on the power spectrum of the filtered signal. Figure 10 shows how the PAPR starts at SNR = 5 dB with about 42.04 dB and steadily progresses before reaching optimization at SNR = 30 dB with about 42.89 dB. This shows that the system can run consistently from SNR = 30 dB.

6 Conclusion

In this research, a small 6-element UCA microphone is proposed to filter audio signals for online calls by combining the MUSIC algorithm and adaptive beamforming technique using the LMS algorithm. The above simulation results and performance evaluation for narrowband sinusoidal signals show that the signal incidence angle estimation process has small beamwidths and small errors, which creates favorable input conditions for signal filtering in the next step. The performance of the LMS algorithm is shown by its fast adaptation speed and simple and effective filtering of the desired signal. The power of the signal after filtering is not significantly lost. This makes it possible to design a microphone model for practical applications. The limitation of this proposal is that the MUSIC algorithm works correctly only when the number of signal sources to be determined is less than the number of elements in the microphone array. In addition, it is necessary to continue to perform simulations and experiments under many different audio signal conditions, such as effects of multipath noise, color noise, etc., and to combine Deep Learning and AI to automate the identification of noise on the fly.

References

1. Schmidt, R.: Multiple emitter location and signal parameter estimation. IEEE Trans. Antennas Propag. **34**(3), 276–280 (1986). https://doi.org/10.1109/TAP.1986.1143830
2. Bo, W.: Realization and simulation of DOA estimation using MUSIC algorithm with uniform circular arrays. Ion: The 2006 4th Asia-Pacific Conference on Environmental Electromagnetics, pp. 908–912. Dalian, China, (2006). https://doi.org/10.1109/CEEM.2006.258099
3. Amine, I.M., Seddik, B.: 2-D DOA estimation using MUSIC algorithm with uniform circular array. In: 2016 4th IEEE International Colloquium on Information Science and Technology (CiSt), pp. 850-853. Tangier, Morocco (2016).https://doi.org/10.1109/CIST.2016.7805007
4. Tran, X.L., Vesely, J., Doan, V.S., Hubacek, P.: UHF/C-band testing of AOA estimation using MUSIC algorithm. In: 2016 New Trends in Signal Processing (NTSP), pp. 1–6 (2016). https://doi.org/10.1109/NTSP.2016.7747792
5. Sun, C., Ding, J.: Application of the DOA algorithms in the uniform circular array antennas. In: 2018 International Conference on Intelligent Transportation, Big Data & Smart City (ICITBS), Xiamen, China, pp. 633–636 (2018). https://doi.org/10.1109/ICITBS.2018.00165
6. Mao, Z., Li, B., Dong, L., Qiao, Y., Sun, H., Li, Y.: An effective algorithm for direction-of-arrival estimation of coherent signals with ULA. In: 2023 5th International Conference on Natural Language Processing (ICNLP), pp. 136–140. Guangzhou, China (2023). https://doi.org/10.1109/ICNLP58431.2023.00031
7. Hakam, A., Shubair, R.M., Salahat, E.: Enhanced DOA estimation algorithms using MVDR and MUSIC. In: 2013 International Conference on Current Trends in Information Technology (CTIT), pp. 172–176. Dubai, United Arab Emirates (2013).https://doi.org/10.1109/CTIT.2013.6749497
8. Tran, C.T., Doan, V.S., Nguyen, T.H., Tran, V.H.: Ứng dụng thuật toán MUSIC nâng cao độ chính xác đo góc trong sonar thụ động. J. Mil. Sci. Technol. **56**, 105–114 (2018)
9. Job, M., Suchit Yadav, R.: High resolution DOA estimation of narrowband signal for MUSIC, MVDR and Beamscan algorithm. In: 2023 11th International Symposium on Electronic Systems Devices and Computing (ESDC), pp. 1–5. Sri City, India (2023). https://doi.org/10.1109/ESDC56251.2023.10149863
10. Vesa, A., Simu, C.: Performances of uniform sensor array antenna in case of DoA estimation using the MUSIC algorithm. In: 2022 International Symposium on Electronics and Telecommunications (ISETC), pp. 1–4. Timisoara, Romania (2022). https://doi.org/10.1109/ISETC56213.2022.10010112
11. Kawitkar, R.: Performance of different types of array structures based on multiple signal classification (MUSIC) algorithm. In: 2009 Fifth International Conference on MEMS NANO, and Smart Systems, pp. 159–161. Dubai, United Arab Emirates (2009). https://doi.org/10.1109/ICMENS.2009.39
12. Kulaib, A.R., Shubair, R.M., Al-Qutayri, M.A., Ng, J.W.P.: Performance evaluation of linear and circular arrays in wireless sensor network localization. In: 2011 18th IEEE International Conference on Electronics, Circuits, and Systems, pp. 579–582. Beirut, Lebanon (2011). https://doi.org/10.1109/ICECS.2011.6122341
13. Huang, Z., Balanis, C.A.: BER performances of ULA and UCA in AWGN. In: 2007 IEEE Antennas and Propagation Society International Symposium, pp. 4196–4199. Honolulu, HI (2007). https://doi.org/10.1109/APS.2007.4396466
14. Haykin, S.O.: Adaptive Filter Theory (5th Edition) Pearson plc (2014)
15. Anjaneyulu, P., Rao, P.V.D.S., Sunehra, D.: Effect of various parameters on minimum mean square error and adaptive antenna beamforming using LMS algorithm. In: 2021 6th International Conference for Convergence in Technology (I2CT), pp. 1–5. Maharashtra, India (2021)

16. Abualhayja'a, M., Hussein, M.: Comparative study of adaptive beamforming algorithms for smart antenna applications. In: 2020 International Conference on Communications, Signal Processing, and their Applications (ICCSPA), pp. 1–5. Sharjah, United Arab Emirates (2021).https://doi.org/10.1109/ICCSPA49915.2021.9385725

17. Aswoyo, B., Milchan, M., Budikarso, A.: Adaptive beamforming based on linear array antenna for 2.3 GHz 5G communication using LMS algorithm. In: 2022 International Electronics Symposium (IES), pp. 436–441. Surabaya, Indonesia (2022). https://doi.org/10.1109/IES 55876.2022.9888682

18. Nand, K., Agarwal, S., Kaur, G.: Algorithms for adaptive beamforming in smart antenna in 5G. In: 2023 3rd International Conference on Intelligent Technologies (CONIT), pp. 1–6. Hubli, India (2023).https://doi.org/10.1109/CONIT59222.2023.10205664

19. Rudander, J., Husøy, T., Orten, P., Walree, P.V.: Comparing RLS and LMS adaptive equalizers for large hydrophone arrays in underwater acoustic communication channels. In: OCEANS 2019 - Marseille, pp. 1–5. Marseille, France (2019). https://doi.org/10.1109/OCEANSE.2019. 8867313

20. Sun, Y., Zhang, J., Yang, X.: Design of experimental adaptive beamforming system utilizing microphone array. In: IET International Radar Conference 2013, pp. 1–5. Xi'an (2013). https:// doi.org/10.1049/cp.2013.0242

21. Morency, M.W., Vorobyov, S.A.: Partially adaptive transmit beamforming for search free 2D DOA estimation in MIMO radar. In: 2015 23rd European Signal Processing Conference (EUSIPCO), pp. 2631–2635. Nice, France (2015).https://doi.org/10.1109/EUSIPCO.2015. 7362861

22. Sun, Y., Yang, X., Guo, L.., Long, T.: Experimental array signal processing demonstration system by utilizing microphone array. In: 2016 CIE International Conference on Radar (RADAR), pp. 1–5. Guangzhou, China (2016). https://doi.org/10.1109/RADAR.2016.8059533

23. Thomas, J.A., Mini, P.R., Kumar, M.N.A.: DOA estimation and adaptive beamforming using MATLAB and GUI. In: 2017 International Conference on Energy, Communication, Data Analytics and Soft Computing (ICECDS), pp. 1890–1896. Chennai, India (2017). https://doi. org/10.1109/ICECDS.2017.8389778

24. Vu, H.S., Truong, K.T., Bang, L.T., Vu, V.Y., Le, M.T.: An investigation of adaptive digital beamforming antenna for gNodeB 5G. In: 2019 International Conference on Advanced Technologies for Communications (ATC), pp. 221–224. Hanoi, Vietnam (2019). https://doi.org/ 10.1109/ATC.2019.8924509

25. Suleesathira, R.: Direction of arrival identification using MUSIC method and NLMS beamforming. In: 2020 15th International Joint Symposium on Artificial Intelligence and Natural Language Processing (iSAI-NLP), pp. 1–6. Bangkok, Thailand (2020). https://doi.org/10. 1109/iSAI-NLP51646.2020.9376838

Non-inverting Buck-Boost DC-DC Converter with Three-Mode Selection Circuit

Van Tuan Nguyen, Quoc Bao Bo, and Xuan Thanh Pham[(✉)]

Hanoi University of Industry, Hanoi, Vietnam
thanhpx@haui.edu.vn

Abstract. For battery-powered applications where high current conversion efficiency and long battery life are required, non-inverting Buck-Boost converters are considered the best option. However, during mode switching, ripples in the output current and voltage can significantly affect the efficiency of the chip. The novel Non-inverting Buck-Boost DC-DC converter proposed in this study with a three-mode selection circuit selects the different operating modes (three modes) by comparing V_{IN} and V_{OUT}. By this way, the DC-DC converter can reduce the output ripple and instability during operation. The proposed chip was developed and implemented on the CMOS 0.18 μm process. In addition, a high peak efficiency of 97% can be achieved under the conditions of a wide input range of 2.5 V - 5 V.

Keywords: Three-Mode Selection Circuit · DC-DC Converter · Integrated Power Management

1 Introduction

With the rapid proliferation of battery-powered devices, effective power management solutions have become an important part of the design to ensure long battery life [1, 2]. Since they offer a wide operating range of input and output voltages, non-inverting Buck-Boost converters are a good choice to better utilise battery capacity [2–8]. There are three options: Boost, Buck and Buck-Boost. The level of the input and output voltages determines these modes. If V_{IN} is lower than V_{OUT}, the converter operates in Boost mode. The converter switches to Buck mode when the V_{IN} exceeds V_{OUT}. The converter enters Buck-Boost mode when V_{IN} approaches or equals V_{OUT}. On the other hand, these converters need to sustain a consistently high-power conversion efficiency across all three modes. However, certain converter architectures, such as those explained in [9–11], as a result of the integration of several converter pairs, phase difference management, and many internal oscillators, the demand on the controller grows. As a result, these complexities lead to inconsistent operation and interruptions in the operation of the converter. Alternative techniques, such as the reverse Buck-Boost approach presented in [12, 13], have already been presented. However, the high switching current resulting from continuous operation in Buck-Boost mode puts significant stress on the device. In

© ICST Institute for Computer Sciences, Social Informatics and Telecommunications Engineering 2024
Published by Springer Nature Switzerland AG 2024. All Rights Reserved
N. Thi Dieu Linh et al. (Eds.): ADHOCNETS 2023, LNICST 558, pp. 15–24, 2024.
https://doi.org/10.1007/978-3-031-55993-8_2

contrast, the Buck-Boost converter in [14] does not employ the Buck-Boost mode. How-ever, switching between Buck and Boost modes causes substantial ripple in the output voltage and hence reduced efficiency. Another method detailed in [15] employs digital control of the converter. This converter switches between Boost and Buck modes. The proposed solution to duty cycle over-lap control decreases voltage ripple and unstable output voltage behavior. However, improving the efficiency of this architecture remains an important goal. This paper presents a DC-DC Buck-Boost converter that achieves good efficiency in all three modes with varying input voltage levels. The proposed con-verter aims to improve conversion efficiency by switching quickly and with minimal delay between Buck, Buck-Boost and Boost modes with minimal delay to keep the circuit operating continuously [16]. This allows smooth transitions between the three modes and minimizes switching and conduction losses. Therefore, the proposed circuit for selecting the three modes helps to quickly detect changes in input voltage and output voltage with low latency and determine the appropriate mode.

2   Circuit Design

2.1   Proposed System

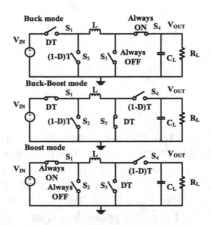

Fig. 1. The Buck-Boost converter's operational principles.

A non-inverting Buck-Boost converter is a switching power supply that can raise (Boost) or decrease (Buck) an input voltage to produce a regulated output voltage, even if the input voltage fluctuates drastically. Figure 1 shows the structure of a non-inverting Buck-Boost converter. The converter runs in Boost mode when the input voltage V_{IN} is lower than the output voltage V_{OUT}. Switch S_1 is always on, while switch S_2 is always off. The control of the power switches S_3 and S_4 leads to this operating mode. On the other hand, the converter operates in Buck mode. When V_{IN} is greater than V_{OUT}, switch S_4 is always ON and switch S_3 is always OFF. The output voltage is kept stable by switching switches S_1 and S_2. The last mode is when V_{IN} is equal or close to V_{OUT} and the converter is set to Buck-Boost mode. In this mode, all switches (S_1-S_3) and (S_2-S_4) are controlled in two groups to regulate the induction cycle (charging and discharging). According to the previous description, the switching behaviour of the power switches and the control circuit allows the converter to adapt to changing input conditions and provide a regulated output.

Figure 2 depicts a visual depiction of the proposed system's block diagram. A power stage and a control circuit are the main components of the converter. The power stage is comprised of four on-chip power switches ($S_{1,2,3,4}$); the transistors used for the switches are larger in size compared to the control circuit. This deliberate choice results in a reduction of the detector current and resistance (R_{ON}) of the transistors to improve efficiency. The control circuit includes a ramp generator, a pulse generator, a soft-start circuit, and a three-mode selection circuit. The operating modes are automatically and quickly determined by using the proposed three-mode selection circuit, which relies on comparing V_{IN} to V_{OUT} and simultaneously outputs the control signals HS_I, LS_I, HS_O, and LS_O, depending on the operating mode. This allows smooth transitions between the three modes and reduces switching and conduction losses. In cases where V_{OUT} is lower than V_{IN}, the converter is set to Boost mode. On the contrary, when V_{OUT} exceeds V_{IN}, the converter is set to Buck mode. When V_{IN} is equal to or close to V_{OUT}, the converter will use Buck-Boost mode.

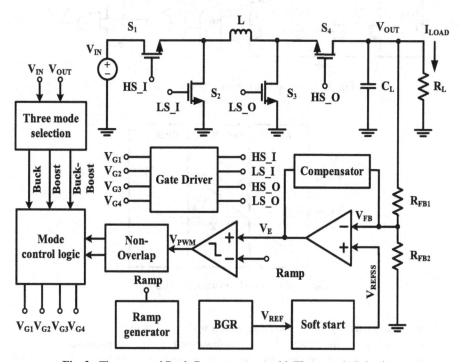

Fig. 2. The proposed Buck-Boost converter with Three-mode Selection.

2.2 Three-Mode Selection Circuit

In practice, the input voltage waveform has a small slope and may fluctuate. The bandgap reference's output voltage is likewise prone to variations, resulting in an unstable condition during transitions between operating modes. This instability during mode switching could result in increased leakage current through the switching transistor, which could lead to lower efficiency or malfunctions that adversely affect output voltage regulation. To eliminate the instability during mode switching and improve the overall performance of the converter, reference [17] presents an approach that uses a fixed output architecture. However, this architecture is not suitable for non-fixed output architectures, which limits the flexibility of the converter. Another technique presented in reference [15] uses a digital controller to monitor the operation of the converter. However, this approach can't work when faced with the challenge of handling high load currents.

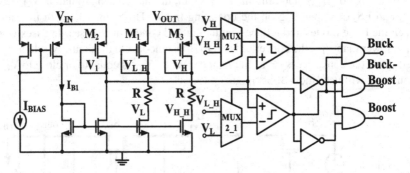

Fig. 3. The proposed three-mode selection circuit.

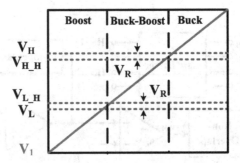

Fig. 4. Three-mode operation diagram.

To achieve the dual goal of operating with a wide load range while achieving high performance, the three-mode selection circuit described in Fig. 3 is proposed as a solution. The core of this three-mode selection circuit consists of two separate blocks. The first block generates a comparison signal from the magnitude values of V_H, V_L and V_1; V_L is designed to be lower than V_H. On the other hand, Conversely, the second block furnishes the signals required to enable the selection among three operational modes:

Buck-Boost, Buck and Boost. As can be seen in Fig. 4, V_{OUT} is converted to V_H, V_{H_H}, V_L and V_{L_H}; similarly, V_{IN} is converted to V_1. For the converter to go from Buck-Boost to Buck mode, the input voltage V_1 must exceed V_H. To return from Buck mode to Buck-Boost mode, V_1 must fall below V_{H_H}. When the converter transitions between Boost and Buck-Boost modes, the same thing happens. The integration of this circuit greatly improves the adaptability and flexibility of the adapter and provides an optimal solution for handling changing load conditions while maintaining optimum performance.

3 Results and Discussions

The proposed chip was developed and implemented on the CMOS 0.18 μm process. The converter utilises off-chip components with a 1μH inductor and a 44 μF capacitor. The function of the converter was verified with an adjustable V_{IN} of 2.5 V to 5 V, V_{OUT} of 3.3 V and a 1 MHz switching frequency. The layout of the proposed chip shows in Fig. 5. The chip has a total area of 455 μm × 380 μm.

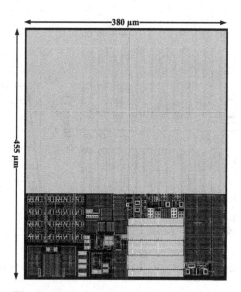

Fig. 5. The layout of the proposed converter.

The simulation results are shown for three modes: Boost, Buck-Boost and Buck. Figure 6 depicts the control voltage of the various transistors in the Buck mode. As mentioned in the previous section, with Buck mode, transistors S_4, S3 is always ON, OFF respectively, and transistors S_1 and S_2 switch over. The output of the converter is 3.3 V, even if V_{IN} is 5 V. Figure 7 depicts the control voltage of the various transistors in the Buck-Boost mode and the respective V_{IN} and V_{OUT}. V_{IN} is close to or equal to V_{OUT}, the Buck-Boost mode is enabled, all transistors switch to control V_{OUT} to 3.3 V. Figure 8 depicts the control voltage of the various transistors in the Boost mode. When the Boost mode is selected,

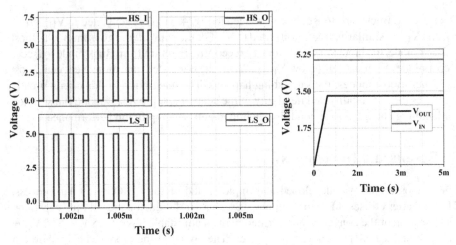

Fig. 6. The simulation results with $V_{IN} = 5$ V, the converter works in Buck mode and $V_{OUT} = 3.3$ V.

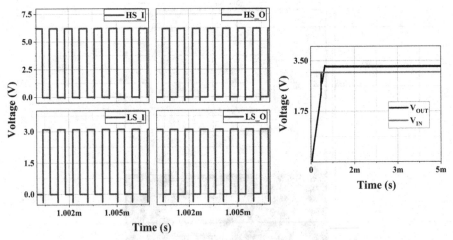

Fig. 7. The simulation results with $V_{IN} = 3.1$ V, the converter works in Buck-Boost mode and $V_{OUT} = 3.3$ V.

transistor S_1 is always ON and S_2 is always OFF and transistors S_3 and S_4 switch over. The input of the converter increases from 2.5 V to the desired output of 3.3 V. The converter's simulation results reveal that V_{IN} is 2.5 V, the converter is in Boost mode, with a V_{OUT} of 3.3 V and a duty cycle of 24.2%. Figure 9 depicts how the converter functions in three modes throughout the whole input voltage range of 2.5 V to 5 V: Boost, Buck-Boost and Buck, with voltage ripple values of 4 mV, 29 mV and 21 mV respectively. The output voltage has an overshoot of 75 mV during the mode change. Figure 10 shows the proposed converter's power conversion efficiency in three different operating modes. The results show that the power level remains consistently high in

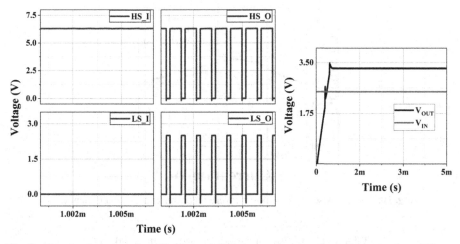

Fig. 8. The simulation results with V_{IN} = 2.5 V, the converter works in Boost mode and V_{OUT} = 3.3 V.

the different modes, even at different load currents from 100 mA to 800 mA. Table 1 gives a detailed overview of the proposed converter's performance compared to previous studies.

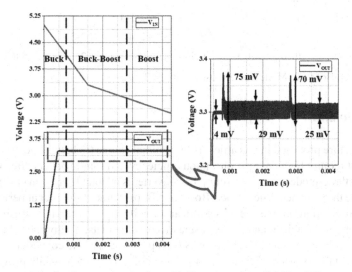

Fig. 9. Converter operation with V_{IN} range from 2.5 V to 5 V.

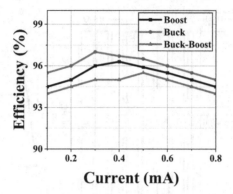

Fig. 10. The proposed Buck-Boost converter's power conversion efficiency.

Table 1. Comparison of performances with other works.

	[13]	[16]	[15]	[14]	[18]	This work
Tech. (μm)	0.18	0.18	-	0.25	0.18	0.18
Modes	A	B	A	A	B	B
Efficiency (%)	89.3	94.8	85.5	91	91	97
Freq (MHz)	0.5	3.2	1	5	2.5	1
Input Range (V)	1.8	3–8	2.5–4.5	2.5–4.5	2.7–5.5	2.5–5
Output (V)	−4	5	3.3	2–4	2–5	3.3
Max. I_{LOAD} (A)	0.005	0.5	0.5	0.4	2	0.8

A: Mode Buck-Boost; B: Mode Buck/Boost and Buck-Boost.

4 Conclusion

The architecture proposed in this article is the optimal choice for battery-powered applications that require high energy conversion efficiency and longer battery life. With the design of a three-mode selection circuit, the converter is adaptable and can easily switch between the three modes: Buck, Buck-Boost and Boost without significant performance degradation. In addition, the use of a soft-start circuit helps to limit the inrush current, which increases reliability and protects sensitive components. The proposed chip was developed and implemented on the CMOS 0.18 μm process. The converter regulation maintains a stable V_{OUT} of 3.3 V over V_{IN} range of 2.5 V to 5 V, while providing an output current range of 100 mA to 800 mA. The maximum efficiency is 97%. The total area of the chip is 455 μm $\times$ 380 μm.

References

1. Oh, J.-W., Jo, J.-W., Kim, Y.-H., Lee, S.-J., Pu, Y.-G.: A 316.5nA quiescent current of DC–DC converter with 92.8% peak efficiency for a IoT application. In: 2023 Fourteenth International Conference on Ubiquitous and Future Networks (ICUFN), pp. 736–739. Paris, France (2023). https://doi.org/10.1109/ICUFN57995.2023.10199436
2. Chen, Y.-Y., Chang, Y.-C., Wei, C.-L.: Mixed-ripple adaptive on-time controlled non-inverting buck-boost DC-DC converter with adaptive-window-based mode selector. IEEE Trans. Circuits Syst. II Express Briefs 69(4), 2196–2200 (2022). https://doi.org/10.1109/TCSII.2021.3139100
3. Bai, Y., Zhu, Z., Yang, Z., Zha, S., Hu, S.: Analysis and comparison of inductor current characteristics for non-inverting buck-boost converter with four-mode modulation. In: 2022 IEEE 5th International Electrical and Energy Conference (CIEEC), pp. 2534–2540. Nangjing, China (2022). https://doi.org/10.1109/CIEEC54735.2022.9846753
4. Ikeda, T., Castellazzi, A., Hikihara, T.: Modulation options for a high-frequency high-efficiency GaN-based non-inverting buck-boost DC-DC converter. In: 2021 IEEE 12th Energy Conversion Congress & Exposition - Asia (ECCE-Asia), pp. 2193–2198. Singapore, Singapore (2021).https://doi.org/10.1109/ECCE-Asia49820.2021.9479297
5. Alajmi, B.N., Abdelsalam, I., Marei, M.I., Ahmed, N.A.: Two stage single-phase EV on-board charger based on interleaved cascaded non-inverting buck-boost converter. In: 2023 IEEE Conference on Power Electronics and Renewable Energy (CPERE), pp. 1–6. Luxor, Egypt (2023). https://doi.org/10.1109/CPERE56564.2023.10119584
6. Wei, A., Lehman, B., Bowhers, W., Amirabadi, M.: A soft-switching non-inverting buck-boost converter. In: 2021 IEEE Applied Power Electronics Conference and Exposition (APEC), pp. 1920–1926. Phoenix, AZ, USA (2021).https://doi.org/10.1109/APEC42165.2021.9487051
7. Xu, C., Liu, L.: A four modes and smooth transition non-inverting buck-boost converter. In: 2021 IEEE 14th International Conference on ASIC (ASICON), pp. 1–4. Kunming, China (2021). https://doi.org/10.1109/ASICON52560.2021.9620338
8. Alajmi, B.N., Marei, M.I., Abdelsalam, I., Ahmed, N.A.: Multiphase interleaved converter based on cascaded non-inverting buck-boost converter. IEEE Access 10, 42497–42506 (2022). https://doi.org/10.1109/ACCESS.2022.3168389
9. Wu, H., Mu, T., Ge, H., Xing, Y.: Full-range soft-switching-isolated buck-boost con-verters with integrated interleaved boost converter and phase-shifted control. IEEE Trans. Power Electron. 31(2), 987–999 (2016). https://doi.org/10.1109/TPEL.2015.2425956
10. Wu, D., Calderon-Lopez, G., Forsyth, A.J.: Discontinuous conduction/current mode analysis of dual interleaved buck and boost converters with interphase transformer. IET Power Electron. 9(1), 31–41 (2016). https://doi.org/10.1049/iet-pel.2014.0924
11. Li, W., Xiao, J., Zhao, Y., He, X.: PWM plus phase angle shift (PPAS) control scheme for combined multiport DC/DC converters. IEEE Trans. Power Electron. 27(3), 1479–1489 (2012). https://doi.org/10.1109/TPEL.2011.2163826
12. Hong, S.-W., Park, S.-H., Kong, T.-H., Cho, G.-H.: Inverting buck-boost DC-DC con-verter for mobile AMOLED display using real-time self-tuned minimum power-loss tracking (MPLT) scheme with lossless soft-switching for discontinuous conduction mode. IEEE J. Solid-State Circ. 50(10), 2380–2393 (2015). https://doi.org/10.1109/JSSC.2015.2450713
13. Shin, S.-H., Hong, S., Kwon, O.-K.: High-efficient inverting buck-boost converter with fully digital-controlled switch width modulation for microdisplays. Elec-tronics Letters 54, 309–311 (2018)
14. Wu, K.-C., Wu, H.-H., Wei, C.-L.: Analysis and design of mixed-mode operation for non-inverting buck-boost DC–DC converters. IEEE Trans. Circ. Syst. II: Express Briefs 62(12), 1194–1198 (2015). https://doi.org/10.1109/TCSII.2015.2469032

15. Tsai, Y.-Y., Tsai, Y.-S., Tsai, C.-W., Tsai, C.-H.: Digital noninverting-buck–boost con-verter with enhanced duty-cycle-overlap control. IEEE Trans. Circ. Syst. II Express Briefs **64**(1), 41–45 (2017). https://doi.org/10.1109/TCSII.2016.2546881
16. Thi Kim Nga, T., et al.: A wide input range buck-boost DC–DC converter using hysteresis triple-mode control technique with peak efficiency of 94.8% for RF energy harvesting applications. Energies, **11**(7), 1618 (2018)
17. Chen, J.-J., Shen, P.-N., Hwang, Y.-S.: A high-efficiency positive buck-boost converter with mode-select circuit and feed-forward techniques. IEEE Trans. Power Electron. **28**(9), 4240–4247 (2013). https://doi.org/10.1109/TPEL.2012.2223718
18. Malcovati, P., Belloni, M., Gozzini, F., Bazzani, C., Baschirotto, A.: A 0.18-μm CMOS, 91%-efficiency, 2-a scalable buck-boost DC–DC converter for LED drivers. IEEE Trans. Power Electron. **29**(10), 5392–5398 (2014). https://doi.org/10.1109/TPEL.2013.2294189

Two Embedding Algorithms in Schur-Based Image Watermarking Scheme

Anh Le-Thi[1(✉)], Bich Pham-Ngoc[2], and Dung Tran-Tien[1]

[1] Hanoi University of Industry, Hanoi, Vietnam
{leanh,trantd}@haui.edu.vn
[2] FPT College, Hanoi, Vietnam
bichpn@fpt.edu.vn

Abstract. Digital watermarking is a potential technique for copyright protection purposes that has been widely developed in recent years. In image watermarking schemes, the embedding algorithm plays an essential role in the process of embedding and extracting information. This paper presents a Schur-based image watermarking scheme with two different embedding algorithms. The first algorithm embeds the watermark into two components of the orthogonal matrix, while the second algorithm considers the embedding element. To increase the security of the proposed scheme, the watermark image (WMI) is encoded by the Arnold transform before it is embedded into the host image. The achieved outcomes reveal that both algorithms have good performance in terms of invisibility and robustness. Besides that, the two embedding algorithms are analyzed and compared by data and illustrative examples to see the difference between them as well as their advantages and disadvantages in the watermarking scheme based on Schur decomposition (SDC).

Keywords: Image watermarking · Schur decomposition · Transform domain · Embedding algorithm · Copyright protection

1 Introduction

With the rapid development of technology, the requirement of protection for copyright has also become an urgent topic that needs to be addressed. Among existing solutions, digital watermarking is considered an effective tool for image copyright protection. It is essentially a process of creating a binding through embedding and extraction formulas amid the origin picture and the watermark. One requirement is that the watermark must be resistant to common image attacks. Robust image watermarking models are frequently implemented by applying matrix transformations. Besides expansions such as DWT, SVD, QR,

Supported by Hanoi University of Industry.

N. Thi Dieu Linh et al. (Eds.): ADHOCNETS 2023, LNICST 558, pp. 25–40, 2024.
https://doi.org/10.1007/978-3-031-55993-8_3

LU, or Hessenberg, Schur analysis is well suited for use in this area. According to [1], the Schur decomposition has the computation complication as $O(8n^3/3)$ and SVD is $O(11n^3)$. It is obvious that the number of computations required for Schur decomposition is less than one-third of SVD required. In addition, in the paper [2], Mohan compared the performance of Schur and SVD and concluded that Schur decomposition has a lower execution time than SVD decomposition. This relation shows that the Schur decomposition will be more widely applied in digital watermarking. Meanwhile, the Schur vector has good scaling invariance, which can enhance the robustness of the watermarking technique. Therefore, there have been many studies on the application of Schur in the watermarking field in recent years. Image watermarking techniques based on the Schur transform usually focus on two main directions: single domain and hybrid domain. On the single domain, the researchers only embed the watermark through the Schur decomposition [3–12]. On the contrary, it is a combination of Schur factorization with other transformations (such as $DWT, DCT, SVD, QHT, NSCT$) in hybrid domain-based watermarking schemes [13–22].

For single domain-based watermarking schemes, the first example is a proposal by Su in 2017 [6]. This study embeds the watermark on two components $U(2, c)$ and $U(3, c)$ of the matrix U with $c = max(Dij)$ (D is the upper triangular matrix. To improve resistance to cropping attacks, embedded blocks are chosen based on a pseudo-random sequence. Thus, the elements of the WMI as R, G, and B were swapped by the AT with K_a. Authors in [10] proposal give positive watermark image (WMI) quality and durability results and ensure system security. Moreover, in [11], before using the Schur transformation to each block, Li divides the black and white WMIs into 8 × 8 blocks. Next, the watermark is shuffled by Arnold and Logistic Map before embedding in the element with the most significant energy $D(1, 1)$ of the upper triangular matrix. $PSNR$ values without attack are in the range of 40 dB–47 dB. Their results were found to be better than other comparable studies; however, low-pass filtering issues and resizing attacks are required to solve in the following research.

For hybrid domain-based watermarking schemes, Karajeh and colleagues published a study based on the DWT-Schur association scheme [14] in 2019. In this proposal, the two-level Haar filter transforms the DWT, and then the Schur is employed to $HL2$. The watermark is then embedded in the diagonal elements of the matrix D. In 2021, Prabha proposed a scheme using LWT (Lift Wavelet Transform) and Schur transformations on the B color channel of the original image [15]. LWT is a fast and efficient transformation. The original image is first transformed through the Haar transform, and then Schur is expanded on the sub-band LL. After being swapped by Arnold, the WMI will be embedded in the U matrix. The results show that the $PSNR$ value reaches 41.1241 dB and the NC value is close to 1.

From the above discussions, it is seen that the choice of location to embed information is very important in the process of building a watermarking scheme because it directly affects the stability of the watermark and the quality of the watermarked image. In other words, the embedding formula and the embedding element largely determine the different performance of watermarking schemes if they use the same matrix transformation. Therefore, in this paper, we propose a blind image watermarking scheme which includes two embedding algorithms. Then, we focus on analyzing their role in Schur-based watermarking schemes. By experimental results and illustrative examples, two embedding algorithms are evaluated and compared in terms of robustness and invisibility. Finally, the advantages and limitations of each algorithm will be presented.

The remainder of the manuscript is organized into four sections: Sect. 2 presents primary Schur decomposition (SDC) and Arnold transform (AT); Sect. 3 shows the image watermarking scheme; The experiments and analysis will be presented in Sect. 4; the final Sect. 5 is conclusion.

2 Preliminary

2.1 Schur Decomposition (SDC)

In SDC, a matrix A of size $n \times n$ is analyzed as the product of three matrices U, D, and U^T as follows.

$$A = UDU^T, \tag{1}$$

here U, D is the orthogonal and upper triangular matrices respectively, and U^T is the transpose matrix of U.

For instance, suppose one matrix A of size 4×4 as follows.

$$A = \begin{bmatrix} 98 & 108 & 108 & 114 \\ 202 & 204 & 203 & 199 \\ 197 & 200 & 199 & 198 \\ 204 & 207 & 207 & 201 \end{bmatrix}$$

By applying Eq. 1, we can reach D and U as below:

$$D = \begin{bmatrix} 713.7100 & 156.8300 & 18.9500 & 3.4027 \\ 0 & -9.8128 & -3.2578 & -5.7126 \\ 0 & 0 & 0.2065 & 0.2476 \\ 0 & 0 & 0 & -2.0990 \end{bmatrix}$$

and

$$U = \begin{bmatrix} -0.2957 & -0.9470 & -0.1168 & 0.0471 \\ -0.5519 & 0.2560 & -0.7644 & -0.2132 \\ -0.5429 & 0.0678 & 0.5824 & -0.6012 \\ -0.5597 & 0.1820 & 0.2506 & 0.7687 \end{bmatrix}$$

As shown in the above example, the biggest values belong to the component $D(1, 1)$ of the matrix D, so it is considered to embed the information. Besides, in the matrix U, two components, $U(2, 1)$ and $U(3, 1)$, have the same sign and are the closest elements. Thus, these two elements are also a good choice.

2.2 Arnold Transform (AT)

AT is applied to swap pixels of the original WMI before embedding with the
purpose of improving the secrecy watermarking approach. The change of location
of a pixel from (x, y) to another location (s, t) [23] is performed by this method,
in Eq. (2).

$$\begin{bmatrix} s \\ t \end{bmatrix} = \begin{bmatrix} 1 & 1 \\ 1 & 2 \end{bmatrix} \begin{bmatrix} x \\ y \end{bmatrix} (mod\ N) \tag{2}$$

here, N is a factor of size $N \times N$ of the watermark picture.

Then, using an inversion of the AT in Eq. (3) to recover the original image.

$$\begin{bmatrix} x \\ y \end{bmatrix} = \begin{bmatrix} 2 & -1 \\ -1 & 1 \end{bmatrix} \begin{bmatrix} s \\ t \end{bmatrix} (mod\ N) \tag{3}$$

In the process of permuting the pixels, the parameter determines the AT's security level. This parameter will not be the same for different image sizes and
depends on the number of repetitions. In this paper, the number of repetitions
is 24 because the WMI size is 32×32. Therefore, the parameter is a number
between 1 and 24.

3 The Proposed Watermarking Scheme

A Schur-based watermarking (SBW) scheme with two different embedding algorithms will be introduced in this part. The first algorithm performs embedding
the watermark into two components $U(2, 1)$ and $U(3, 1)$ of the orthogonal matrix
U. The first algorithm uses these two components because they are the closest
[8]. The second algorithm selects the first component $D(1, 1)$ of D to imbed
information because of its energy concentration [20]. To be fair, both algorithms
are implemented on the same color channel and the same size of the block. The
scheme consists of two main processes, namely the embedding phase and the
extracting phase, as follows.

3.1 Embedding Phase

The embedding procedure of the image watermarking is presented as follows.

- First step:
  - AT technique is applied to permute the WMI.
  - Then, converting the permuted image into a one-dimensional binary array
    w_i.
- Second step
  - R, G and B is created by dividing the host image.
  - Next, B is split into 4×4 non-overlapping blocks.
- Third step:
  - Each block is assigned to a matrix A.

- SDC is executed on the matrix A of each block by Eq. 1 to acquire the matrices U and D.
- Fourth step:
  - Embedding a watermark bit into the matrices U or D based on two algorithms as follows.
    * (a) Algorithm 1:
      If $(w_i = 0)$ and $(|U(2,1)| > |U(3,1)|)$, then

$$\begin{cases} U'(2,1) = sign(U(2,1) * (U_{avg} - T/2) \\ \\ U'(3,1) = sign(U(3,1) * (U_{avg} + T/2) \end{cases} \tag{4}$$

      If $(w_i = 1)$ and $(|U(2,1)| \leq |U(3,1)|)$, then

$$\begin{cases} U'(2,1) = sign(U(2,1) * (U_{avg} + T/2) \\ \\ U'(3,1) = sign(U(3,1) * (U_{avg} - T/2) \end{cases} \tag{5}$$

      where sign(x) represents the sign of x, $U_{avg} = (|U(2,1)| + |U(3,1)|)/2$, $|x|$ means the absolute value of x, and T is one threshold value.
    * (b) Algorithm 2:
      If $(w_i = 0)$, then

$$D'(1,1) = \begin{cases} D(1,1) - \lambda + \frac{1}{4}\sigma, \lambda \in [0, \frac{3}{4}\sigma) \\ \\ D(1,1) - \lambda + \frac{5}{4}\sigma, \lambda \in [\frac{3}{4}\sigma, \sigma) \end{cases} \tag{6}$$

      If $(w_i = 1)$, then

$$D'(1,1) = \begin{cases} D(1,1) - \lambda - \frac{1}{4}\sigma, \lambda \in [0, \frac{1}{4}\sigma) \\ \\ D(1,1) - \lambda + \frac{3}{4}\sigma, \lambda \in [\frac{1}{4}\sigma, \frac{3}{4}\sigma) \end{cases} \tag{7}$$

      where σ indicates quantification step and $\lambda = mod(D(1,1), \sigma)$
- Fifth step:
  - Inverse SDC and repeating from the thrid step to the fifth step until all blocks are embedded.
- Sixth step:
  - Rebuild watermarked elements to get the watermarked image.

3.2 Extracting Phase

Figure 1 shows the extraction procedure. In our image watermarking scheme, both the original image and the watermark do not need to be considered in the watermark extraction phase, so this is a blind watermarking scheme. The procedure of the extracting stage is presented as follows.

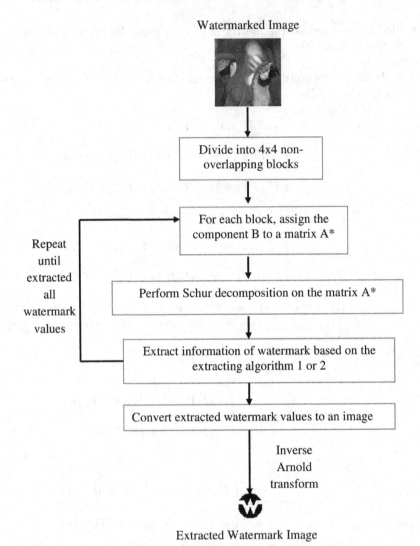

Fig. 1. Extraction process.

- First step:
  - R, G, and B is created by dividing the watermarked image.
  - Next, B is split into 4×4 non-overlapping blocks.
- Second step:
  - Each block is assigned to a matrix A^*.
  - SDC is applied on the matrix A^* of each block by Eq. (1) to acquire U^* and D^*
- Third step:
  - Extracting the information bit of watermark has been established on Algorithm 1 and Algorithm 2:

* (a) Algorithm 1:

$$w_i^* = \begin{cases} \text{"0"} & , \quad U^*(2,1) \leq U^*(3,1) \\ \\ \text{"1"} & , \quad \text{elsewhere} \end{cases} \tag{8}$$

* (b) Algorithm 2:

$$w_i^* = \begin{cases} \text{"0"} & , \quad \lambda^* < \frac{1}{2}\sigma \\ \\ \text{"1"} & , \quad \text{elsewhere} \end{cases} \tag{9}$$

where $\lambda^* = mod(D^*(1,1), \sigma)$
• Repeating both steps 2 and 3 until all watermark values.
– Forth step:
  • The extracted watermark values are converted to an image.
  • Getting the final extracted WMI by using Inverse AT.

4 Experimental Analysis

In this section, a comparison of Algorithm 1 and Algorithm 2 will be presented based on the results of invisibility tests and robustness tests. Previously, the simulation setting, which includes evaluation criteria, image data, and parameters setting, will be introduced.

4.1 Simulation Setting

Evaluation Criteria. To measure the implementation quality of our watermarking scheme, we use the peak signal-to-noise ratio ($PSNR$) and normalized correlation (NC). $PSNR$ is determined in Eq. 10:

$$PSNR = 10\log_{10}\frac{255^2}{MSE}, \tag{10}$$

here, MSE (mean square error) is formulated as follows

$$MSE = \frac{1}{MN}\sum_{i=0}^{M-1}\sum_{j=0}^{N-1}(H(i,j) - H'(i,j))^2 \tag{11}$$

NC is applied to evaluate the resemblance between the original and extracted watermarks. It is constantly not greater than one and can be computed by Eq. (12):

$$NC = \frac{\sum_{j=1}^{4}\sum_{x=1}^{m}\sum_{y=1}^{n}(W(x,y,j)W'(x,y,j))}{\sqrt{\sum_{j=1}^{4}\sum_{x=1}^{m}\sum_{y=1}^{n}(W(x,y,j))^2}\sqrt{\sum_{j=1}^{4}\sum_{x=1}^{m}\sum_{y=1}^{n}(W'(x,y,j))^2}}, \tag{12}$$

here $W(x,y,j)$ and $W'(x,y,j)$ represent the value of pixel (x,y) in element j of the original and extracted watermarks, respectively. And, $m \times n$ is the watermark size.

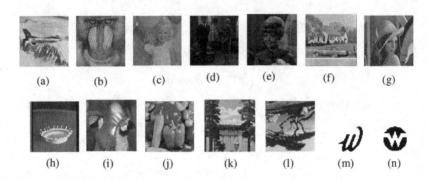

Fig. 2. The host images: (a) avion, (b) baboon, (c) Balloon, (d) couple, (e) Girl, (f) house, (g) lena, (h) milkdrop, (i) parrots, (j) peppers, (k) sailboat, (l) tree. The watermarks: (m) w1, (n) w2.

Image Data and Parameters. To evaluate the performance of the watermarking model, twelve color images with sizes of 512×512 and 256×256 from [24] are utilized as host images. The original watermarks are displayed in Fig. 2 with characteristics: two gray-scale and size of 32×32.

In embedding algorithms, selecting a suitable parameter value is extremely necessary. To balance between robustness and imperceptibility, the threshold T of Algorithm 1 is estimated to be 0.04, and the quantification step σ of Algorithm 2 is set to 70 in our experiments.

Besides, to investigate the efficiency of the two proposed algorithms, we perform the comparison with two other approaches that were published in 2022, namely Soualmi [12] and Sun [22]. While Soualmi [12] *et al.* examined a blind image watermarking scheme that has been established on Schur decomposition and chaotic sequence (CS).

4.2   Invisibility Experiment

In this subsection, the watermarks w1 and w2 are embedded into twelve color images to estimate the invisibility of the image after embedding. Then, the $PSNR$ values are calculated based on Eq. 10 to give a comparison of four algorithms as shown in Table 1. The results in this table indicate that the values of $PSNR$ of Soualmi [12] *et al.* are higher than other algorithms for both watermarks. The average PSNR value of this algorithm is larger than 60dB for all tested images. A reason for this result is that Soualmi *et al.* only hides the watermark in one element $D(2, 1)$ of D by adding 1 to this element for all blocks. Thus, the distance between the pixel value after embedding and the original value is not large. Meanwhile, the algorithm of Sun [22] *et al.* gives the lowest result among the four algorithms since the authors embedded information in the whole first column of Q. Therefore, all elements of the pixel matrix after embedding are modified, leading to a reduction in the watermark's quality.

In addition, this table displays that the values of $PSNR$ in Algorithm 1 are greater than that of Algorithm 2 except in the scenarios of the "baboon" picture. This shows that Algorithm 1 gives better quality of the watermarked images than Algorithm 2. $PSNR$ values are in the range of 50.4527 dB and 58.1620 dB when Algorithm 1 (Alg1) is applied, while they are always around 51 dB when Algorithm 2 (Alg2) is used. These results can be explained as follows.

Table 1. $PSNR$ values of the two algorithms without attacks.

Image	w1				w2			
	Soualmi [12]	Sun [22]	Alg1	Alg2	Soualmi [12]	Sun [22]	Alg1	Alg2
Girl	62.5318	38.2071	58.1143	51.6357	62.1344	38.9001	58.1620	51.5537
avion	63.1120	39.4210	52.9759	51.5691	63.5017	39.1266	53.0076	51.4619
baboon	62.7699	38.7309	50.5138	51.5093	62.4586	38.8233	50.4527	51.4408
House	61.3142	36.5586	51.9829	51.6655	61.7209	36.4508	52.2222	51.4720
milkdrop	64.0081	40.1102	55.8592	51.4481	63.8999	40.2160	56.0307	51.3932
peppers	64.2173	38.9233	55.1237	51.5927	64.3216	38.7567	54.8419	51.5912
sailboat	62.5605	37.1538	52.2410	51.6451	63.0025	37.3214	52.1667	51.4180
lena	61.7249	38.2170	53.9790	51.4801	61.6510	38.0571	54.1249	51.4239
Balloon	64.1126	40.1256	54.1353	51.5559	64.3021	40.4012	54.0019	51.4442
couple	65.0410	38.5241	57.1718	51.8779	64.9712	38.6318	56.7774	51.7497
Parrots	61.2536	38.3096	53.6720	51.6619	61.3324	38.4177	54.0833	51.6928
tree	62.9002	37.8993	52.1963	51.3993	63.1806	37.9054	52.0995	51.3839

First, although Algorithm 1 modifies the value of $U(2,1)$ and $U(3,1)$ of the matrix U by Eq. 4 and Eq. 5,only the middle two rows are changed in the achieved matrix after embedding. Meanwhile, Algorithm 2 only uses one element $D(1,1)$ of the matrix D for embedding, but it changes the value of all the elements of the resulting matrix A'. Figure 3 is an example to illustrate this argument. In this instance, A is the 6th block of "baboon". It is easy to see that after the achieved elements are converted to unsigned 8-bit pixel values, the matrix A'_{int} of Algorithm 2 has more difference from Algorithm 1 compared to the matrix.

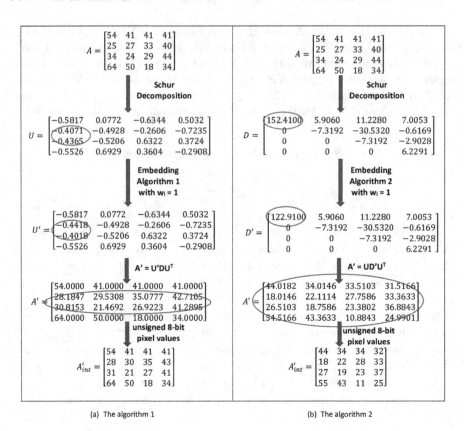

(a) The algorithm 1   (b) The algorithm 2

Fig. 3. An example indicates the difference between the Algorithm 1 and the Algorithm 2 regarding invisibility.

Table 2. The rate of unchanged blocks of the two algorithms.

Image	Size of image	Algorithm 1		Algorithm 2	
		Number of unchanged blocks	Percentage (%)	Number of unchanged blocks	Percentage (%)
Girl	512 × 512	8176	49.90	2623	16.00
avion	512 × 512	8209	50.10	2859	17.45
baboon	512 × 512	8213	50.13	2712	16.55
House	512 × 512	8113	49.52	3134	19.13
milkdrop	512 × 512	8135	49.65	2426	14.81
peppers	512 × 512	7992	48.78	2446	14.93
sailboat	512 × 512	8091	49.38	3026	18.47
lena	512 × 512	8019	48.94	2620	15.99
Balloon	256 × 256	2059	50.27	743	18.14
couple	256 × 256	2064	50.39	669	16.33
Parrots	256 × 256	2065	50.41	668	16.31
tree	256 × 256	2016	49.22	519	12.67

Second, the rate of change of pixel values after embedding from the original value affects the quality of the watermarked picture. Digital watermarking is an approach to create the binding between the host image and the watermark through embedding and extraction formulas. Each watermark bit of the host image will be embedded in a block and extracted on the same block in the extraction phase. However, blocks are not always changed through embedding. For example, if $w_i = 0$ and a block has $|U(2,1)| \leq |U(3,1)|$, they do not satisfy the conditions of Eq. 4 and Eq. 5. Therefore, there is not any change in this case, and $U'(2,1) = U(2,1)$ and $U'(3,1) = U(3,1)$. It means that pixel values of this block after embedding are the same as the original values. The watermark bit in the extraction phase will be performed via Eq. 8, and because of $|U^*(2,1)| \leq |U^*(3,1)|$, $w_i^* = 0$. In other words, the watermark bit is still exactly extracted in this case. Table 2 counts some unchanged blocks of twelve host images when applying Algorithm 1 and Algorithm 2, and the watermark is w1. For 512×512 images, the total number of blocks is 16384 blocks, and 4096 blocks for 256×256 images. Accordingly, the rate of unchanged blocks is calculated. As displayed in Table 2, the rate of unchanged blocks of Algorithm 1 is much larger than that of Algorithm 2. Thus, the $PSNR$ values of Algorithm 1 are bigger than those of Algorithm 2.

4.3   Robustness Experiment

To compare the efficiency of the two algorithms regarding robustness, nine common types of attacks are applied to watermarked images. These attacks consist of Gaussian noise, salt & pepper noise, blurring, sharpening, rotation, resizing, cropping, mean filter, and $JPEG$ compression. After that, the watermarks are extracted based on Eq. 8 and Eq. 9. Moreover, we have calculated NC values of two previous algorithms, namely Soualmi [12], and Sun [22] under these attacks to assess the superiority of the proposed method. NC values are calculated via Eq. 12.

Figure 4 displays the results of four algorithms when the watermarked images are "Balloon" and "Milkdrop" in term of robustness. As shown in Fig. 4, the algorithm of Soualmi [12] et al. is less robust against most attacks. Extracted watermarks can not be recognized under many attacks, such as Gaussian noise, rotation, scaling, and mean filter. The reason for this result is that Soualmi [12] et al. did not apply any parameter in the embedding formula. Therefore, this algorithm can not ensure a balance of invisibility and robustness. As a result, although this algorithm has image's good quality and high embedding capacity, it is weak against common image attacks.

Figure 4 also indicates that the algorithm of Sun [22] *et al.* has good resistance to most attacks. In [22], the quaternion combines the split color channels, so the correlation between the color channels and the synchronization of watermark embedding is not lost. After that, the watermark is embedded and extracted blindly by modifying the relative relationship between multiple coefficient pairs. Therefore, although the algorithm of Sun [22] *et al.* can meet the robustness requirement, it has low image quality as analyzed in Sect. 4.2.

In addition, Fig. 4 shows that Algorithm 2 has the best robustness in comparison with three other algorithms. Algorithm 1 and Algorithm 2 can also extract information efficiently because the watermarks can be recognized in most cases. NC values of Algorithm 2 are bigger than those of Algorithm 1 and the algorithm of Sun [22], except for adding salt & pepper noise. It means that Algorithm 2 is more robust against attacks than Algorithm 1. In particular, Algorithm 2 is quite stable under attacks such as Gaussian noise and $JPEG$ compression. One of the reasons is that the constraints of Algorithm 1 are easier to change than those of Algorithm 2. In other words, the relationship between $U(2,1)$ and $U(3,1)$ is easily broken under the impact of attacks. This can be explained by an example in Fig. 5 as follows.

In Fig. 5, matrix A is the 3rd block of the original image "Balloon", and the watermark bit $w_i = 1$. In the embedding stage, after decomposing the matrix A by Schur decomposition, we receive $U(2,1) = 0.4977$, $U(3,1) = 0.4968$, $D(1,1) = 585.79$, and so $\lambda = mod(D(1,1), \sigma) = 25$. Because $|U(2,1)| > |U(3,1)|$, by using Eq. 5 of the algorithm 1, we have $U'(2,1) = U(2,1) = 0.4977$ and $U'(3,1) = U(3,1) = 0.4968$. Hence, the matrix A'_{int} keeps the same values as matrix A. Meanwhile, after applying Eq. 7 of Algorithm 2, we find out $D'(1,1) = 613.29$ and $\lambda' = 53$. As a result, the A'_{int} is obtained as in the figure. Under the attack "Gaussian noise 0.003", the matrix A^* of the 3rd block of the watermarked image is modified on some elements for both algorithms, highlighted in red. For Algorithm 1, we get $U^*(2,1) = 0.4908$ and $U^*(3,1) = 0.4967$, so $|U(2,1)| < |U(3,1)|$. It means that the relationship of $U(2,1)$ and $U(3,1)$ have been changed. Based on Eq. 8, we have $w_i^* = 0$. Therefore, this result does not match the original bit w_i. On the contrary, Algorithm 2 gives $w_i^* = w_i = 1$ since $\lambda^*(= 50) > 0.5\sigma(= 35)$ according to Eq. 9.

Attack	Parameter	Watermarked image is "Balloon"				Watermarked image is "milkdrop"			
		Soualmi [12]	Sun [22]	Algorithm 1	Algorithm 2	Soualmi [12]	Sun [22]	Algorithm 1	Algorithm 2
Gaussian noise	0.001	0.7452	0.9547	0.9489	0.9964	0.7510	0.9650	0.9707	0.9971
	0.003	0.6571	0.9068	0.9137	0.9906	0.6892	0.9219	0.9339	0.9971
Salt & Pepper noise	0.005	0.9508	0.9884	0.9834	0.9084	0.9489	0.9707	0.9534	0.9060
	0.01	0.8812	0.9669	0.9499	0.8148	0.8765	0.9679	0.9359	0.8437
JPEG	8x8	0.8234	0.9547	0.8564	0.9986	0.8009	0.9441	0.8106	0.9990
	16x16	0.8376	0.9823	0.8509	0.9986	0.8289	0.9842	0.8445	0.9990
Cropping	25%								
	50%								
Blurring	0.2	0.9120	0.9804	0.9993	0.9993	0.9289	0.9902	0.9990	0.9990
	0.5	0.8773	0.8996	0.9630	0.9935	0.8871	0.9029	0.8337	0.9895
Sharpening	0.2	0.9850	0.9945	0.9993	0.9993	0.9762	0.9931	0.9990	0.9990
	0.5	0.9503	0.9826	0.9819	0.9964	0.9318	0.9835	0.9551	0.9971
Rotation	5°	0.7002	0.9324	0.9237	0.9509	0.7136	0.9110	0.8925	0.9001
	10°	0.6786	0.8871	0.8985	0.9257	0.6872	0.8568	0.8462	0.8467
Scaling	1/2	0.7809	0.9532	0.8772	0.9680	0.7823	0.9420	0.8525	0.9454
	2	0.8315	0.9917	0.9697	0.9978	0.8440	0.9932	0.9338	0.9962
Mean Filter	2x2	0.8663	0.8995	0.8820	0.9384	0.7582	0.8356	0.7989	0.8448
	3x3	0.8217	0.9213	0.9406	0.9673	0.8188	0.8872	0.9209	0.9416

Fig. 4. The extracted watermarks and NC values of four algorithms under nine different types of attacks.

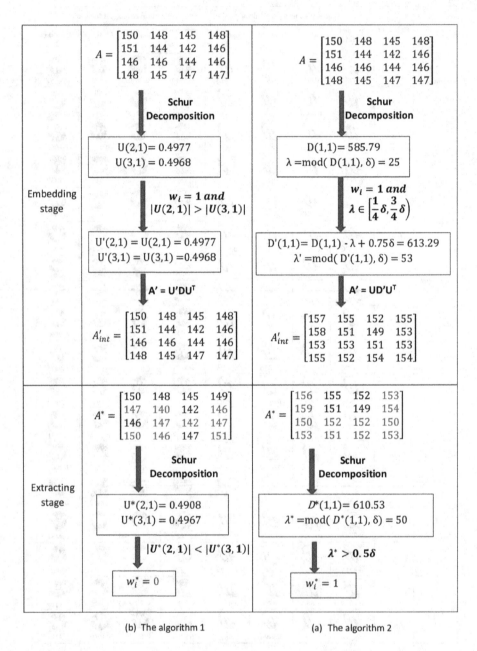

Fig. 5. A comparison of the instability between the Algorithm 1 and Algorithm 2.

5   Conclusion

This paper introduced a blind image watermarking scheme that has been established on Schur decomposition with two different embedding algorithms. In the first algorithm, the watermark was embedded into $U(2,1)$ and $U(3,1)$ of matrix U by modifying their relation. Meanwhile, the second algorithm selects a suitable position to embed in matrix D that is the first element $D(1,1)$. In the experiments, both algorithms are applied on the same condition of the host images, the watermarks, and the size of the blocks. The results have pointed out that in the case of evaluation of the watermarked image's quality, Algorithm 1 performs better than Algorithm 2; however, Algorithm 1 is less effective in the aspect of robustness. Besides, in comparison with previous studies, the achieved results indicated that our proposed algorithms can better balance the watermarked image's quality and the extracted watermark's robustness.

Acknowledgment. This research is funded by the Hanoi University of Industry, and thanks to Nha Phuong-Thi, who supported us during the process.

References

1. Golub, G.H., Van Loan, C.F.: Matrix Computations. Johns Hopkins University Press, Baltimore (2013)
2. Mohan, B.C., Swamy, K.V., Kumar, S.S.: A Comparative performance evaluation of SVD and Schur Decompositions for Image Watermarking. In: IJCA Proceedings on International Conference on VLSI, Communications and Instrumentation (ICVCI), vol. 14, pp. 25–29 (2011)
3. Su, Q., Niu, Y., Liu, X., Zhu, Y.: Embedding color watermarks in color images based on Schur decomposition. Opt. Commun. **285**(7), 1792–1802 (2012)
4. Mohammad, A.A.: A new digital image watermarking scheme based on Schur decomposition. Multimed. Tools Appl. **59**, 851–883 (2012). https://doi.org/10.1007/s11042-011-0772-7
5. Liu, F., Yang, H., Su, Q.: Color image blind watermarking algorithm based on Schur decomposition. Appl. Res. Comput. **34**(10), 3085–3089 (2017)
6. Su, Q., Chen, B.: An improved color image watermarking scheme based on Schur decomposition. Multimed. Tools Appl. **76**, 24221–24249 (2017). https://doi.org/10.1007/s11042-016-4164-x
7. Su, Q., Zhang, X., Wang, G.: An improved watermarking algorithm for color image using Schur decomposition. Soft Comput. **24**(1), 445–460 (2020). https://doi.org/10.1007/s00500-019-03924-5
8. Su, Q., Su, L., Wang, G., Li, L., Ning, J.: A novel colour image watermarking scheme based on Schur decomposition. Int. J. Embed. Syst. **12**(1), 31–38 (2020)
9. Hsu, L.Y., Hu, H.T.: A reinforced blind color image watermarking scheme based on Schur decomposition. IEEE Access **7**, 107438–107452 (2019). https://doi.org/10.1109/ACCESS.2019.2932077
10. Liu, D., Yuan, Z., Su, Q.: A blind color image watermarking scheme with variable steps based on Schur decomposition. Multimed. Tools Appl. **79**, 7491–7513 (2020)
11. Liu, D., Su, Q., Yuan, Z., Zhang, X.: A color watermarking scheme in frequency domain based on quaternary coding. Vis. Comput. **37**, 2355–2368 (2021)

12. Soualmi, A., Alti, A., Laouamer, L.: A novel blind medical image watermarking scheme based on Schur triangulation and chaotic sequence. Concurr. Comput.: Pract. Exp. **34**(1), 6480 (2022)
13. Li, J., Yu, C., Gupta, B.B., Ren, X.: Color image watermarking scheme based on quaternion Hadamard transform and Schur decomposition. Multimed. Tools Appl. **77**, 4545–4561 (2018). https://doi.org/10.1007/s11042-017-4452-0
14. Karajeh, H., Khatib, T., Rajab, L., et al.: A robust digital image watermarking scheme based on DWT and Schur decomposition. Multimed. Tools Appl. **78**, 18395–18418 (2019). https://doi.org/10.1007/s11042-019-7214-3
15. Prabha, K., Shatheesh Sam, I.: Lifting scheme and Schur decomposition based robust watermarking for copyright protection. In: Sheth, A., Sinhal, A., Shrivastava, A., Pandey, A.K. (eds.) Intelligent Systems. AIS, pp. 143–151. Springer, Singapore (2021). https://doi.org/10.1007/978-981-16-2248-9_15
16. Ye, G., Pan, C., Dong, Y., Jiao, K., Huang, X.: A novel multi-image visually meaningful encryption algorithm based on compressive sensing and Schur decomposition. Trans. Emerg. Telecommun. Technol. **32**(2), e4071 (2021)
17. Barouqa, H., Al-Haj, A.: Watermarking E-government document images using the discrete wavelets transform and schur decomposition. In: 2021 7th International Conference on Information Management (ICIM), pp. 102–106. IEEE (2021)
18. Abdullah, M.J.: The Trade-off between robustness and impercepbility performance of watermarking technique with DWT and Schur decomposition for medical images. J. Theor. Appl. Inf. Technol. **100**(1) (2022). ISSN 1992-8645
19. Marjuni, A., Nurhayati, O.D.: Robustness improvement against a non-geometrical attacks of lifting scheme-based image watermarking through singular value and Schur decompositions. Int. J. Intell. Eng. Syst. **14** (2021)
20. Li, J.Y., Zhang, C.Z.: Blind watermarking scheme based on Schur decomposition and non-subsampled contourlet transform. Multimed. Tools Appl. **79**, 30007–30021 (2020). https://doi.org/10.1007/s11042-020-09389-1
21. Hu, F., Cao, H., Chen, S., Sun, Y., Su, Q.: A robust and secure blind color image watermarking scheme based on contourlet transform and Schur decomposition. Vis. Comput. 1–20 (2022). https://doi.org/10.1007/s00371-022-02610-2
22. Sun, Y., Su, Q., Chen, S., Zhang, X.: A double-color image watermarking algorithm based on quaternion Schur decomposition. Optik **269**, 169899 (2022)
23. Satish, A., Prasad, E.V., Tejasvi, R., Swapna, P., Vijayarajan, R.: Image scrambling through two level Arnold transform. In: Alliance International Conference on Artificial Intelligence and Machine Learning (AICAAM) (2019)
24. University of Granada, Computer Vision Group, CVG-UGR Image Database. https://decsai.ugr.es/cvg/dbimagenes/c512.php. Accessed December 2022

Metaheuristics-Based Hyperparameter Tuning for Convolutional Neural Networks

Tong Van Luyen and Nguyen Van Cuong$^{(\boxtimes)}$

Faculty of Electronic Engineering, Hanoi University of Industry, Hanoi 100000, Vietnam
cuongnv@haui.edu.vn

Abstract. Convolutional neural networks have made remarkable strides in the field of deep learning, achieving outstanding successes. However, to ensure the efficiency and high performance of these networks, it is crucial to optimize their hyperparameters. This paper presents a novel approach that focuses on optimizing hyperparameters for convolutional neural networks. The proposed approach leverages the binary bat algorithm, which is recognized as one of the most efficient algorithms among nature-inspired metaheuristic algorithms. By utilizing this approach, a set of optimal hyperparameters can be obtained, enabling the construction of convolutional neural network models that exhibit superior performance for specific applications. To demonstrate the effectiveness of this approach, the study employs it to determine hyperparameters such as the learning rate of optimizers and the number of filters in each convolutional layer. The objective is to build optimal models for the task of handwritten Chinese character classification. The empirical results obtained demonstrate the remarkable capabilities of the proposed approach. The models generated through this method exhibit higher performance in terms of classification accuracy and convergence ability when compared to the LeNet-5 model, as well as models based on Hyperband, Random Search, and Bayesian Optimization.

Keywords: Hyperparameter optimization · Convolutional neural networks · Binary bat algorithm · Metaheuristic algorithms · Handwritten Chinese character classification

1 Introduction

The convolutional neural network (CNN) has emerged as a prominent network within the realm of deep learning. Its significant advancements across diverse domains such as computer vision and natural language processing have captured substantial attention from both academic and business communities. Remarkable achievements, including facial recognition, autonomous vehicles, automated supermarkets, intelligent medical therapies, and pattern classification, have shattered previous limits and expanded the realm of what was once considered unattainable [1].

The convolution layer, the pooling layer, and the fully connected (FC) layer are the fundamental components of CNNs. It can effectively complete a variety of visual tasks

N. Thi Dieu Linh et al. (Eds.): ADHOCNETS 2023, LNICST 558, pp. 41–54, 2024.
https://doi.org/10.1007/978-3-031-55993-8_4

by properly stacking these layers in a deep network. The performance of a CNN is heavily dependent on various factors, such as the configuration of convolutional layers, the number of filters utilized, filter sizes, stride values, dropout probabilities, batch sizes, and the number of training epochs. The regularization technique and activation function selection both have a big impact on how well the network performs [2, 3]. Although it necessitates a thorough grasp of the used CNNs and their hyperparameter value settings, manual testing is a conventional way of identifying the proper hyperparameters to obtain high-performance CNNs. However, manual tuning becomes impractical for many problems due to several factors such as a large number of hyperparameters, complex models, time-consuming evaluations, and non-linear interactions among hyperparameters. Consequently, these factors have prompted extensive research into automatic optimization techniques for hyperparameters, commonly referred to as hyperparameter optimization (HPO). HPO's primary goal is to automate the process of hyperparameter tuning and enable users to successfully deploy CNN models with the best hyperparameters to real-world issues [2–5].

Numerous metaheuristic optimization techniques have been developed in recent years to address challenging computing issues. Particle swarm optimization, genetic algorithms, the whale optimization algorithm, grey wolf optimizer, and the bat algorithm are a few of them [6–9]. When compared to traditional optimization techniques, these algorithms are preferred by academics because of their flexibility and improved capacity to handle a variety of issues. Furthermore, it has been established that no metaheuristic algorithm can operate broadly enough to address every optimization issue. In other words, while some issues can be solved with the current algorithms, not all of them can. One of these new metaheuristic optimization algorithms among the aforementioned algorithms is the bat algorithm. This algorithm employs artificial bats as search agents to conduct the optimization process, simulating the natural pulse loudness and emission rate observed in real bats. The algorithm takes inspiration from the echolocation behavior exhibited by bats. It has been demonstrated that this algorithm may deliver results that are comparable to those of other algorithms, such as particle swarm optimization [6, 10, 11]. The binary bat algorithm (BBA) was introduced to address problems characterized by discrete binary search spaces, such as dimensionality reduction, feature selection, and signal processing. This distinguishes it from the original version of the bat algorithm, which was designed for solving problems with continuous real search spaces [6, 12–15].

To find the best hyperparameters, it is essential to use suitable optimization techniques. Due to the fact that many HPO problems fall under the category of NP-hard problems or are non-convex or non-differentiable optimization problems, conventional optimization techniques may not be effective for solving HPO problems [2, 4, 16, 17]. BBA is one of the most effective metaheuristic-based approaches, and it can solve the above problems. Therefore, this paper utilizes BBA to propose an HPO approach for CNN models. Particularly for large datasets or complex models with many hyperparameters, this approach aids deep learning developers in reducing the amount of effort spent tuning the hyperparameters. Moreover, the proposed approach improves the performance of CNN models. The efficiency of the proposal will be verified by optimizing hyperparameters for CNN models which are used to classify handwritten Chinese characters.

The rest of this paper is structured as follows. The next section proposes an HPO approach to optimize hyperparameters for CNN models. Section 3 evaluates the performance of the proposed approach via several scenarios before concluding the paper in Section 4.

2 Proposed Approach

The primary function of deep learning is the solution to optimization problems. An optimization method is employed to initialize and optimize the weight parameters of a deep learning model, aiming to minimize the objective function or maximize the accuracy until a minimum value or maximum value, respectively, is approached [4]. Similar to this, hyperparameter optimization approaches aim to improve the architecture of a deep learning model by identifying the best combinations of hyperparameters. This section presents a description of the fundamental concepts behind the hyperparameter optimization problem and outlines the proposed algorithm designed for CNN models.

2.1 Hyperparameter Optimization Problem

Deep learning model designers can find the best hyperparameters for their models by efficiently scanning the hyperparameters space utilizing optimization techniques. The exploration of hyperparameter combinations encompasses four key components: an estimator (a regressor or classifier) coupled with its objective function, a search space (also known as the configuration space), a search or optimization technique, and an evaluation function utilized to evaluate the performance of different hyperparameter configurations [4].

The domain of a hyperparameter can be classified into different types, including categorical (e.g., optimizer type), binary (e.g., early stopping), discrete (e.g., number of clusters), or continuous (e.g., learning rate). In actual applications, continuous and discrete hyperparameters' domains are typically constrained [4]. On the other side, conditionality can occasionally be contained in the hyperparameter configuration space. A conditional hyperparameter, also known as a hyperparameter that changes dependent on the value of another hyperparameter, may need to be used or tuned [18].

Generally, the objective of a hyperparameter optimization problem is to attain [4]:

$$\mathbf{h}* = \arg\min_{\mathbf{h}\in\mathbf{H}} f(\mathbf{h}), \tag{1}$$

where the objective function to be minimized is denoted as $f(\mathbf{h})$, $\mathbf{h}$ represents a hyperparameter vector. The optimum value of $f(\mathbf{h})$ is achieved with the hyperparameter vector $\mathbf{h}*$. The search space $\mathbf{H}$ encompasses all possible values that the hyperparameter vector can take. The objective of hyperparameter optimization is to fine-tune the hyperparameters within given resource constraints, aiming to achieve optimal or near-optimal model performance. Various evaluation metrics such as accuracy, root mean square error, F1-score, and false alarm rate can be utilized to assess the model's performance [4].

For CNN models, the search space $\mathbf{H}$ includes hyperparameters, including the number of filters, filter sizes within convolutional layers, the number of nodes in FC layers, activation functions, optimizers, and learning rate. Considering that CNN models necessitate the optimization of m distinct hyperparameters, with each hyperparameter having n_i choices within the categorical and discrete domain in the i - th search space H_i for $i = 1, 2, \ldots, m$. Hence, the search space can be expressed as:

$$
\mathbf{H} = \begin{matrix} H_{1,1} & H_{1,2} & \ldots & H_{1,n_1} \\ H_{2,1} & H_{2,2} & \ldots & H_{2,n_2} \\ \ldots & \ldots & \ldots & \ldots \\ H_{m,1} & H_{m,2} & \ldots & H_{m,n_m} \end{matrix} . \tag{2}
$$

The hyperparameter vector $\mathbf{h}* = [h_1, h_2, \ldots, h_m]^T$ comprises of m optimized hyperparameters. To obtain $\mathbf{h}*$, the index vector $\mathbf{k} = [k_1, k_2, \ldots, k_m]^T$, which consists of m values mapping to search space $\mathbf{H}$, needs to be optimized. Each value in $\mathbf{k}$ should be less than or equal to the corresponding number of choices in the respective search space H_i. For instance, if the first row of the search space H_1 has n_1 choices, then k_1 should be less than or equal to n_1, and the first optimized hyperparameter h_1 is H_{1,k_1}. Consequently, effective optimization algorithms should be employed to address HPO problems, enabling the determination of the index vector and subsequent identification of optimized hyperparameters.

2.2 Proposed Algorithm

The proposed algorithm is derived from the basic BBA (refer to [6] for details) for the purpose of determining the optimal hyperparameter vector $\mathbf{h}*$. Nevertheless, alternative metaheuristics can also be employed in conjunction with the proposed algorithm, instead of utilizing BBA exclusively. The flowchart illustrating the algorithm is presented in Fig. 1, and its description is provided below:

Initialization (a red border block):
Initially, it is essential to determine the type of learning (supervised or unsupervised) and identify the datasets to be used. Subsequently, the search space $\mathbf{H}$ needs to be defined, encompassing hyperparameters such as the number of filters, filter sizes in convolutional layers, and the range of choices or upper and lower limits for each hyperparameter. Additionally, considerations should be made regarding the inclusion of early stopping as a hyperparameter. Given that the optimization problem aims to minimize the objective function, the selection of this function relies on performance metrics evaluated on test datasets. The objective function can be formulated as:

$$
\text{Accuracy:} f = \frac{1}{accuracy_{test}}, \tag{3}
$$

$$
\text{Loss:} f = loss_{test}. \tag{4}
$$

Next, the population size and the number of iterations are initialized, and the dimension (d) of a single solution (bat's position) in BBA is calculated as follows:

$$
d = \sum_{i=1}^{m} \lceil \log_2 n_i \rceil. \tag{5}
$$

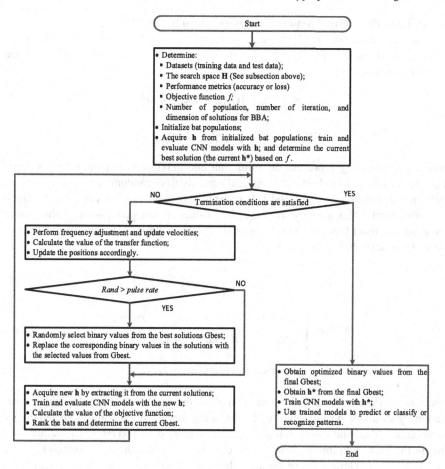

Fig. 1. The flowchart of the proposed algorithm.

The rounding up operation to the nearest number is denoted by $\lceil \bullet \rceil$. The binary bat populations are randomly initialized, and each bat's position $\mathbf{s}$ is represented as a binary number vector, which needs to be converted into a decimal number vector denoted as $\mathbf{k}$. For each element k_i in $\mathbf{k}$ for $i = 1, 2, \ldots, m$, k_i is formulated as:

$$k_i = \left\lceil \frac{n_i}{2^{\lceil \log_2 n_i \rceil} - 1} \text{int}(\mathbf{s}) \right\rceil, \tag{6}$$

where $\lceil \bullet \rceil$ represents the rounding to the nearest number while int $(\bullet)$ signifies converting to an integer. Subsequently, the hyperparameter vector $\mathbf{h}$ is acquired by mapping $\mathbf{k}$ into the search space $\mathbf{H}$. Using this hyperparameter vector, CNN models are constructed, trained, and tested to evaluate their performance based on the objective function described in (3) or (4). Through this process, the current best hyperparameter vector can be identified by considering the performance metrics.

Determining the optimal hyperparameters (green border blocks):

The search operation of BBA is implemented. For the p - th bat with $p = 1, 2, \ldots, numPop$, the velocity V_p^{iter} and the frequency Q_p at the $iter$ - th iteration are updated as follows:

$$Q_p = Q_{min} + (Q_{max} - Q_{min})rand, \tag{7}$$

$$V_p^{iter} = V_p^{iter-1} + (\mathbf{S}_p^{iter-1} - G_{best})Q_p. \tag{8}$$

Here, Q_{min} and Q_{max} represent the minimum and maximum frequency, respectively. G_{best} denotes the current best solutions, and $rand$ signifies random values drawn from a uniform distribution between 0 and 1. In order to update the positions of bats or enforce their movement within a binary space, velocity values are mapped to binary values using a V-shaped transfer function. This transfer function, employed to update the position of the p - th, is described as follows:

$$F_{transfer}\left(V_p^{iter}\right) = \left|\frac{2}{\pi} \arctan\left(\frac{2}{\pi} V_p^{iter}\right)\right|, \tag{9}$$

$$\mathbf{S}_p^{iter} = \begin{cases} (\mathbf{S}_p^{iter-1})^{-1} & \text{if } rand < F_{transfer}(V_p^{iter}) \\ \mathbf{S}_p^{iter-1} & \text{if } rand \geq F_{transfer}(V_p^{iter}) \end{cases}, \tag{10}$$

$$\mathbf{S}_p^{iter}(j) = G_{best}(j) \text{ if } rand > pulse\ rate, \tag{11}$$

where $(\bullet)^{-1}$ denotes binary numbers' complements. If $pulserate$ is lower than $rand$, the binary numbers in $\mathbf{s}$ are modified by replacing them with randomly selected binary values from G_{best}, where $pulserate$ indicates bats' pulse emission rates. This adjustment directs the local solution, $\mathbf{s}$, towards the current best solution G_{best}, using (11) with $j = 1, 2, \ldots, d$. During the process of obtaining a new hyperparameter vector from the current solution, $\mathbf{h}$ can be derived using the same methodology as explained earlier. The optimization process continues until the termination conditions are met. Based on experimental evaluations, this process finishes after executing 20 iterations.

Constructing and testing CNN models with optimized hyperparameters (a blue border block):

The best hyperparameter vector $\mathbf{h}*$ is derived from the optimal solution represented by binary numbers. Subsequently, the optimized CNN models are constructed and trained using $\mathbf{h}*$. Eventually, the trained model is utilized for various tasks such as prediction, classification, or pattern recognition.

3 Performance Evaluation

This section presents a comprehensive evaluation of the effectiveness of our proposed approach. To begin, we define the datasets, relevant parameters, and the search space $\mathbf{H}$ utilized in our experiments, ensuring a clear and well-defined foundation for our evaluations. Next, we showcase the convergence capability of the proposed approach, emphasizing its ability to efficiently converge to optimal solutions. Through illustrative demonstrations and convergence plots, we provide evidence of its effectiveness in finding superior hyperparameters for convolutional neural network models. Moreover, we conduct a thorough comparative analysis to assess how our proposed approach fares against other state-of-the-art methods, including Hyperband, Random Search (RS), and Bayesian Optimization (BO). By quantitatively comparing their performances on various metrics, such as classification accuracy and convergence speed, we aim to identify the strengths and weaknesses of each method.

3.1 Datasets and Parameter Setup

This study uses the CASIA offline database which includes plain gray-scale images of isolated handwritten Chinese characters [19]. Specifically, a subset of the HWDB1.1 dataset is used, and it includes 20 Chinese characters written by about 300 writers (with minor differences for some categories). The test set contains about 50 randomly selected images per category, while the remaining images (approximately 240) form the training set.

The performance of metaheuristic algorithms is closely influenced by two factors: the population size and the maximum number of iterations [20, 21]. Through experimental analysis, it has been determined that a population size of 20 and a maximum number of iterations of 20 yield favorable results. As for the remaining parameters, they are set based on recommendations provided in [6]: *pulserate* $= 0.5$; $Q_{min} = 0$; $Q_{max} = 2$. The termination condition for the algorithm is reached when all iterations have been executed. The simulation results in all scenarios represent the average values obtained from 20 independent runs.

This study validates the proposed approach by applying it to optimize the hyperparameters of the baseline model, namely the LeNet-5 model. The LeNet-5 model is composed of three convolutional layers and two fully connected layers, including the output layer, as illustrated in Fig. 2.

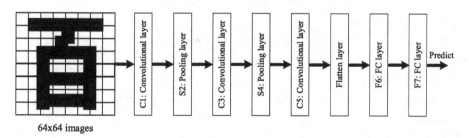

Fig. 2. The LeNet-5 model for handwritten Chinese character classification problems.

The search space **H**, as defined in (12), encompasses various hyperparameters. It includes the number of filters in the three convolutional layers (C1-C3) represented by the first three rows, the number of hidden neurons in the first fully connected layer (F6) denoted by the fourth row, different optimizers listed in the fifth row, and the learning rate mentioned in the last row. Each hyperparameter has four possible choices, resulting in a solution dimension (d) of 12, as calculated using (5). The performance metric used in this study is accuracy, so the objective function is chosen as (3).

$$\mathbf{H} = \begin{matrix} 32 & 64 & 96 & 128 \\ 64 & 96 & 128 & 192 \\ 96 & 128 & 192 & 256 \\ 256 & 512 & 1024 & 1536 \\ \text{Adamax} & \text{SGD} & \text{RMSprop} & \text{Adam} \\ 0.0001 & 0.01 & 0.001 & 0.005 \end{matrix}. \tag{12}$$

Table 1 displays the hyperparameters utilized in both the proposed approach-based model and the LeNet-5 model. The input of CNN models is 64 x 64 gray-scale images, and the output is the prediction of Chinese characters written in input images. Besides, L2 regularization penalties, dropout layers, and scheduler are used to prevent overfitting.

Table 1. Hyperparameters of CNN models.

	LeNet-5 model	Proposed approach-based model
Number of filters in C1	6	Optimization
Number of filters in C2	16	Optimization
Number of filters in C3	120	Optimization
Number of neurons in F6	84	Optimization
Optimizer	SGD	Optimization
Learning rate	0.01	Optimization
Filter size	5	3
Activation function	Tanh	ReLu
	The Softmax function is followed by F7	
Number of neurons in F7	20	
Loss	Categorical cross-entropy	
Pooling layer	Max pooling	
Stride and Padding	1	
Regularizer	L2 with the regularization factor of 0.0005	
Dropout (precede F6 and F7)	0.5	
Scheduler	Halve the learning rate every 3 epochs	
Batch size	100	

3.2 Convergence Ability

We evaluate both the convergence capability and the accuracy of the optimized CNN models on test datasets in this subsection. Figure 3 and Fig. 4 illustrate the values of the objective function and classification accuracy on test datasets over 20 iterations. The results are the average values of 20 independent experiments. It can be seen that the proposed approach converges rapidly within the first 3 iterations, and the accuracy has reached greater than 95.65%. From the 4th iteration onwards, the accuracy insignificantly increases, about 95.8%. Figure 5 demonstrates some Chinese handwritten characters which are classified by a CNN model with optimized hyperparameters. According to the results, the lowest classification accuracy is the character 依, with 99.47% while almost characters are classified with 100% accuracy. The hyperparameters optimized by the proposed approach are summarized in Table 2.

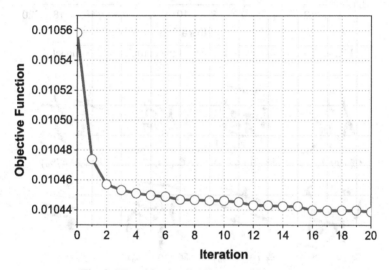

Fig. 3. The objective function over 20 iterations.

3.3 Comparative Analysis

This subsection compares the proposed approach to Hyperband, RS, and BO which are popular and efficient approaches for HPO [3, 4]. Besides, the LeNet-5 model is used as the reference model in this comparison. Figure 6 and Fig. 7 compare the accuracy of optimized CNN models that utilize different approaches. The results indicate that the proposed approach-based optimized model had higher accuracy than other approaches, and the model utilizing the proposed approach demonstrates a significant convergence trend starting from the seventh epoch onwards. At this epoch, the models based on the proposed approach, Hyperband, RS, BO, and the LeNet-5 model achieved accuracies of **95.45%**, 94.66%, 94.97%, 89.69%, and 59.68%, respectively.

The accuracies of trained models at the twentieth epoch and optimized hyperparameters are summarized in Table 2 and Table 3, respectively. The proposed approach

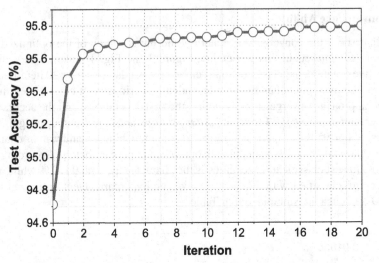

Fig. 4. The classification accuracy of the optimized CNN model.

依 (99.47%)   磨 (99.47%)   嚏 (99.47%)   松 (99.47%)

冠 (99.47%)   寺 (99.47%)   屑 (99.47%)   产 (99.47%)

下 (99.47%)   碌 (99.47%)   哄 (99.47%)   青 (99.47%)

毡 (99.47%)   乾 (99.47%)   朱 (99.47%)   烫 (99.47%)

Fig. 5. The classification accuracy for Chinese handwritten characters.

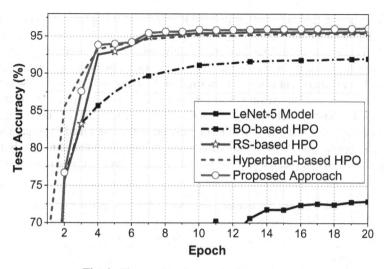

Fig. 6. The comparative graph of the accuracy.

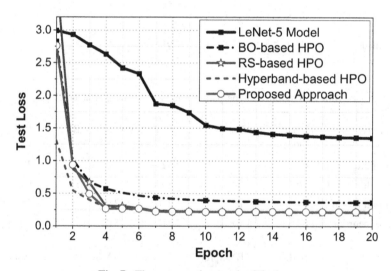

Fig. 7. The comparative graph of the loss.

outperformed all other methods with an impressive accuracy of 96.12%. This indicates that the proposed approach effectively fine-tuned the hyperparameters, leading to a highly accurate CNN model. The hyperparameter settings for the proposed approach involved significantly higher numbers of filters in C1 (128), C2 (64), C3 (192), and neurons in F6 (1024) compared to the LeNet-5 model. This increase in model complexity allows the proposed approach to extract more sophisticated features and achieve superior accuracy. Hyperband and RS also demonstrated competitive performances with accuracies of 95.43% and 95.54%, respectively. Their hyperparameter configurations revealed a balance between model complexity and accuracy, with a moderate number of filters and neurons. Both approaches utilized RMSprop as the optimizer and a learning rate of 0.001, which contributed to their strong performances. BO, on the other hand, achieved an accuracy of 92.02%, showing slightly lower performance compared to the other approaches. Its hyperparameter settings were more conservative, with a relatively lower number of filters and neurons compared to the proposed approach, Hyperband, and RS. BO employed the Adam optimizer with a smaller learning rate of 0.0001. In contrast, the LeNet-5 model obtained the lowest accuracy of 72.91%. This is expected as the LeNet-5 model is a basic architecture and lacks the fine-tuned hyperparameters of the other approaches. Its hyperparameter configuration consisted of relatively fewer filters and neurons, and it employed the SGD optimizer with a learning rate of 0.01.

Table 2. The classification accuracy of different approaches.

Approach	Accuracy (%)
Proposed approach	96.12
Hyperband	95.43
RS	95.54
BO	92.02
LeNet-5 model	72.91

Table 3. Optimized hyperparameters of different approaches.

Hyperparameter	LeNet-5 model	Proposed approach	Hyperband	RS	BO
Number of filters in C1	6	128	32	64	128
Number of filters in C2	16	64	192	96	64
Number of filters in C3	120	192	256	256	256
Number of neurons in F6	84	1024	512	512	1536
Optimizer	SGD	RMSprop	Adam	RMSprop	Adam
Learning rate	0.01	0.001	0.001	0.001	0.0001

Overall, the results reveal that the choice and tuning of hyperparameters significantly impact the accuracy of CNN models. The proposed approach stands out as the most effective method, showcasing the importance of comprehensive hyperparameter optimization in achieving state-of-the-art performance. Hyperband and RS demonstrate competitive performances, highlighting their potential in finding good hyperparameter settings with fewer evaluations. Meanwhile, BO, despite being less accurate in this study, remains a valuable approach due to its probabilistic nature and potential for exploration in high-dimensional spaces. The findings provide valuable insights into the selection and tuning of hyperparameters in CNN models, aiding researchers and practitioners in making informed decisions for model optimization in real-world applications.

4 Conclusion

This paper has proposed a novel approach for finding optimal hyperparameters in CNN models. The efficacy of this approach has been demonstrated by optimizing hyperparameters for a CNN model used in handwritten Chinese character classification. The results clearly indicate that the proposed approach achieves higher classification accuracy compared to other popular and efficient methods named Hyperband, RS, and BO, when tested under similar experimental conditions. These findings have highlighted the potential of our proposed approach as a promising solution for hyperparameter optimization problems. For future work, it would be beneficial to explore the application of this approach to more complex CNN models or even consider its applicability to other types of neural networks, such as recurrent neural networks. Additionally, experimenting with diverse datasets could provide valuable insights into the versatility and robustness of the proposed approach across different problem domains. By extending the evaluation to a wider range of scenarios, we can better understand its capabilities and limitations, which will contribute to its broader adoption and potential improvements in the field of hyperparameter optimization.

References

1. Li, Z., Liu, F., Yang, W., Peng, S., Zhou, J.: A survey of convolutional neural networks: analysis, applications, and prospects. IEEE Trans. Neural Netw. Learn. Syst. Inst. Electr. Electron. Eng. pp. 1–21 (2021)
2. Bacanin, N., Bezdan, T., Tuba, E., Strumberger, I., Tuba, M.: Optimizing convolutional neural network hyperparameters by enhanced swarm intelligence metaheuristics. Algorithms 13(3), 67 (2020)
3. Akay, B., Karaboga, D., Akay, R.: A comprehensive survey on optimizing deep learning models by metaheuristics. Artif. Intell. Rev. 55(2), 829–894 (2021)
4. Yang, L., Shami, A.: On hyperparameter optimization of machine learning algorithms: theory and practice. Neurocomputing 415, 295–316 (2020)
5. Thuc, K.X., et al.: A metaheuristics-based hyperparameter optimization approach to beamforming design. IEEE Access 11, 52250–52259 (2023)
6. Mirjalili, S., Mirjalili, S.M., Yang, X.-S.: Binary bat algorithm. Neural Comput. Appl. 25(3), 663–681 (2014)
7. Dokeroglu, T., Sevinc, E., Kucukyilmaz, T., Cosar, A.: A survey on new generation metaheuristic algorithms. Comput. Ind. Eng. 137, 106040 (2019)
8. Yoo, Y.: Hyperparameter optimization of deep neural network using univariate dynamic encoding algorithm for searches. Knowl.-Based Syst. 178, 74–83 (2019)
9. Wang, Y., Zhang, H., Zhang, G.: CPSO-CNN: An efficient PSO-based algorithm for fine-tuning hyper-parameters of convolutional neural networks. Swarm Evol. Comput. 49, 114–123 (2019)
10. Luyen, T.V., Cuong, N.V.: An effective beamformer for interference suppression without knowing the direction. Int. J. Electr. Comput. Eng. 13(1), 601–610 (2023)

11. Kha, H.M., et al.: An efficient beamformer for interference suppression using rectangular antenna arrays. J. Commun. **18**(2), 116–122 (2023)

12. Luyen, T.V., Cuong, N.V., Duy, L.: An effective beamformer for interference mitigation. In: Anh, N.L., Koh, SJ., Nguyen, T.D.L., Lloret, J., Nguyen, T.T. (eds.) Intelligent Systems and Networks. LNCS, vol. 471, pp. 630–639. Springer, Singapore (2022). https://doi.org/10.1007/978-981-19-3394-3_73

13. Liu, F., Yan, X., Lu, Y.: Feature selection for image steganalysis using binary bat algorithm. IEEE Access **8**, 4244–4249 (2019)

14. Ghanem, W.A.H.M., et al.: Cyber intrusion detection system based on a multiobjective binary bat algorithm for feature selection and enhanced bat algorithm for parameter optimization in neural networks. IEEE Access **10**, 76318–76339 (2022)

15. Luyen, T.V., et al.: Null-steering beamformers for suppressing unknown direction interferences in sidelobes. J. Commun. **17**(8), 600–607 (2022)

16. Nakisa, B., Rastgoo, M.N., Rakotonirainy, A., Maire, F., Chandran, V.: Long short term memory hyperparameter optimization for a neural network based emotion recognition framework. IEEE Access **6**, 49325–49338 (2018)

17. Sabar, N.R., Turky, A., Song, A., Sattar, A.: An evolutionary hyper-heuristic to optimise deep belief networks for image reconstruction. Appl. Soft Comput. **97**, 105510 (2020)

18. Luo, G.: A review of automatic selection methods for machine learning algorithms and hyper-parameter values. Netw. Model. Anal. Health Inform. Bioinform. **5**, 1–16 (2016)

19. Liu, C.L., Yin, F., Wang, D.H., Wang, Q.F.: Online and offline handwritten Chinese character recognition: benchmarking on new databases. Pattern Recogn. **46**(1), 155–162 (2013)

20. Li, Q., Liu, S.Y., Yang, X.S.: Influence of initialization on the performance of metaheuristic optimizers. Applied Soft Comput. **91**, 106193 (2020)

21. Kha, H.M., et al.: A null synthesis technique-based beamformer for uniform rectangular arrays. In: 2022 International Conference on Advanced Technologies for Communications (ATC), pp. 13–17 (2022)

Antenna Array Pattern Nulling via Convex Optimization

Tong Van Luyen[1]([✉]) [iD], Phan Dang Hung[2], Hoang Manh Kha[1], and Nguyen Van Cuong[1] [iD]

[1] Faculty of Electronic Engineering, Hanoi University of Industry, Hanoi, Vietnam
luyentv@haui.edu.vn
[2] Information Technology Center, Hanoi University of Industry, Hanoi, Vietnam

Abstract. This paper introduces a novel approach for achieving antenna array pattern nulling through the application of convex optimization techniques. Nulling, the suppression of unwanted interference sources or jamming signals, is a critical aspect of modern wireless communication and radar systems. Leveraging the power of convex optimization, we propose an approach that offers precise control over null placement while maintaining the main lobe and suppressing the sidelobe to enhance the resilience and reliability of such systems.

Keywords: Array Pattern Synthesis · Pattern Nulling · Convex Optimization · Beamforming · Interference Suppression

1 Introduction

Wireless communication and radar systems are continually evolving to meet the demands of a connected world and the challenges of modern warfare. Among the many critical aspects of these systems, the ability to suppress interference and jamming signals is of paramount importance. Antenna arrays, comprising multiple radiating elements, have proven to be a powerful tool for achieving this goal. However, the efficient nulling of undesired sources in the received signal pattern remains a complex and critical task [1–3].

Recently, the design of antenna arrays for interference suppression relied on meta-heuristics or nature-inspired optimization such as bat algorithms [4–6], particle swarm optimization [7], grey wolf optimization [8]. When the issue sizes are moderate, these global optimization strategies are extremely flexible and produce good results [9], but as the issue sizes grow, their processing time increases noticeably [10]. Besides, convex optimization has emerged as a transformative tool for addressing a wide range of optimization problems, including those related to antenna array pattern synthesis [11]. Convex optimization (CO) techniques offer a mathematically rigorous and systematic approach to pattern nulling. By formulating the nulling problem within the framework of convex optimization, we can leverage powerful algorithms to achieve precise control over the nulls in the antenna pattern. This approach enables us to adapt rapidly to

N. Thi Dieu Linh et al. (Eds.): ADHOCNETS 2023, LNICST 558, pp. 55–62, 2024.
https://doi.org/10.1007/978-3-031-55993-8_5

changing interference scenarios, optimize null placement, and mitigate unwanted signals effectively [12, 13].

In this paper, we explore the concept of antenna array pattern nulling via convex optimization. We delve into the theoretical foundations of convex optimization and its application to the nulling problem. Through a series of case studies, we demonstrate how convex optimization techniques can be employed to create robust and adaptive nulling solutions that meet stringent interference suppression requirements.

Furthermore, we highlight the advantages of this approach, including its capacity to handle various interference scenarios, accommodate dynamic environments, and optimize array parameters for nulling while preserving desired signal strength. As we embark on this journey, our aim is to provide researchers and engineers with a comprehensive understanding of the principles, methodologies, and practical implementations of antenna array pattern nulling via convex optimization. The innovations in this domain hold the potential to significantly enhance the resilience and reliability of wireless communication and radar systems in the face of ever-evolving interference challenges.

2 Antenna Array Pattern Nulling Formulation

In this paper, uniform rectangular arrays with half-wavelength dipoles has been investigated in Fig. 1. The array pattern can be expressed as [14]:

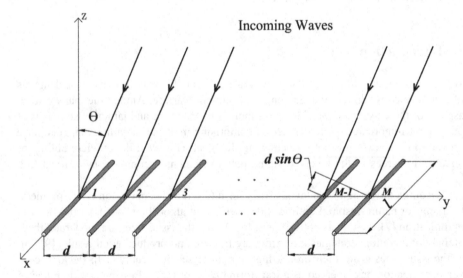

Fig. 1. A linear half-wave dipole array with uniformly spaced elements

$$P(\theta) = EF(\theta) \cdot AF(\theta) = EF(\theta) \sum_{m=1}^{M} w_m e^{j(m-1)kd \sin(\theta)} \quad (1)$$

where

- EF is the element factor of the dipole and AF is the array factor of the array
- w_m is the complex weight at the element $(m)^{th}$

Vectorization form of this pattern can be described as:

$$P(\theta) = EF(\theta)s(\theta)w \quad (2)$$

where:

s: steering vectors

w: complex weights

To obtain patterns nulling, w can be found by solving optimization problems described with typical mathematical forms as [15]:

$$\begin{aligned} &\text{minimize } f_0(x) \\ &\text{subject to } f_i(x) \le b_i, i = 1, \dots, I, \end{aligned} \quad (3)$$

where: the variable of the problem is the vector $x = (x_1, x_2, \dots, x_{Nx})$, fitness function is $f_0(x) : \mathbb{R}^{Nx} \to \mathbb{R}$, and the functions $f_i(x) : \mathbb{R}^{Nx} \to \mathbb{R}$ are the (inequality) constraint functions with the constant limits, or bounds $b_1, b_2, \dots, b_I$ corresponding to each constraint function. The vector $x*$ is an optimal solution to the problem (3) if and only if among all the vectors that satisfy the constraints, it has the smallest fitness value: for any u with $f_1(u) \le b_1, \dots, f_I(u) \le b_I$, then $f_0(u) \ge f_0(x*)$. In the later section, a convex optimization-based approach will be proposed to find optimized weights to conduct required pattern nulling.

3 Proposed Antenna Array Pattern Nulling

The optimal weight vector for the problem (3) utilizing CO-based approach is expressed as:

$$w_0 = w_{ref} - \Delta, \quad (4)$$

w_{ref}: reference weight vector, such as weights using Chebyshev method

w_0: optimal weight vector

Δ: the perturbation of the weight vector

Optimized pattern with imposed null, maintained main lobe and suppressed sidelobes as presented as:

$$P_o(\theta) = EF(\theta)s(\theta)w_0 = EF(\theta)s(\theta)(w_{ref} - \Delta) \quad (5)$$

$$\Leftrightarrow P_o(\theta) = EF(\theta)s(\theta)w_{ref} - EF(\theta)s(\theta)\Delta \quad (6)$$

$$\Leftrightarrow P_o(\theta) = EF(\theta)AF_{ref}(\theta) - EF(\theta)s(\theta)\mathbf{\Delta} \tag{7}$$

To impose K nulls in the directions of $\theta_k = [\theta_1, \ldots, \theta_K]$ with $k = 1, \ldots, K, P_o(\theta_k)$ is set equal to zero, and the resultant equations are then written as:

$$\mathbf{S}\Delta = \mathbf{v_{ref}} \tag{8}$$

where

$$\mathbf{S} = \begin{bmatrix} s(\theta_1)_1 & \cdots & s(\theta_1)_M \\ s(\theta_2)_1 & \cdots & s(\theta_2)_M \\ \vdots & \ddots & \vdots \\ s(\theta_K)_1 & \cdots & s(\theta_K)_M \end{bmatrix}.$$

$$\mathbf{\Delta} = [\Delta_1, \ldots, \Delta_M]^{\mathrm{T}}$$

$$\mathbf{v_{ref}} = \left[AF_{ref}(\theta)_1, \ldots, AF_{ref}(\theta_K)\right]^{\mathrm{T}}$$

Then, optimization problem can be expressed as:

$$\begin{aligned} &\text{minimize } \|\mathbf{\Delta}\| \\ &\text{subject to } \mathbf{S}\Delta - \mathbf{v_{ref}} = 0 \end{aligned} \tag{9}$$

This problem can be solved by CVX toolbox in [16] to obtain the optimal weight of the desired pattern.

4 Numerical Results

The performance of the proposed approach for sidelobe control is evaluated in this section through several scenarios. The proposal is introduced and evaluated for the receiver, and for the transmitter, it will also go through a similar development process. All scenario simulations use the following parameters if not specified:

The array includes 20 half-wavelength dipoles. The approach based on the Nature-Inspired Algorithm (NIO) is used as the one to compare to our proposed approach. The NIO-based approach utilizes the bat algorithm as in the paper [6]. The important parameters for the bat algorithm: the population is 500; the maximum number of iterations is 100; and the penalty parameter is 10000. The reference pattern is calculated by using the Chebyshev method-based weights with the side lobe level (SLL) of -30 dB. The illustrative results for all scenarios are taken as an average of over 50 simulations in MATLAB 2023a with an Intel® Xeon® Intel® Gold 5115 processor.

4.1 Pattern Nulling Ability

In this scenario, the anti-interference ability of the proposed solution will be verified. First, we assume interference occurs at 14°. The optimal radiation pattern shown in Fig. 2 indicates that the main beam and side beam levels are preserved approximately as well as the reference radiation pattern while placing a strong null point at 14°. The null point depth of −232.5 dB for the proposed approach is about 150 dB deeper than the NIO-based approach. To achieve that optimal radiation pattern, the convex optimization approach requires 6 iterations to converge with the fitness function value of 0.089 as shown in Fig. 3. For the proposed approach, the time required to find the optimal solution for this fitness function is 0.441 s. Meanwhile, the NIO-based approach requires 11.8 s, more than 26.5 times the calculation time of the proposed approach. This is also possible because the computational complexity of convex optimization is $O\big((M)^{3.5} log\,(\varepsilon^{-1})\big)$, where ε is the tolerance of the primal-dual interior-point method, while that of NIO is $O(maxIter \times pop \times range \times M)$, where $maxIter$ is the maximum number of iterations, pop is the population size, $range$ is the number of degrees used in fitness function (e.g., 181 when the angle range is from −90° to 90° with step 1°).

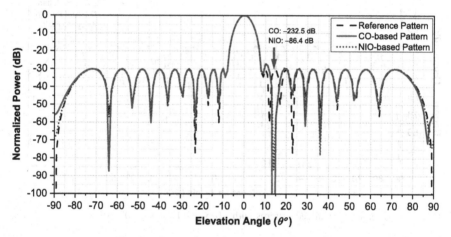

Fig. 2. Normalized patterns with a single null.

When interferences appear to fluctuate over an angular range, interference suppression over a wide range is really necessary. Figure 4 illustrates the ability to suppress interferences appearing in an angle range from −50° to −20°. The results show that the CO-based radiation pattern is capable of suppressing the sidelobe in the interference region mostly to less than 85 dB while it is only 55 dB for that based on NIO. The CO-based approach's ability to control the peak sidelobe level is also better than that based on NIO.

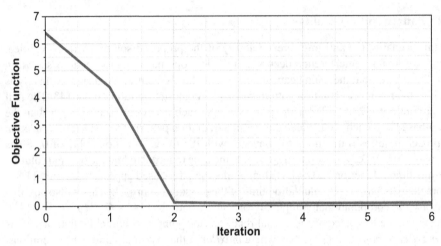

Fig. 3. The fitness function versus the number of iterations.

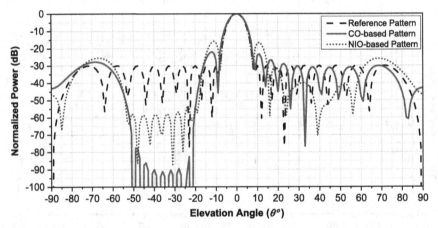

Fig. 4. Normalized patterns with a broad null from $-50°$ to $-20°$.

4.2 Performance with Increasing Antennas

When we increased the number of antennas, we observed a noteworthy trend in the fitness function value in Fig. 5. Starting at the value of 2.13 and steadily decreasing, it reached its lowest point at 0.41 with 75 antennas before rising slightly again. This decrease in the fitness function value indicates a significant improvement in the efficiency of wireless power transfer system as more antennas are added. It suggests that the proposed approach effectively optimizes the power beamforming process, resulting in reduced energy losses and enhanced power transfer efficiency.

In parallel, Fig. 6 shows the fitness function versus the number of iterations. The number of iterations, representing the computational effort required, exhibited a pattern of stability after an initial decline. With 25 iterations for 20 antennas and then consistently at 7 iterations for higher antenna counts, it demonstrates that our approach

maintains computational efficiency even with larger-scale systems. The proposed approach showcases impressive performance as the number of antennas increases. It not
only achieves substantial gains in wireless power transfer efficiency, as evidenced by
the decreasing fitness function values, but also maintains computational efficiency with
a consistent and low number of iterations. These findings underscore the scalability and
effectiveness of our approach in addressing the challenges of wireless power transfer in
complex electromagnetic environments.

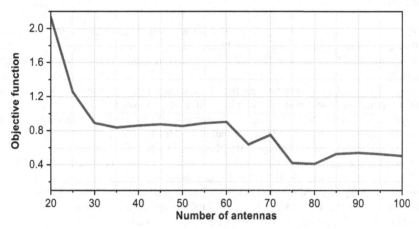

Fig. 5. The fitness function versus the number of antennas.

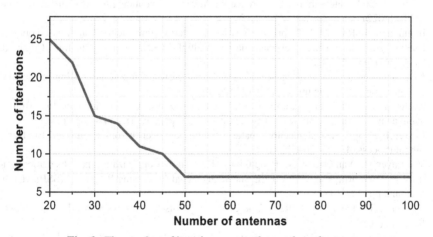

Fig. 6. The number of iterations versus the number of antennas.

5 Conclusion

In this paper, we have explored the application of convex optimization techniques for
antenna array pattern nulling, shedding light on their efficacy in mitigating interference
sources while maintaining the integrity of desired signals. The key takeaways from this

study underscore the significance of convex optimization as a valuable tool in the realm of antenna array design.

Acknowledgment. This research is supported by Hanoi University of Industry [Grant number: 25–2023-RD/HĐ-ĐHCN].

References

1. Yingjie, J.G., Ziolkowsk, R.W.: Advanced Antenna Array Engineering for 6G and Beyond Wireless Communications. Wiley-IEEE Press (2022)
2. Jiang, W., Luo, F.L.: 6G Key Technologies: A Comprehensive Guide. Wiley-IEEE Press (2023)
3. Guo, Y.J., et al.: Circuit type multiple beamforming networks for antenna arrays in 5G and 6G terrestrial and non-terrestrial networks. IEEE J. Microwaves **1**(3), 704–722 (2021)
4. Luyen, T.V., Cuong, N.V.: An effective beamformer for interference suppression without knowing the direction. Int. J. Electr. Comput. Eng. (IJECE). **13**(1), 601–610 (2023)
5. Tong, V.L., Hoang, M.K., Duong, T.H., Pham, T.Q.T., Nguyen, V.T., Truong, V.B.G.: An approach of utilizing binary bat algorithm for pattern nulling. In: Solanki, V.K., Hoang, M.K., Lu, Z.(, Pattnaik, P.K. (eds.) Intelligent Computing in Engineering. AISC, vol. 1125, pp. 963–973. Springer, Singapore (2020). https://doi.org/10.1007/978-981-15-2780-7_101
6. Luyen, T.V., et al.: An efficient ULA pattern nulling approach in the presence of unknown interference. J. Electromagn. Waves Appl. **35**(1), 1–18 (2020)
7. Kha, H.M., et al.: A null synthesis technique-based beamformer for uniform rectangular arrays. In: 2022 International Conference on Advanced Technologies for Communications (ATC) (2022)
8. Indumathi, G., Rani, S.N.: Hybrid grey wolf optimization with cuckoo search-based optimal channel estimation for energy efficient massive multiple input multiple output. Int. J. Commun. Syst. **35**(7), e5106 (2022)
9. Kha, H.M., et al.: An efficient beamformer for interference suppression using rectangular antenna arrays. J. Commun. **18**, 116–122 (2023)
10. Zhang, Y.X., et al.: Antenna array directivity maximization with sidelobe level constraints using convex optimization. IEEE Trans. Antennas Propag. **69**(4), 2041–2052 (2021)
11. Lebret, H., Boyd, S.: Antenna array pattern synthesis via convex optimization. IEEE Trans. Signal Process. **45**(3), 526–532 (1997)
12. Van Luyen, T., Van Cuong, N., Bang Giang, T.V.: Convex optimization-based sidelobe control for planar arrays. In: 2023 IEEE Statistical Signal Processing Workshop (SSP), Hanoi, Vietnam, pp. 304-308 ()
13. Nguyen, L.D., Duong, T.Q.: Real Time Convex Optimisation for 5G Networks and Beyond. IET, UK (2022)
14. Balanis, C.A.: Antenna Theory: Analysis and Design, 4th edn., pp. 348–360. John Wiley and Sons, Hoboken (2016)
15. Boyd, S.P., Vandenberghe, L.: Convex Optimization. Cambridge University Press, Cambridge (2004)
16. Grant, M., Boyd, S.: CVX: MATLAB software for disciplined convex programming, version 2.0 beta (2013). http://cvxr.com/cvx/

Wireless Communications

Interference Suppression Approaches Utilizing Phase-Only Control and Metaheuristic Algorithms: A Comparative Study

Le Thi Trang[1,2] , Nguyen Van Cuong[1] , and Tong Van Luyen[1(✉)]

[1] Hanoi University of Industry, Hanoi, Vietnam
luyentv@haui.edu.vn
[2] Electric Power University, Hanoi, Vietnam

Abstract. This paper evaluates interference suppression solutions using beam-forming (BF) techniques based on phase control of the excitation signal for each element in the antenna array and metaheuristic algorithms. The metaheuristic algorithms investigated in this study include BA Algorithm (BA), Hybrid Particle Swarm Optimization-Gray Wolf Optimization (HPSOGWO), Multi-Verse Optimizer (MVO), and Jaya. Nulls are placed in the interfering directions on the radiation pattern of the equally spaced linear half-wavelength antenna array (Half-wave Dipole Uniformly spaced Linear Array-HDULA). The evaluation results have demonstrated that the interference suppression solutions based on meta-heuristic algorithms are capable of suppressing sidelobes, maintaining the main lobe, and accurately imposing nulls in any interference direction. Furthermore, this evaluation has also shown that the solutions utilizing BA, HPSOGWO, and MVO outperform the Jaya-based ones in terms of computation time and null depth levels.

Keywords: Metaheuristic algorithms · Beamforming · Interference suppression · Null-steering · Half-wave dipole uniformly spaced linear array

1 Introduction

Today, the evolution of the fifth-generation (5G) mobile network has reached new heights, boasting expanded coverage, increased information traffic, reduced latency, and connection density with enormous bandwidth. This remarkable progress is proving to be a crucial driving force behind the development of the Internet of Things, ushering in an era where billions of sensors can seamlessly connect over the Internet [1–3]. However, amidst these advancements, a significant challenge that looms large for 5G networks is interference. The promise of 5G lies in its potential to deliver incredibly faster internet speeds compared to its predecessor, 4G. This leap is achieved through the utilization of wider bands and higher frequencies. Unfortunately, this progress also brings with it the vulnerability of high-frequency bands to interference and signal weakness when confronted with obstacles like buildings or trees. The deployment of 5G signals introduces

N. Thi Dieu Linh et al. (Eds.): ADHOCNETS 2023, LNICST 558, pp. 65–85, 2024.
https://doi.org/10.1007/978-3-031-55993-8_6

particular obstacles that need to be overcome to fully exploit the potential of this state-of-the-art technology. One notable issue is the vulnerability of 5G waves, which operate in the millimeter wave (mmWave) range, to being weakened or absorbed by physical structures. This characteristic can lead to signal loss or a reduction in strength as the waves pass through buildings and other obstacles. Interference from various electronic devices is another concern in 5G networks. With the expectation of supporting a multitude of devices concurrently, there is a risk of bandwidth contention and interference from other electronic gadgets within the environment. Additionally, when numerous base stations and connected devices are in close proximity, signals may interfere with each other, resulting in compromised performance and reduced connection speeds. To overcome these problems and challenges, it is crucial to focus on research and development efforts to create new technologies that enhance the network's ability to suppress interference. Improving performance and connection speed during the deployment and operation of 5G networks is paramount importance.

The effectiveness of 5G in the Internet of Things hinges on three pivotal elements: ensuring secure communication, enhancing overall performance, and achieving smooth transmission of substantial data volumes devoid of disruptions [4, 5]. To accomplish this, fast-response interference suppression solutions are essential for 5G wireless communication technology [6]. In the realm of information network processing, an integrated interference suppression solution holds paramount importance.

Several popular interference suppression solutions are available today, offering various advantages and capabilities. These solutions encompass various technologies such as digital encryption, error correction codes, information filtering, channel code usage, improved Multiple Input Multiple Output (MIMO) technology, the Maximum Ratio Combining (MRC) method, digital signal processing techniques, multi-user MIMO (MU-MIMO), and BF techniques. The beauty of these solutions lies in their versatility, as they can be combined and tailored according to the specific requirements and conditions of the information network, ensuring the highest performance and reliability [4, 7–9]. This paper places special emphasis on evaluating the interference suppression solution using BF. In the context of 5G mobile communication systems, BF assumes a vital role, boasting numerous advantages such as extended coverage, improved signal transmission quality, enhanced spectrum usage, and effective interference suppression capabilities.

The BF technique involves controlling the signal of each antenna element based on a predefined principle. The primary purpose of this control operation is to shape and direct the beam of the antenna array, achieving specific objectives such as generating and steering the main beam in a designated direction, modifying the sidelobe level, and establishing a "Null" region. The configuration and control of the antenna array's beams are effectively tailored to suit the communication system's requirements [10, 11]. In general, the received signal from each element can be adjusted in terms of magnitude, phase, or both magnitude and phase. Different control techniques, each with unique benefits and drawbacks, have been extensively utilized in practical applications. This paper focuses on a method that sets the "Null" region through phase adjustment and optimizes it using a metaheuristic algorithm to address specific limitations. This approach presents enhanced complexity and attractiveness for phase arrays since it leverages existing controls without incurring additional costs. Furthermore, correcting the main beam's direction can be easily accomplished through phase weight adjustments [12, 13].

Metaheuristic techniques like BA, HPSOGWO, MVO, and Jaya have been utilized to address continuous optimization challenges. These algorithms are non-derivative methods and are known for their simplicity, adaptability, and capability to avoid getting trapped in local optima. They operate in a stochastic manner, beginning the optimization process by generating random solutions. Unlike Gradient search techniques, metaheuristics do not require the calculation of derivatives for the search space. They are both flexible and easy to comprehend due to their straightforward concepts and ease of implementation. These algorithms can be easily customized to suit specific problems. Moreover, owing to their inherent randomness, these techniques function like a black box, steering clear of local optima and efficiently exploring the search space. They achieve a balance between two critical processes: exploration and exploitation. During the exploration phase, the algorithms extensively explore potential search spaces, and subsequently, they conduct a local search in the identified promising areas [14].

BA is an optimization algorithm that draws inspiration from the foraging behavior of BAs in their natural environment. It mimics their use of echolocation techniques to detect prey, avoid obstacles, and determine locations in the darkness. During the search process, BAs interact and learn from each other by modifying their positions and velocities. By utilizing this process, BA becomes capable of finding optimal solutions for optimization problems. Introduced by Xin-She Yang in 2010, the algorithm has proven successful in solving a wide range of engineering problems [14–16]. HPSOGWO combines the exploration capability of Grey Wolf Optimizer (GWO) and the exploitation ability of Particle Swarm Optimization (PSO) to achieve enhanced performance in discovering optimal solutions [17]. It utilizes a population of agents to create a search space. The search process involves interactions among the agents, where PSO is employed to adjust their velocities and GWO is used to update their positions. MVO is a unique nature-inspired algorithm that draws inspiration from three cosmological concepts: white holes, black holes, and wormholes. It constructs mathematical frameworks based on these ideas to execute exploration, exploitation, and localized investigation within optimization challenges. The study outcomes have demonstrated the encouraging capacity of MVO to adeptly address practical issues encompassing unfamiliar search domains [18]. Jaya, on the other hand, is a relatively recent metaheuristic algorithm with a straightforward structure, needing only the population size and termination conditions for optimization. Due to these two characteristics, Jaya has found extensive applications in solving various optimization problems. However, when dealing with complex optimization problems, Jaya may become susceptible to getting stuck in local minima because of its single learning strategy and limited population information [19].

After the introduction, we will move on to the problem formulation. In this section, we will detail the specific issue that this research is focusing on. There will be a detailed description of how interference reduction will be performed using metaheuristic algorithms as well as phase control of the excitation signal for each element in the antenna array. Important aspects of the problem will be analyzed and outlined, ensuring that the reader has a clear view of the scope and goals of the research.

2 Problem Formulation

This paper will consider HDULA with a three-dimensional radiation pattern, depicted in Fig. 1, and an equidistant linear array of M uniformly spaced elements positioned along the axis y as illustrated in Fig. 2. Throughout the paper, the azimuth angle ϕ will be considered at $90°$.

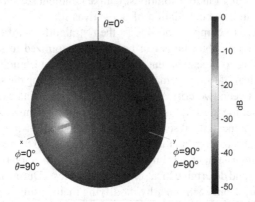

Fig. 1. 3D radiation pattern of a dipole antenna with a length equal to half of a wavelength.

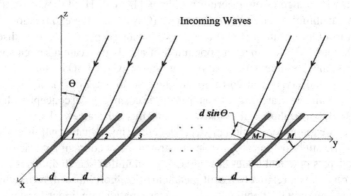

Fig. 2. The dipole antenna array comprises M elements.

The array factor of the HDULA can be represented as shown in references [20] and [21]:

$$AF(\theta) = \sum_{m=1}^{M} w_m e^{j(m-1)dk\sin(\theta)} \tag{1}$$

where:

- $w_m = a_m e^{j\delta_m}$: the complex current (or complex weight) excited at the m array element.

- a_m : the amplitude of the current at the m array element.
- δ_m: the phase of the current at the m array element.
- M : the total number of array element antennas in the array.
- $k = \frac{2\pi}{\lambda}$: the wave numbers.
- λ: the wavelength.
- $d = \frac{\lambda}{2}$: the distance between adjacent elements.

The expression for the array factor in Eq. (1) is as follows:

$$AF(\theta) = \sum_{m=1}^{M} a_m e^{j((m-1)dk \sin(\theta)+\delta_m)} \tag{2}$$

where $EF(\theta)$ is the array element pattern and $l = \frac{\lambda}{2}$ is the length of dipole.

This paper will use the technique of setting null as the phase control of the weights to obtain the optimal radiation pattern for interference suppression. The block diagram of interference suppression solutions based on beamformer is illustrated in Fig. 3, where the total number of elements in the array M is an even integer (M = 2N). Through the center of the antenna array, the amplitudes of the weights are chosen as an even symmetric function ($a_{-n} = a_n$), and the phase of the weights is chosen as an odd symmetric function ($\delta_{-n} = -\delta_n$) [22, 23]. As a result, through the main beam direction ($\theta = 0$), an antisymmetrical pattern is formed. So, when $a_{-n} = a_n$ and $\delta_{-n} = -\delta_n$, the array coefficient in (2) can be rewritten as:

$$AF(\theta) = 2 \sum_{n=1}^{N} a_n \cos(knd \sin(\theta) + \delta_n) \tag{3}$$

The radiation pattern of the array $P(\theta)$ is calculated by the principle of multiplication, which is the product of the radiation pattern of the element $EF(\theta)$ and the array coefficient $AF(\theta)$[20]:

$$P(\theta) = EF(\theta)AF(\theta) \tag{4}$$

An optimization problem has the following form:

$$\begin{aligned}
\text{minimize} \quad & f(\mathbf{x}), \quad \mathbf{x} = (x_1, \dots, x_d)^T \in \mathbb{R}^d \\
\text{subject to} \quad & g_i(\mathbf{x}) = 0, \quad i = 1, \dots, K \\
& h_j(\mathbf{x}) \leq 0, \quad j = 1, \dots, N
\end{aligned} \tag{5}$$

where $\mathbf{x}$ is the optimal variable vector to be found for the problem, the function $f(\mathbf{x})$ is the objective function, and the functions $g_i(\mathbf{x})$ with $i = 1, \dots, K$ and $h_j(\mathbf{x})$ with $j = 1, \dots, N$ are bound functions. A vector $\mathbf{x}*$ is said to be optimal or a solution to the problem if it has the smallest objective function value among the vectors satisfying the conditions of the constraint functions. That is, for any vector $\mathbf{z}$ where $g_1(\mathbf{z}) = 0, \dots, g_k(\mathbf{z}) = 0$ and $h_1(\mathbf{z}) \leq 0, \dots, h_n(\mathbf{z}) \leq 0$, then $f(\mathbf{z}) \geq f(\mathbf{x}*)$[15, 23].

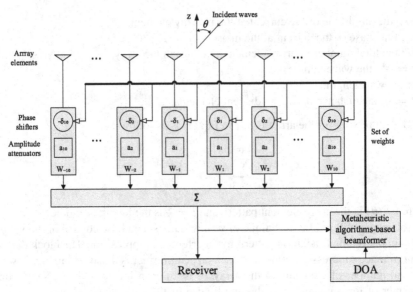

Fig. 3. Block diagram of beamformer based interferences suppression solutions with M = 2N

One of the ways to solve this optimization problem is to apply the Penalty Method [24]. Then, the constrained optimization problem (5) is transformed into the unconstrained optimization problem [15]:

$$\text{minimize } f(\mathbf{x}) + P_e(\mathbf{x}) \tag{6}$$

where $P_e(\mathbf{x})$ is the penalty component, defined as follows:

$$P_e(\mathbf{x}) = \sum_{i=1}^{K} \xi_i |g_i(\mathbf{x})| + \sum_{j=1}^{N} \upsilon_j \max\left(0, h_j(\mathbf{x})\right)^2 \tag{7}$$

The penalty parameters, or penalty coefficients, in this instance are $\xi_i > 0$ and $\upsilon_j > 0$. By transforming the constrained optimization problem into an unconstrained optimization problem, the penalty function method has the advantage of removing constraints. The new objective function specifically includes all binding functions. But as a result, there are more free parameters (penalty parameters) than values that must be identified in order to address the issue [15]. To simplify the implementation, assume that $\xi = \xi_i$ for every i and $\upsilon = \upsilon_j$ for every j. The new objective function can be rewritten as follows:

$$F(\mathbf{x}, \xi, \upsilon) = f(\mathbf{x}) + \xi \sum_{i=1}^{K} |g_i(\mathbf{x})| + \upsilon \sum_{j=1}^{N} \max\left(0, h_j(\mathbf{x})\right)^2 \tag{8}$$

It is evident that, when the equality constraint $g_i(\mathbf{x})$ is satisfied, their influence or contribution to the objective function is zero. However, when violated, they are penalized by multiplying the penalty parameter ξ, and their contribution to the objective function increases significantly. Likewise, they are also true for the inequality constraints $h_j(\mathbf{x})$[15].

However, choosing the right values for penalty parameters can help solve the problem efficiently. Deciding which values are appropriate is a matter of concern. If the penalty parameters are too small, they can lead to insufficient penalties for violations; conversely, when the penalty parameters are too large, they can lead to excessive fines, from which the solution $\mathbf{x}$ too satisfies the condition the constraint functions instead of minimizing the objective function [15]. In this paper, the penalty parameter chosen is 10000.

According to the goal and requirements of the interference suppression solution, the beamformer is able to resist interference while maintaining the direction and width of the main beam and keeping the auxiliary beam at a pre-specified level. This means that the problem to be solved is a constrained optimization problem. Based on the above analysis, this problem can be expressed as an unconstrained optimization problem with a similar objective function (8) as follows:

$$F(\mathbf{x}, \xi) = f(\mathbf{x}) + \xi \sum_{i=1}^{K} |g_i(\mathbf{x})| \tag{9}$$

$$\Leftrightarrow F(\mathbf{w}, \xi) = f(\mathbf{w}) + P_e(\mathbf{w}) \tag{10}$$

where:

$$f(\mathbf{w}) = \sum_{\theta=-90°, \theta \neq \theta_i}^{\theta=90°} |P_o(\mathbf{w}, \theta) - P_d(\mathbf{w}, \theta)|^2 \tag{11}$$

$$P_e(\mathbf{w}) = \xi \sum_{i=1}^{N_i} |P_o(\mathbf{w}, \theta_i)|^2 \tag{12}$$

- The variable vector $\mathbf{x}$ is mapped by the weight vector $\mathbf{w}$;
- $f(\mathbf{w})$ is used to maintain the main beam's direction and width and keep the sub-beam at a pre-specified level;
- $P_e(\mathbf{w})$ is used to set nulls in the directions of the noisy signal on the radiation pattern;
- $P_o(\mathbf{w}, \theta)$ is the optimal radiation pattern obtained by optimization algorithms at θ.
- $P_d(\mathbf{w}, \theta)$ is the radiation pattern with the main beam and the desired SLL specified in advance at θ;
- $P_o(\mathbf{w}, \theta_i)$ is the optimal radiation pattern at θ;
- N_i is the total number of directions of the interfering signal;
- θ is the direction of the ith interferences signal with $i = 1, \ldots, N_i$

The final objective function of the issue can be restated as:

$$F(\mathbf{w}, \xi) = \sum_{\theta=-90°, \theta \neq \theta_i}^{\theta=90°} |P_o(\mathbf{w}, \theta) - P_d(\mathbf{w}, \theta)|^2 + \xi \sum_{i=1}^{N_i} |P_o(\mathbf{w}, \theta_i)|^2 \tag{13}$$

The existence of other antenna elements in the array has an impact on the radiation properties of the antenna elements during electromagnetic energy transmission in the array, including impedance and radiation pattern. Mutual coupling (MC: Mutual Influence) is the name given to this influence. In an adaptive array, taking into account the interaction effect is crucial since it has a direct impact on the array's effectiveness and performance, including the primary beam direction, SLL, and NDL. Therefore, the terms mutual impedance, coupling matrix, S parameter, or embedded element radiation (Embedded Element Pattern) have been used to describe the features of the interaction [20]. In order to analyze the interaction effect in HDULA in this paper, mutual impedance will be used.

For mutual impedance, if the source voltage $V = [V_1, V_2, ..., V_M]^T$ is taken, the input currents (excitation weight) $I = [I_1, I_2, ..., I_M]^T$ will be calculated using the following equation:

$$ZI = V \tag{14}$$

It can be determined using the induced electromotive force method, which is described in references, using Z as the mutual impedance matrix [20] and [21]:

$$Z = \begin{bmatrix} Z_{11} & Z_{12} & ... & Z_{1M} \\ Z_{21} & Z_{22} & ... & Z_{2M} \\ ... & ... & ... & ... \\ Z_{M1} & Z_{M2} & ... & Z_{MM} \end{bmatrix} \tag{15}$$

The mutual impedance (Z_{mn}) between element m and element n in the array is specified according to the information provided in references [20, 21, 24]:

$$Z_{mn} = \begin{cases} 73.129 + 42.546j & \text{if } m = n \\ 30[2C_i(u_0) - C_i(u_1) - C_i(u_2)] - 30j[2S_i(u_0) - S_i(u_1) - S_i(u_2)] & \text{if } m \neq n \end{cases} \tag{16}$$

where: $u_0 = 2\pi d$, $u_1 = 2\pi\sqrt{d^2 + 0.25} + \pi$; $u_2 = 2\pi\sqrt{d^2 + 0.25} - \pi$; the distance between the dipole elements is denoted as d, and C_i and S_i are given by:

$$C_i(u) = \int_\infty^u \frac{\cos(x)}{x} dx$$

$$S_i(u) = \int_\infty^u \frac{\sin(x)}{x} dx \tag{17}$$

Based on Eqs. (7), (8), and (9), it is clear that the mutual impedance matrix $Z_{mn} \neq 0$ is non-diagonal, as $Z_{mn} \neq 0$ when $m \neq n$. Hence, the effective input currents I may not be identical to the voltages V. This leads to certain distortions in the array's pattern, affecting the nulls as well.

By applying noise suppression using an adaptive beamformer based on various nature-inspired algorithms. The adaptive beamformer requires global optimization algorithms to function properly. In this paper, algorithms BA, HPSOGWO, MVO, and Jaya will be applied to develop adaptive BF algorithms based on BA, HPSOGWO, MVO, and Jaya. To do so, the following steps will be performed:

- Map the location of the individual with the weight vector (including amplitude and phase), which are the variables to look for in the optimization process.
- Determine the search size of an instance: This value is equal to the product of the total number of weights and the number of binary bits representing a value.
- Limit the search value range of parameters.

Thus, the algorithm flowchart of an adaptive beamformer based on Jaya, HPSOGWO, BA, and MVO can be illustrated as Fig. 4, 5, 6 and 7, where the termination condition is the maximum number of iterations of the algorithm [25].

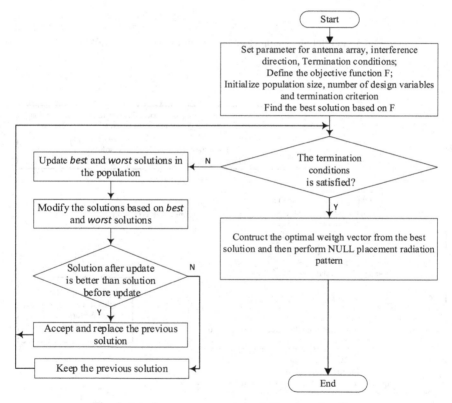

Fig. 4. Interferences suppression solutions based on Jaya

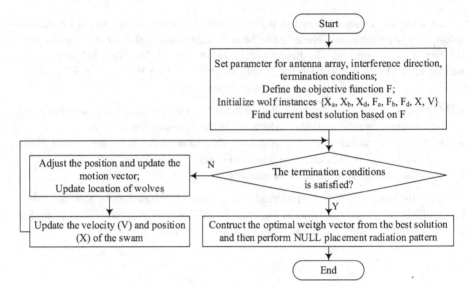

Fig. 5. Interferences suppression solutions based on HPSOGWO

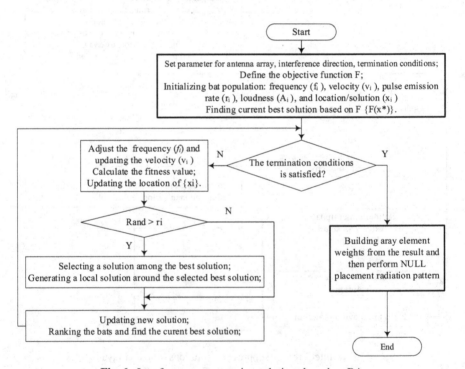

Fig. 6. Interferences suppression solutions based on BA

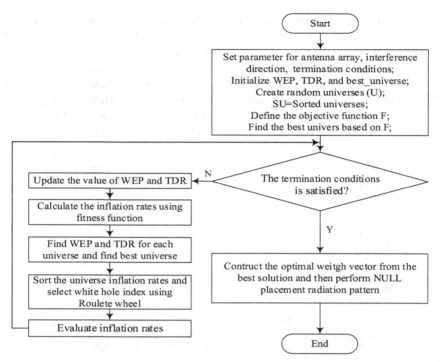

Fig. 7. Interferences suppression solutions based on MVO

After the problem is presented and analyzed, we perform eight simulation scenarios to evaluate interference suppression solutions using BF techniques based on phase control of the excitation signal for each element in the antenna array and metaheuristic algorithms. Eight simulation scenarios are presented, including convergence rate, placing single null, multiple nulls, and broad nulls on the radiation pattern in an ideal case, the impact of interference, steering the main beam, and the final scenario to evaluate the effectiveness of the solution as increasing the number of antenna elements will be done through the technique of setting null by phase adjustment based on BA, HPSOGWO, MVO, and Jaya algorithms.

3   Numerical Results

To evaluate interference suppression solutions using BF techniques based on phase control of the excitation signal for each element in the antenna array and metaheuristic algorithms, the study will investigate seven scenarios. The significant weight distribution in the Chebyshev array results in an optimized radiation pattern that effectively balances the sidelobe levels in the pattern and achieves a beamwidth for the first null point of the main beam in equally spaced arrays [26]. As a result, in this communication, the Chebyshev array factor has been selected as the desired pattern to regulate the *Sidelobe Level (SLL)* and beamwidth of the main beam. Initially, a Chebyshev array pattern exhibiting a SLL of 30 dB has been employed, consisting of 20 half-wave-dipole elements with an inter-element spacing of $\lambda/2$. The step size of the theta angle in (1) is 1°. The smaller θ is, the more accurate the main beam direction and the null point will be, but the time to find the optimal solution will increase.

In Fig. 8, it can be seen that the pop $= 50$, 100, 150, and 200 cases almost all reach the same objective function value at the loop of 50 and quickly reach $F \leq 2$. However, a large number of instances means increased computation time. Therefore, $pop = 100$ and $iter = 50$ will be selected for simulation for the remaining scenarios. The step size of a random walk is 0.01; boundary frequency values: $f_{min} = 0$ and $f_{max} = 1$.

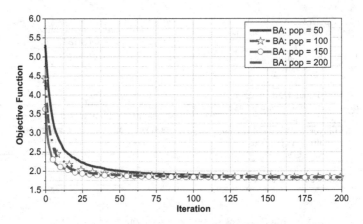

Fig. 8. Objective function of BA based solutions with different population sizes

Scenarios 1 and 2, named "Convergence Rate," were utilized to measure the convergence time of the objective function using the BA, HPSOGWO, MVO, and Jaya algorithms. Moving on, Scenarios 3 to 6 were used to assess the null steering capability of the waveform generator based on the BA, HPSOGWO, MVO, and Jaya algorithms in an ideal scenario disregarding mutual coupling effects. Expanding the evaluation, Scenario 6 was used to investigate the influence of mutual coupling, specifically employing the MVO algorithm. Scenario 7 focuses on main beam steering; the last scenario is used to evaluate the solution's effectiveness by increasing the number of antenna elements using the technique of setting null by phase adjustment based on the MVO algorithm. The simulation results for all scenarios are depicted in Figs. 8, 9, 10, 11, 12, 13, 14, 15, 16, 17, 18 and Tables 1 and 2.

A. *Convergence rate*

In Scenario 2, the convergence rate of the beamformer generator is evaluated using four algorithms: BA, HPSOGWO, MVO, and Jaya. Since the complexity of the algorithms is the same, the computation time and number of iterations to achieve a target objective function value are the parameters used to assess and compare these algorithms. The objective function values for each algorithm are illustrated in Fig. 9. The time taken for all four solutions to reach a target objective function value $(F < = 2.5)$ is 0.216 s for BA, 0.738 s for HPSOGWO, 1.364 s for MVO, and 3.659 s for Jaya, respectively. These evaluations were conducted on an Intel(R) Xeon(R) CPU @ 2.20GHz with

13 GB of RAM. The number of iterations for all four solutions to reach an equal objective function value $(F < = 2.5)$ is 7, 12, 17, and 150 iterations, respectively, for BA, HPSOGWO, MVO, and Jaya algorithms. It is evident that BA converges faster compared to HPSOGWO, even faster than MVO, but significantly faster than Jaya. With such fast computation times, BA, HPSOGWO, and MVO can be considered promising solutions for real-time applications in wireless communication systems.

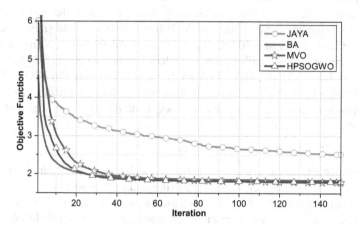

Fig. 9. Objective function of interferences suppression solutions with different algorithms

B. *Ability to eliminate single-interferences*

In Scenario 3, the radiation pattern is optimized with a single null. This null can be placed at any angle, and in this case, it is chosen at the peak of the second sidelobe (14°). The individuals were initialized as Chebyshev array weights with an SLL of −30dB.

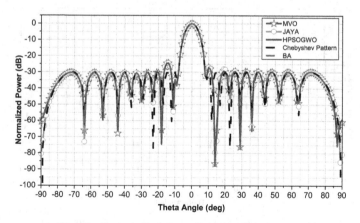

Fig. 10. Optimized patterns with a single null at 14°

In [11], Haupt made a significant discovery that the phase has a more substantial impact on the main beam compared to the amplitude, and introducing slight phase perturbations during nulling will not significantly degrade the main beam. Additionally, a smaller phase weighting range leads to a faster convergence rate. Hence, during the simulation process for all radiation pattern adjustment scenarios, the phase weight variations were confined to the range from −0.1 to 0.1 radians. Figure 10 displays the optimized radiation patterns with a single null obtained using the BA, HPSOGWO, MVO, and Jaya algorithms. These algorithms successfully retain almost all the characteristics of the original Chebyshev pattern, such as the half-power beamwidth *(HPBW = 7.64°)* and *Sidelobe Level (SLL)* of −30 dB, except for a few sidelobes exhibiting an approximate maximum SLL of −20 dB. Notably, the depth of the null point (NDL) at 14° is −87.8 dB, −87.8 dB, −85 dB, and −79.5 dB, respectively, for HPSOGWO, MVO, BA, and Jaya algorithms. These results clearly demonstrate the high effectiveness of interference suppression achieved by accurately placing null points at interference directions using metaheuristic algorithms.

C. *Ability to eliminate Multiple-interferences*

In Scenario 4, the radiation pattern is optimized with multiple individual nulls located at angles −48°, 20°, and 40°, corresponding to the peaks of the next three sidelobes after the main beam in the Chebyshev array radiation pattern. Figure 11 displays the optimized radiation patterns with multiple nulls obtained using the BA, HPSOGWO, MVO, and Jaya algorithms. These algorithms effectively preserve almost all the characteristics of the original Chebyshev pattern, including the half-power beamwidth (HPBW = 7.64°) and Sidelobe Level (SLL) of −30 dB, with only a few sidelobes exhibiting an approximate maximum SLL of −20 dB. The NDL at −48°, 20°, and 40° is presented in Table 1, demonstrating that all NDL values are deeper than −73 dB and all SLL values are lower than −20 dB, while the HPBW remains close to the Chebyshev pattern. These results further illustrate the interference suppression and cancellation capabilities of metaheuristic algorithms in this scenario.

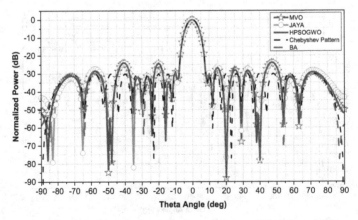

Fig. 11. Optimized patterns with three nulls at −48°, 20°, and 40°

Table 1. Null Depth Level in Fig. 11

Parameters	BA (dB)	HPSOGWO (dB)	MVO (dB)	Jaya (dB)
NDL at:−48°	−74.2	−79.5	−79.5	−74.2
NDL at: 20°	−79.5	−87.8	−88	−79.5
NDL at: 40°	−73.6	−78.2	−77.8	−77.7

D. *Ability to eliminate Broad-interferences*

In interference suppression applications, a broad null becomes essential when the Directions of Arrival (DOA) of interferences slightly vary with time, are not precisely known, or when continuous null steering is required to achieve an appropriate signal-to-noise ratio. To showcase the capability of broad interference suppression, in Scenario 4, a pattern has been generated with an imposed broad null covering the target sector of [30°, 40°]. This pattern is depicted in Fig. 12.

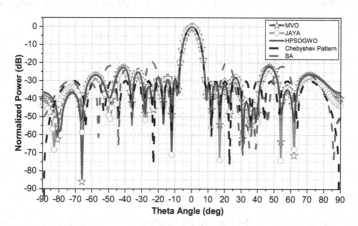

Fig. 12. The optimized patterns exhibit a broad null spanning from 30° to 40°

The main beamwidth remains nearly unchanged, and the maximum Sidelobe Level (SLL) is approximately −20 dB. The results demonstrate that the BA pattern outperforms HPSOGWO, MVO, and Jaya in terms of *NDL,* with wide null and NDL values reaching a minimum of < −53.9 dB, −41.3 dB, 40.9 dB, and 40.9 dB, respectively, for the BA, HPSOGWO, MVO, and Jaya patterns.

E. *Patterns with Mutual Coupling*

Scenario 6 is used to explore the impact of mutual coupling on the radiation pattern optimized by MVO.

To achieve this, the influence of mutual coupling is computed using the mutual impedance matrix presented in Sect. 2, and Fig. 13 illustrates the simulation results for the case of placing multiple nulls simultaneously, with results summarized in Table 2.

The results have indicated that the nulls have been successfully placed at the desired positions, but with a shallower NDL and more challenging control of the sidelobes at around −30 dB, although the main lobe is still maintained.

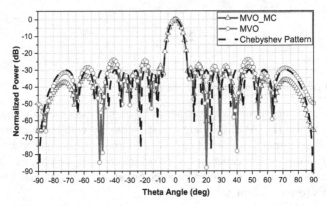

Fig. 13. The optimized pattern (with nulls at angles −48°, 20°, and 40°) accounting for mutual coupling effects

Table 2. Null Depth Level in the Fig. 13

Parameters	Null at: −48°		Null at: 20°		Null at: 40°	
Algorithm	MVO	MVO-MC	MVO	MVO-MC	MVO	MVO-MC
NDL (dB)	−79	−48.8	−88	−60.6	−78.3	−48.6

F. *The radiation pattern when steering the main beam*

The beamformer can also steer the main beam in any direction in space. To achieve this, before proceeding with the search for optimal weights, the Chebyshev radiation pattern in the objective function needs to be steered in the desired direction. In this scenario, the main beam is steered towards $\theta^0 = 10^0$ while setting various types of nulls, as illustrated in Fig. 14.

The results indicate that interference suppression solutions based on metaheuristic algorithms can still perform well, as presented in the cases above. Specifically, the main beam is preserved almost similarly to the main beam of the Chebyshev radiation pattern, and the majority of the SLL is controlled at around −30 dB, except for some sidelobes at approximately −20 dB due to the odd-symmetry nature of the phase-only control technique.

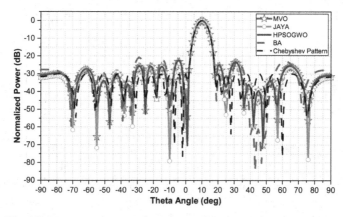

Fig. 14. The optimized radiation patterns when steering the main beam.

G. *Change the number of antenna elements in the antenna array to evaluate the solution*

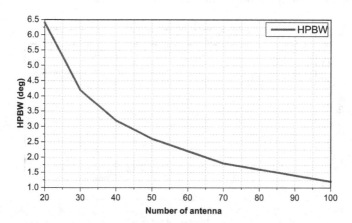

Fig. 15. HPBW versus the number of array antenna elements

Scenario 8 is designed to comprehensively evaluate the impact of varying the number of antenna elements in the array on essential performance parameters, namely HPBW, FNBW, NDL, and MaxSLL. The results of this scenario are displayed in four graphs that unravel the dynamic relationship between key performance metrics (HPBW, FNBW, NDL, and MaxSLL) and antenna element counts, providing an in-depth analysis. About the multifaceted interaction between antenna array size and BF performance. We investigate the relationship between each parameter and the number of antenna elements, which varies from 20 to 100 elements with penalty parameters is 10000 and based on the MVO algorithm.

Figure 15 and 16, which depict the relationship between antenna elements and HPBW and FNBW, respectively, contribute significantly to our comprehension. Within these

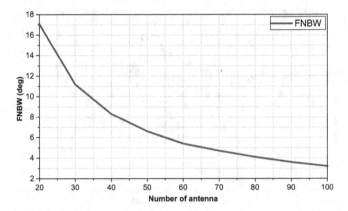

Fig. 16. FNBW versus the number of array antenna elements

visuals, an intriguing pattern comes to the fore: both HPBW and FNBW exhibit a tendency to narrow, signalling the enhanced capabilities of larger arrays in terms of more precise main lobe concentration and improved angular precision.

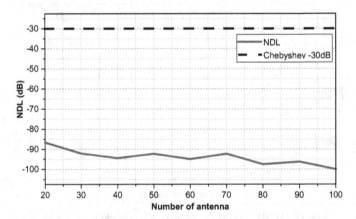

Fig. 17. NDL versus the number of array antenna elements

Observing the graph in Fig. 17, we discern a noteworthy trend: as the number of antenna elements increases, the null point depth experiences a consistent improvement. This trend underscores the pivotal role of spatial diversity in array configurations, where a larger number of elements empowers BF algorithms to more precisely nullify interference and noise from specific angles. The upward trajectory of null point depth with growing array size holds immense promise for enhancing signal clarity, target localization, and noise suppression in a wide array of applications.

In Fig. 18, as the number of antenna elements increases, the graph shows a marked decrease at the maximum side-beam level. This phenomenon highlights the benefit of a larger antenna array in reducing signal leakage and unwanted radiation away from the main lobe.

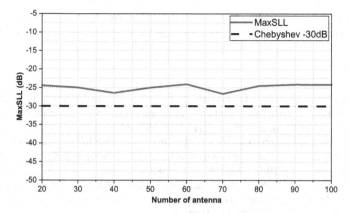

Fig. 18. MaxSLL versus the number of array antenna elements

While a larger antenna array delivers improvements in null point depth, sidelobe reduction, and angular precision, there is a point of diminishing returns. Beyond a certain array size, the benefits may become marginal, and concerns such as hardware complexity, cost, and signal processing burden come to the fore. Industries such as telecommunications, aerospace, and defense have distinct metrics based on their unique requirements. Therefore, the pursuit of an optimal array size necessitates a holistic approach, balancing technical advancements, practical constraints, and specific needs. In conclusion, four graphs provide a panoramic view of the intricate synergy between performance metrics and the number of antenna elements in BF. As researchers and practitioners look for better BF solutions, this relationship acts as a guide, showing them how to find array configurations that make the most of null point depth, sidelobe suppression, angular accuracy, and null beamwidth. This will shape the future of signal enhancement and noise suppression.

4 Conclusion

In this study, we looked at how to get rid of interference using metaheuristic algorithms and controlling the excitation signal's phase only for each antenna element in the array. The interference suppression capability was demonstrated through eight scenarios, including convergence rate, placing single null, multiple nulls, and broad nulls on the radiation pattern in an ideal case, the impact of interference, steering the main beam, and increasing the number of antenna elements. The results demonstrate that the solution can precisely apply the aforementioned nulls to any arbitrary interference direction while maintaining low sidelobe levels and the main lobe in both circumstances of mutual coupling. Moreover, solutions based on BA, HPSOGWO, and MVO demonstrate superior efficiency compared to Jaya-based ones in terms of computation time, pattern nulling, and sidelobe suppression during antenna array radiation pattern synthesis. In this paper, we examine this solution within the context of 5G. However, the outcomes also highlight its potential applicability and suitability for future 6G technology. In the future, solutions for unknown interference directions based on different optimization techniques, such as convex optimization or deep learning, will be further explored.

References

1. Wang, D., Chen, D., Song, B., Guizani, N., Yu, X., Du, X.: From IoT to 5G I-IoT: the next generation IoT-based intelligent algorithms and 5G technologies. IEEE Commun. Mag. **56**(10), 114–120 (2018). https://doi.org/10.1109/MCOM.2018.1701310
2. Quy, V.K., Hau, N.V., Anh, D.V., Ngoc, L.A.: Smart healthcare IoT applications based on fog computing: architecture, applications and challenges. Complex Intell. Syst. **8**(5), 3805–3815 (2022). https://doi.org/10.1007/s40747-021-00582-9
3. Khanh, Q.V., Hoai, N.V., Manh, L.D., Le, A.N., Jeon, G.: Wireless communication technologies for IoT in 5G: vision, applications, and challenges. Wirel. Commun. Mob. Comput. **2022**, 1–12 (2022). https://doi.org/10.1155/2022/3229294
4. Chettri, L., Bera, R.: A comprehensive survey on internet of things (IoT) toward 5G wireless systems. IEEE Internet Things J. **7**(1), 16–32 (2020). https://doi.org/10.1109/JIOT.2019.2948888
5. Kha, H.M., Luyen, T.V., Cuong, N.V.: An efficient beamformer for interference suppression using rectangular antenna arrays. J. Commun. **18**(2), 116–122 (2023)
6. Siddiqui, M.U.A., Qamar, F., Ahmed, F., Nguyen, Q.N., Hassan, R.: Interference management in 5G and beyond network: requirements, challenges and future directions. IEEE Access **9**, 68932–68965 (2021). https://doi.org/10.1109/ACCESS.2021.3073543
7. Shafique, K., Khawaja, B.A., Sabir, F., Qazi, S., Mustaqim, M.: Internet of things (IoT) for next-generation smart systems: a review of current challenges, future trends and prospects for emerging 5G-IoT scenarios. IEEE Access **8**, 23022–23040 (2020). https://doi.org/10.1109/ACCESS.2020.2970118
8. Luyen,T.V., Cuong, N. V., Giang, T.V.B.: Convex optimization-based sidelobe control for planar arrays. In: 2023 IEEE Statistical Signal Processing Workshop (SSP), Hanoi, Vietnam, pp. 304–308 (2023)
9. Zhu, X., Qi, F., Feng, Y.: Deep-learning-based multiple beamforming for 5G UAV IoT networks. IEEE Netw. **34**(5), 32–38 (2020). https://doi.org/10.1109/MNET.011.2000035
10. Trees, H.L.V.: Optimum Array Processing: Part IV of Detection, Estimation, and Modulation Theory. Wiley, New York (2002)
11. Haupt, R.L.: Antenna Arrays: A Computational Approach. John Wiley & Sons, Hoboken (2010)
12. Kha,H.M., Luyen, T.V., Cuong, N.V.: A null synthesis technique-based beamformer for uniform rectangular arrays. In: 2022 International Conference on Advanced Technologies for Communications (ATC), pp. 13–17 (2022)
13. Luyen,T.V., et al.: An efficient ULA pattern nulling approach in the presence of unknown interference. J. Electromagn. Waves Appl., 1–18 (2021)
14. Agrawal, P., Abutarboush, H.F., Ganesh, T., Mohamed, A.W.: Metaheuristic algorithms on feature selection: a survey of one decade of research (2009–2019). IEEE Access **9**, 26766–26791 (2021). https://doi.org/10.1109/ACCESS.2021.3056407
15. Yang, X.-S.: Nature-Inspired Optimization Algorithms, pp. 141–154. Elsevier, Oxford (2014)
16. Thuc, K.X., Kha, H.M., Cuong, N.V., Luyen, T.V.: A Metaheuristic-based hyperparameter optimization approach to beamforming design. IEEE Access **11**, 52250–52259 (2023). https://doi.org/10.1109/ACCESS.2023.3277625
17. Singh, N., Singh, S.B.: Hybrid algorithm of particle swarm optimization and grey wolf optimizer for improving convergence performance. J. Appl. Math. **2017**, 2030489 (2017). https://doi.org/10.1155/2017/2030489

18. Mirjalili, S., Mirjalili, S.M., Hatamlou, A.: Multi-Verse optimizer: a nature-inspired algorithm for global optimization. Neural Comput. Appl. **27**(2), 495–513 (2016). https://doi.org/10.1007/s00521-015-1870-7

19. Rao,R.V.: Jaya: a simple and new optimization algorithm for solving constrained and unconstrained optimization problems. Int. J. Ind. Eng. Comput. (2016). https://www.scilit.net/article/c9341fa01676ca42c8b2157ec8847c37

20. Balanis, C.A.: Antena Theory: Analysis and Design. Wiley, Hoboken (2016)

21. Orfanidis,S.J.: Electromagnetic waves and antennas (2016)

22. Shore, R.: A proof of the odd-symmetry of the phases for minimum weight perturbation phase-only null synthesis. IEEE Trans. Antennas Propag. **32**(5), 528–530 (1984). https://doi.org/10.1109/TAP.1984.1143351

23. Luyen,T.V., et al.: An approach of utilizing binary bat algorithm for pattern nulling. In: Solanki, V., Hoang, M., Lu, Z., Pattnaik, P. (eds.) Intelligent Computing in Engineering. Advances in Intelligent Systems and Computing, vol. 1125. Springer, Singapore (2020). https://doi.org/10.1007/978-981-15-2780-7_101

24. Yeniay, Ö.: Penalty function methods for constrained optimization with genetic algorithms. Math. Comput. Appl. **10**, 45–56 (2005). https://doi.org/10.3390/mca10010045

25. Tong, L., Nguyen, C., Le, D.: An effective beamformer for interference mitigation. In: Anh, N.L., Koh, S.J., Nguyen, T.D.L., Lloret, J., Nguyen, T.T. (eds.) Intelligent Systems and Networks. Lecture Notes in Networks and Systems, vol. 471, pp. 630–639. Springer, Singapore (2022). https://doi.org/10.1007/978-981-19-3394-3_73

26. Dolph, C.L.: A current distribution for broadside arrays which optimizes the relationship between beam width and side-lobe level. Proc. IRE **34**(6), 335–348 (1946). https://doi.org/10.1109/JRPROC.1946.225956

Reconfigurable Intelligent Surface-Aided Wireless Communication Considering Interference Suppression

Tong Van Luyen[1]([✉]) [iD], Le Van Thai[1], Nguyen Minh Tran[2],
and Nguyen Van Cuong[1] [iD]

[1] Hanoi University of Industry, Hanoi, Vietnam
luyentv@haui.edu.vn
[2] Department of Electrical and Computer Engineering, Sungkyunkwan University, Suwon, South Korea

Abstract. As the demand for efficient wireless communication grows, radio frequency (RF) wireless communication emerges as a promising solution, facilitated by recent advancements in signal processing. A pivotal technology driving the efficacy of RF wireless communication is the reconfigurable intelligent surface (RIS). RIS enables passive beamforming and beam focusing, eliminating the need for power-hungry active components. In the era of the Internet of Things, electromagnetic environments are teeming with a multitude of devices, increasing the likelihood of interference. In response to this challenge, this paper presents a novel approach that leverages reconfigurable intelligent surfaces to focus power beams precisely on receivers while suppressing interference. Our research results demonstrate that this approach, based on least squares, outperforms nature-inspired optimization methods. The proposed technique not only enhances the efficiency of wireless communication but also ensures interference-free operation in complex electromagnetic environments. This study contributes to the growing body of knowledge in RF wireless communication and reconfigurable intelligent surfaces, offering a robust solution for the emerging IoT landscape.

Keywords: Reconfigurable intelligent surface · Wireless communication · Interference Suppression · Least squares

1 Introduction

The rapid advancement of wireless communication and power transfer technologies has brought forth a new era of connectivity and energy harvesting. In this context, Reconfigurable Intelligent Surfaces (RIS), also known as intelligent reflecting surfaces or metasurfaces, have emerged as a promising technology to revolutionize wireless communication and wireless communication systems. By actively controlling the electromagnetic (EM) waves in real-time, RIS offers the potential to enhance the efficiency and reliability of wireless communication systems while mitigating interference issues [1].

© ICST Institute for Computer Sciences, Social Informatics and Telecommunications Engineering 2024
Published by Springer Nature Switzerland AG 2024. All Rights Reserved
N. Thi Dieu Linh et al. (Eds.): ADHOCNETS 2023, LNICST 558, pp. 86–98, 2024.
https://doi.org/10.1007/978-3-031-55993-8_7

Besides, the field of wireless communication has witnessed substantial progress in recent years, with various technologies such as magnetic resonance coupling, inductive coupling, and microwave-based power transfer gaining prominence. These technologies have enabled wireless charging solutions for a range of applications, including smartphones, electric vehicles, and biomedical devices. However, challenges persist, particularly regarding the efficiency and distance limitations of these systems [2, 3].

In wireless communication, RIS has shown promise in enhancing signal quality, extending coverage, and reducing interference. In the context of wireless communication, RIS presents a novel opportunity to improve power transfer efficiency and mitigate interference. Meanwhile, interference from external sources and neighboring devices is a critical concern in wireless communication systems. These sources can significantly degrade power transfer efficiency and, in some cases, pose safety risks. Various methods have been proposed to address interference issues, including beamforming, interference cancellation techniques, and spatial modulation. However, integrating RIS into wireless communication systems for interference suppression represents a relatively unexplored area of research [4, 5].

This paper explores the integration of RIS into wireless communication systems and investigates the crucial aspect of interference suppression. The objective is to propose a reconfigurable intelligent surface-aided wireless communication approach that not only maximizes power transfer efficiency but also effectively suppresses interference from nearby sources. This approach encompasses four steps: (i) Estimate channels between the transmitter, receiver, and the RIS; (ii) Determine the directions of receivers; (iii) Find the optimal reflection coefficient vectors; and (iv) Conduct pattern nulling. By simulation, we have proven that the proposed approach can well form the power beam toward receivers while suppressing interference. Therefore, this research will hold significant implications for various applications, including IoT, electric vehicle charging, and remote powering, where efficient and interference-free wireless communication is essential.

The rest of the paper is organized as follows. Section 2 presents the system model. In the next Section, we thoroughly explain the four-step proposed approach. Section 4 shows the simulation results before concluding in Sect. 5.

2 System Model

We consider an RF wireless communication system with one transmitter, one receiver, and one RIS. The three-dimensional spatial model of the considered system is given in Fig. 1. The transmitter sends an EM power beam to the receiver with the assistance of the RIS. The RIS is a planar array with size of MN and is located at the origin of the system's global coordinate. The position of the unit cell (m, n) in the RIS is $\mathbf{q}_{m,n}^{\text{RIS}} = \left(q_{m,n}^{\text{RIS,x}}, q_{m,n}^{\text{RIS,y}}, q_{m,n}^{\text{RIS,z}} \right)^T$. The transmitter is position at $\mathbf{q}^{\text{Tx}} = \left(q^{\text{Tx,x}}, q^{\text{Tx,y}}, q^{\text{Tx,z}} \right)^T$, while the receiver is freely mobile with the location of $\mathbf{q}^{\text{Rx}} = \left(q^{\text{Rx,x}}, q^{\text{Rx,y}}, q^{\text{Rx,z}} \right)^T$. The transmitter sends an EM power beam to the receiver with the assistance of the RIS. The distance between the transmitter and the unit cell (m, n) in the RIS can be derived as [6].

$$d_{m,n}^{\text{Tx-RIS}} = r^{\text{Tx-RIS}} - \left(\boldsymbol{\delta}^{\text{RIS-Tx}} \right)^T \mathbf{q}_{m,n}^{\text{RIS}}, \tag{1}$$

where $r^{\text{Tx--RIS}}$ is the distance between the transmitter and the center of the RIS, $\delta^{\text{Tx--RIS}} = \left(\sin\theta^{\text{Tx--RIS}}\cos\phi^{\text{Tx--RIS}}, \sin\theta^{\text{Tx--RIS}}\sin\phi^{\text{Tx--RIS}}\right)^{T}$ is the u-v representation of the direction from Tx toward RIS.

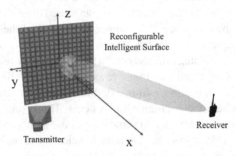

Fig. 1. RIS-aided wireless communication system model [6].

The channel gain between the unit cell (m, n) of the RIS and the transmitter can be given as [6]:

$$h_{m,n}^{\text{Tx - RIS}} = \frac{\lambda\sqrt{G_{m,n}^{\text{Tx - RIS}}G_{m,n}^{\text{RIS - Rx}}}}{4\pi d_{m,n}^{\text{Tx - RIS}}}\exp\left(-j\frac{2\pi}{\lambda}d_{m,n}^{\text{Tx - RIS}}\right),\tag{2}$$

where λ is the wavelength of the EM wave. $G_{m,n}^{\text{RIS - Tx}}$ and $G_{m,n}^{\text{RIS - Rx}}$ are the gains of a unit cell (m, n) of the RIS towards the transmitter and receiver, respectively. $d_{m,n}^{\text{Tx - RIS}}$ is the distance between the transmitter and the unit cell (m, n) in the RIS. In the same way, we can derive the channel gain between the unit cell (m, n) of the RIS and the receiver as:

$$h_{m,n}^{\text{RIS - Rx}} = \frac{\lambda\sqrt{G_{m,n}^{\text{RIS - Rx}}G_{m,n}^{\text{Rx - RIS}}}}{4\pi d_{m,n}^{\text{RIS - Rx}}}\exp\left(-j\frac{2\pi}{\lambda}d_{m,n}^{\text{RIS - Rx}}\right),\tag{3}$$

The unit cell of the RIS is designed with a special design structure. It is equipped with a control element (e.g., a PIN diode) to manipulate the amplitude and phase of the impinging EM wave. The unit cell receives the EM wave from the transmitter and adjusts its amplitude and phase with the control element. Then, the manipulated EM wave is reflected and re-radiated to the air [6]. The total received signal at the receiver can be given as:

$$y = \left(\sum_{m=0}^{M-1}\sum_{n=0}^{N-1} h_{m,n}^{\text{Tx - RIS}}h_{m,n}^{\text{RIS - Rx}}\Gamma_{m,n} + h^{\text{Tx - Rx}}\right)x^{\text{Tx}},\tag{4}$$

where $\Gamma_{m,n}$ is reflection coefficient of the unit cell (m, n). $h^{\text{Tx - Rx}}$ is the direct channel between the transmitter and the receiver. x^{Tx} is the transmitted wave from the transmitter. The additive white Gaussian noise caused by the thermal noise of the receiver circuit is ignored in (4) since the noise level is negligible compared to the received signal in the wireless communication system.

3 RIS Channel and DOT Estimation

3.1 Channel Estimation

To enable adaptive beamforming, the channel state information needs to be acquired by channel estimation method. Several existing channel estimation methods have been developed for the RIS-aided system [3–6]. In this paper, we present a fundamental efficient channel estimation algorithm based on the least square method. We first introduce an orthogonal training matrix as the training pilots of the RIS system. Any orthogonal matrix can be used to train the RIS, however, we use Hadamard matrix in this work. We can build the Hadamard matrix with the size of 2^k by using the following equation.

$$\mathbf{Q}_2 = \begin{bmatrix} 1 & amp; 1 \\ 1 & amp; -1 \end{bmatrix}, \quad \mathbf{Q}_{2^k} = \begin{bmatrix} \mathbf{Q}_{2^{k-1}} & amp; \mathbf{Q}_{2^{k-1}} \\ \mathbf{Q}_{2^{k-1}} & amp; -\mathbf{Q}_{2^{k-1}} \end{bmatrix}. \tag{5}$$

Hence, with the number of unit cells of the RIS (i.e., MN) being the power of 2, the training matrix $\mathbf{G}$ is $\mathbf{Q}_{MN}$. To realize the direct channel between Tx and Rx (i.e., $h^{\text{Tx–Rx}}$), we add one more training vector with all -1 value to the training matrix such that.

$$\mathbf{G} = [\mathbf{Q}_{MN}; -\mathbf{1}], \tag{6}$$

where $\mathbf{1} \in \mathbf{Z}^{MN}$ is unit vector of all 1.

To this end, we rewrite the total receive signal in (4) in matrix form as follows.

$$\bar{y} = \mathbf{\Gamma}^T \mathbf{h} + h^{\text{Tx–Rx}}, \tag{7}$$

where $\bar{y} = \frac{y}{x^{\text{Tx}}}$, $\mathbf{h}$ and $\mathbf{\Gamma}$ are, respectively, the channel gain vector and reflection coefficient vector with size of MN, obtained by vectorization of $h^{\text{Tx–RIS}}_{m,n} h^{\text{RIS–Rx}}_{m,n}$ and $\Gamma_{m,n}$. After training the RIS with the training matrix $\mathbf{G}$, we obtain the received signal vector (i.e., $\bar{y}$) as

$$\begin{aligned} \bar{y} &= \mathbf{G}\mathbf{h} + h^{\text{Tx–Rx}} \\ &= \mathbf{G}\bar{\mathbf{h}}, \end{aligned} \tag{8}$$

where $\bar{\mathbf{h}} = \left[\mathbf{h}; h^{\text{Tx–Rx}}\right]$. The problem in (8) becomes a linear problem, and a solution can be acquired by the least square estimator such as

$$\hat{\mathbf{h}} = \frac{\overline{\mathbf{G}}^T \bar{y}}{\overline{\mathbf{G}}^T \overline{\mathbf{G}}}. \tag{9}$$

The solution in (9) is the estimated channel or the channel state information (CSI) of the RIS-aided system.

3.2 RIS-Based DoT Estimation

Direction of transmission (DoT) is the direction of reflected beam from the RIS toward the desired receiver. Note that the channel information includes the direction of the transmitter toward RIS (i.e., δ^{Tx-RIS}) and the direction of the RIS toward the receiver (i.e., δ^{RIS-Rx}). Under the far-field assumption, the channel gains between RIS and the receiver are sparse in the angular domain. To reveal the sparsity of the channel gains, we use the two-dimension discrete Fourier transform (2D-DFT) to transform the channel gains into the angular domain. The 2D-DFT of $\hat{h}_{m,n}$ for $m = 1, \ldots, M$ and $n = 1, \ldots, N$ can be derived as:

$$\mathcal{F}\left(\hat{h}_{m,n}\right)_{k,l} = \frac{1}{MN} \sum_{m=1}^{M} \sum_{n-1}^{N} \hat{h}_{m,n} \exp\left(-j2\pi\left(\frac{k}{M}m + \frac{l}{N}n\right)\right), \quad (10)$$

for $k = 1, \ldots, M$ and $l = 1, \ldots, N$.

The point that matches to the DoT results in the maximum value of the 2D-DFT. Thus, we can realize the maximum point such as

$$k^*, l^* = \operatorname*{argmax}_{\substack{k = 1, \ldots, M \\ l = 1, \ldots, N}} \mathcal{F}\left(\hat{h}_{m,n}\right)_{k,l}. \quad (11)$$

Then, the tuple $\left(\frac{k^*}{M}, \frac{l^*}{N}\right)$ corresponds to the u-v representation of the DoT. By simple mathematical transformation, one can obtain the azimuth and elevation angles of the DoT.

4 Proposed Approach

Due to the imperfection of the manufacturing and experimental setting, the beam may not exactly be directed in the desired direction, which reduces the power received at the receiver. Moreover, in practical scenarios, the RIS should perform adaptive beam tracking according to the position of the mobile receiving devices. Besides, RIS beams may interfere with other transmitters/receivers, or they may be interfered with by others. In order to tackle this, we propose a four-step scheme allowing us to localize the receiver, focus the power on the receiver direction, and suppress interferences. The procedure of this scheme is presented in Fig. 2. These steps are presented in the next sections.

Each step is explained as follows:

- **Estimate the channel**: The channel will be estimated by training the RIS. Note that the total received signal is changed according to the reflection coefficient vector as mentioned in (4). By sending the signal with L (e.g., 256 in this paper) independent patterns based on the Hadamard matrix as training pilots, L channels between each unit cell of the RIS are estimated by multiplying the received signals with the inversion of L transmitting patterns. The final optimal channel can be obtained by applying the least square estimator [6].
- **Determine the direction of the receiver**: Based on the estimated channel, the direction of the receiver can be derived.

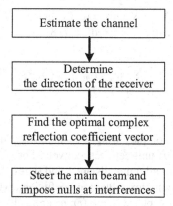

Fig. 2. The four-step proposed scheme.

- **Find the optimal complex reflection coefficient vector:** To form the main beam towards the receiver with the constraint of imposing nulls at the direction of interferences, the least squares method is adopted to calculate the optimal complex reflection coefficient vector. This step is described in detail below.
- **Steer the main beam and impose nulls at interferences:** After obtaining the optimal complex reflection coefficient vectors, these vectors can be applied to the RIS. Therefore, the main beam can be focused on the receiver direction and interferences can be suppressed by imposing nulls at the direction of the jammers.

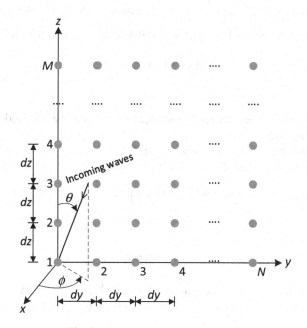

Fig. 3. A RIS with $M \times N$ unit cells.

Considering a RIS with $M \times N$ unit cells as shown in Fig. 3. The scattering field from the RIS can be theoretically expressed as [7, 8]:

$$E(\phi, \theta) = \sum_{m=0}^{M-1} \sum_{n=0}^{N-1} w_{m,n} \Gamma_{m,n} f_{m,n}(\phi, \theta) e^{j(m\psi_z + n\psi_y)}, \qquad (12)$$

where:

- $w_{m,n} = A_{m,n} e^{j\alpha_{m,n}}$ is the complex weights, where $A_{m,n}$ and $\alpha_{m,n}$ are the amplitude and the phase of the (m, n) unit cell, respectively. For simplicity, in this paper, the amplitude and the phase of all unit cells are 1 and 0, respectively;
- $\Gamma_{m,n} = a_{m,n} e^{j\delta_{m,n}}$ is the complex reflection coefficient, where $a_{m,n}$ and $\delta_{m,n}$ are the reflection amplitude and the phase of the (m, n) unit cell, respectively;
- $f_{m,n}(\phi, \theta)$ is the element factor of the unit cell at (ϕ, θ);
- $\psi_z = \kappa d_z \cos(\theta)$; $\psi_y = \kappa d_y \sin(\theta) \sin(\phi)$; $\kappa = 2\pi/\lambda$; $d_z = d_y = \lambda/2$.

The scattering EM wave from the RIS can be controlled and formed by adjusting the reflection amplitude $(a_{m,n})$ and phase $(\delta_{m,n})$ of each unit cell. Therefore, the scattering field can be expressed in the matrix form [9]:

$$E(\phi, \theta) = \mathbf{f}(\phi, \theta) \mathbf{s}(\phi, \theta) \Gamma \qquad (13)$$

where:

- $\mathbf{s}(\phi, \theta) = \left[s(\phi, \theta)_1, \ldots, s(\phi, \theta)_{MN} \right]$: the steering vector of the RIS;
- $\Gamma = [\Gamma_1, \ldots, \Gamma_{MN}]^T$: the complex reflection coefficient vector;
- $\mathbf{f}(\phi, \theta)$: the vector of element factor which is assumed to be 1 in this paper.

Assuming that the optimal complex reflection coefficient vector is as follows:

$$\Gamma_\mathbf{o} = \Gamma_\mathbf{ref} - \mathbf{x}, \qquad (14)$$

where:

- $\Gamma_\mathbf{ref}$: the reference reflection coefficient vector which can be obtained by using the Chebyshev method;
- $\Gamma_\mathbf{o}$: the optimal reflection coefficient vector;
- $\mathbf{x}$: the perturbation of the reflection coefficient vector.

The optimal scattering field can be rewritten as:

$$E_o(\phi, \theta) = \mathbf{s}(\phi, \theta) \Gamma = \mathbf{s}(\phi, \theta)(\Gamma_\mathbf{ref} - \mathbf{x},), \qquad (15)$$

$$\Leftrightarrow E_o(\phi, \theta) = \mathbf{s}(\phi, \theta) \Gamma_\mathbf{ref} - \mathbf{s}(\phi, \theta)\mathbf{x}. \qquad (16)$$

To impose K nulls in the directions of $(\phi, \theta)_k = \left[(\phi, \theta)_1, \ldots, (\phi, \theta)_K \right]$ with $k = 1, \ldots, K$, $E_o(\phi, \theta)$ is set equal to zero, and the resultant equations are then written as:

$$\mathbf{s}(\phi, \theta)\mathbf{x} = \mathbf{s}(\phi, \theta)\Gamma_\mathbf{ref}, \qquad (17)$$

$$\Leftrightarrow \mathbf{Sx} = \mathbf{E_{ref}}, \tag{18}$$

where:

$$\mathbf{S} = \begin{bmatrix} s(\phi_1, \theta_1)_1 & s(\phi_1, \theta_1)_2 & \cdots & s(\phi_1, \theta_1)_{MN} \\ s(\phi_2, \theta_2)_1 & s(\phi_2, \theta_2)_2 & \cdots & s(\phi_2, \theta_2)_{MN} \\ \vdots & \vdots & \ddots & \vdots \\ s(\phi_K, \theta_K)_1 & s(\phi_K, \theta_K)_2 & \cdots & s(\phi_K, \theta_K)_{MN} \end{bmatrix}, \tag{19}$$

$$\mathbf{x} = [x_1, \ldots, x_{MN}]^T, \tag{20}$$

$$\mathbf{E_{ref}} = [\mathbf{s}(\phi_1, \theta_1)\mathbf{\Gamma_{ref}}, \ldots, \mathbf{s}(\phi_K, \theta_K)\mathbf{\Gamma_{ref}}]^T \tag{21}$$

Equation (18) can be solved by applying the method of least squares (LS):

$$\mathbf{x} = \mathbf{S}^\dagger \left(\mathbf{SS}^\dagger \right)^{-1} \mathbf{E_{ref}}. \tag{22}$$

Substituting (22) into (14), the optimal complex reflection coefficient vector is obtained, and the optimal pattern is formed.

5 Numerical Results

The performance of the proposed approach is evaluated through several scenarios by simulation in this section.

5.1 Parameter Setup

All scenario simulations use the following parameters if not specifically specified:

- A horn antenna works as an EM source. The RIS includes 16×16 unit cells. The receiver is equipped with a single antenna. The direction of interferences and jammers is assumed to be known in advance;
- The target operating frequency is chosen as 5.8 GHz in the industrial, scientific, and medical band;
- The reference coefficient vector is obtained by using the Chebyshev method with the side lobe level (SLL) of -20 dB;
- The illustrative results for all scenarios are taken as an average of over 50 simulations in MATLAB 2023a with an Intel® Xeon® Intel® Gold 5115 processor;
- Besides demonstrating the ability of the proposed approach, this approach is also compared to the interference suppression solution based on the bat algorithm which is mentioned as the nature-inspired optimization (NIO) method in this paper. In the same manner in the paper [10, 11], the fitness function is built as (23). Some important parameters are set as in [10, 11]: the penalty parameter ξ is 1000; the population is 500; the number of iterations is 100.

$$F(\mathbf{\Gamma}, \phi_k, \theta_k, \xi) = \sum_{\phi \neq \phi_k, \phi = -90°}^{\phi = 90°} \left[|E_o(\phi, \theta_k) - E_{ref}(\phi, \theta_k)|^2 \right] + \xi \sum_{k=1}^{K} \left[|E(\phi_k, \theta_k)|^2 \right] \tag{23}$$

where: $E_{ref}(\phi, \theta_k)$, $E_o(\phi, \theta_k)$, and $E(\phi_k, \theta_k)$ are the reference field, the optimal field at (ϕ, θ_k), and the optimal field at (ϕ_k, θ_k), respectively.

5.2 Wireless Communication with the Capacity to Suppress Interferences

This subsection presents the ability to focus the main beam towards the receivers and to impose null at the direction of interferences. After estimating the channels between the transmitter and the RIS and between the RIS and the receiver based on the least square estimator, the direction of the receiver can be attained based on the estimated channels. From that, RIS is capable of steering the beam to the receiver direction. Figure 4 shows the 2D pattern of the RIS with the main beam towards the receiver at $(\phi, \theta) = (0°, 90°)$ and with a null imposed at the direction of the interference $(\phi_k, \theta_k) = (25°, 90°)$. It is clear that the main beam of the LS-based pattern is precisely steered towards the receiver and the proposed approach sets a strong null at an interference with -326.78 dB which is more than 250 dB deeper than the null for the NIO-based pattern. Besides, the proposed approach-based pattern can well maintain the SLL as the reference pattern. Figure 5 displays the amplitude and phase distribution matrix of reflection coefficients for the RIS for the scenario in Fig. 4.

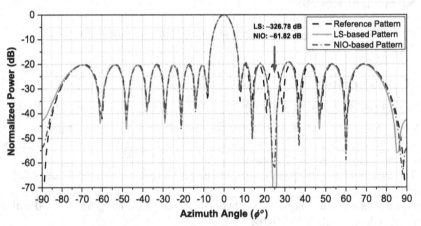

Fig. 4. The 2D pattern of the RIS with the main beam at $(\phi, \theta) = (0°, 90°)$ and an interference at $(\phi_k, \theta_k) = (25°, 90°)$.

However, in reality, the interferences may be present in a wide range or an interference that appears continuously overtime over an angular range. To solve this problem, interference suppression in a wide range is really essential. The next scenario assumes interferences in the range from $-45°$ to $-35°$. Figure 6 indicates that the proposed approach suppresses radiation at $(\phi_k, \theta_k) = [-45° : -35°, 90°]$ while it still maintains the main beam towards the receiver. The null depth levels of the LS-based pattern are almost deeper than -65 dB, and the proposed approach outperforms the NIO-based approach in terms of not only sidelobe control but also interference suppression ability. When the receiver changes position, the receiver's direction relative to the RIS also changes.

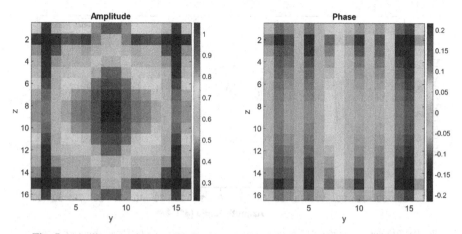

Fig. 5. Amplitude and phase distribution matrix of reflection coefficients for the RIS.

Therefore, the proposed approach needs to be to steer the beam flexibly in space towards the desired direction. To demonstrate this ability, Figs. 7 and 8 show the 2D and 3D pattern of the RIS in the case of the receiver at $(\phi, \theta) = (10°, 80°)$ and interferences at $(\phi_k, \theta_k) = ([40° : 50°], 80°)$, respectively. The LS-based pattern still shows that it is able to steer the main beam toward the receiver while suppressing interferences and it outperforms the NIO-based pattern in every aspect. Similar to this beam steering scenario, Fig. 9 shows the results of steering the main beam towards $(\phi, \theta) = (40°, 60°)$ and suppressing the interference that appears at $(\phi_k, \theta_k) = ([0° : 10°], 60°)$. The results demonstrate that the proposed approach is really effective when the main beam is not only steered toward the $(\phi, \theta) = (0°, 90°)$ direction but also toward many other directions.

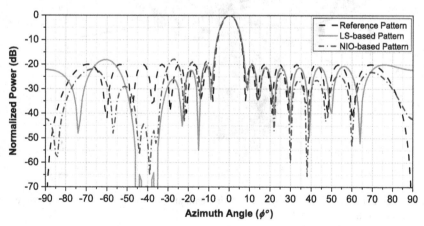

Fig. 6. The 2D pattern of the RIS with the main beam at $(\phi, \theta) = (0°, 90°)$ and interferences at $(\phi_k, \theta_k) = [-45° : -35°, 90°]$.

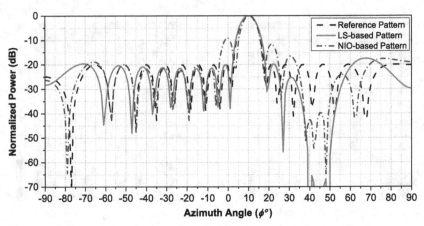

Fig. 7. The 2D pattern of the RIS with the main beam at $(\phi, \theta) = (10°, 80°)$ and interferences at $(\phi_k, \theta_k) = ([40° : 50°], 80°)$.

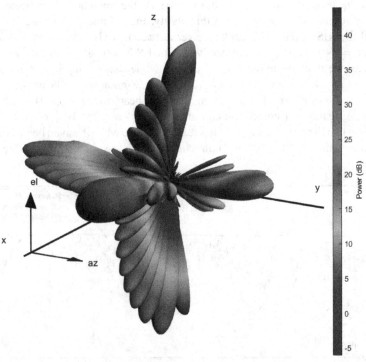

Fig. 8. The 3D pattern of the RIS with the main beam at $(\phi, \theta) = (10°, 80°)$ and interferences at $(\phi_k, \theta_k) = ([40° : 50°], 80°)$.

Fig. 9. The 3D pattern of the RIS with the main beam at $(\phi, \theta) = (40°, 60°)$ and interferences at $(\phi_k, \theta_k) = ([0° : 10°], 60°)$.

6 Conclusion

In this paper, an approach based on the method of least squares for RIS-aided wireless communication is proposed. This study makes a contribution to the ever-growing body of knowledge in RF wireless communication and RIS. It offers a robust and practical solution tailored to the demands of the emerging IoT landscape, where efficient and interference-free wireless communication is paramount. Specifically, the four-step proposed approach, which includes: (i) estimate the channel; (ii) determine the direction of the receiver; (iii) find the optimal complex reflection coefficient vector; (iv) and steer the main beam and impose nulls at interferences, is applied and verified via some scenarios. The proposed approach with the ability to steer the main beam towards the receiver and suppress interferences has shown outperformance relative to the NIO-based approach with respect to both sidelobe control and interference suppression ability. In future works, a system with multiple antennas in the transmitter and the receiver; or applying RIS-aided wireless communication to integrated sensing and communication in 6G wireless communication systems should be considered.

Acknowledgment. This research is supported by Hanoi University of Industry [Grant number: 29–2023-RD/HĐ-ĐHCN].

References

1. Xie, L., Shi, Y., Hou, Y.T., Lou, A.: Wireless power transfer and applications to sensor networks. IEEE Wireless Commun. **20**(4), 140–145 (2013)
2. Kamalinejad, P., Mahapatra, C., Sheng, Z., Mirabbasi, S., Leung, V.C., Guan, Y.L.: Wireless energy harvesting for the internet of things. IEEE Commun. Mag. **53**(6), 102–108 (2015)
3. Choi, K.W., et al.: Simultaneous wireless information and power transfer (SWIPT) for internet of things: novel receiver design and experimental validation. IEEE Internet Things J. **7**(4), 2996–3012 (2020)
4. Cui, T.J., Qi, M.Q., Zhao, J., Cheng, Q.: Coding metamaterials, digital metamaterials and programmable metamaterials. Light Sci. Appl. **3**(e218) (2014)
5. Li, Y.B., et al.: Transmission-type 2-bit programmable metasurface for single-sensor and singlefrequency microwave imaging. Sci. Rep. **6**(23731) (2016)
6. Nguyen, M.T.: Reconfigurable intelligent surface beam focusing for performance enhancement of wireless power transfer systems: a theoretical and experimental study. Ph.D. dissertation, Department of Electrical and Computer Engineering, Sungkyunkwan University, South Korea (2022)
7. Yang, H., et al.: A programmable metasurface with dynamic polarization, scattering and focusing control. Sci. Rep. **6**(1) (2016)
8. Kha, H.M., et al.: An efficient beamformer for interference suppression using rectangular antenna arrays. J. Commun. **18**(2), 116–122 (2023)
9. Kha, H.M., et al.: A null synthesis technique-based beamformer for uniform rectangular arrays. In: 2022 International Conference on Advanced Technologies for Communications (ATC), pp. 13-17 (2022)
10. Tong, L., Nguyen, C., Le, D.: An effective beamformer for interference mitigation. In: Anh, N.L., Koh, SJ., Nguyen, T.D.L., Lloret, J., Nguyen, T.T. (eds.) Intelligent Systems and Networks. Lecture Notes in Networks and Systems, vol. 471, pp. 630–639. Springer, Singapore (2022). https://doi.org/10.1007/978-981-19-3394-3_73
11. Luyen, T.V., et al.: An efficient ULA pattern nulling approach in the presence of unknown interference. J. Electromagn. Waves Appl. **35**(1), 1–18 (2020)

Nature-Inspired Algorithms-Based Beamforming for Advanced Antenna Systems

Tong Van Luyen[1](✉) , Nguyen Thi Van Anh[2] , Nguyen Van Cuong[1] ,
Tran Hai Duong[2] , and Le Thi Trang[1]

[1] Hanoi University of Industry, Hanoi, Vietnam
luyentv@haui.edu.vn

[2] Faculty of Electronic Engineering, Hanoi University of Industry, Hanoi, Vietnam

Abstract. In pursuit of enhancing the signal processing capabilities of antenna arrays for directed signal transmission and reception in spatial contexts, novel methodologies have been developed for advanced antenna systems. Leveraging cutting-edge technologies such as beamforming (BF) and multiple-input and multiple-output (MIMO) within smart antenna systems has emerged as a compelling strategy for elevating the quality of service, capacity, and coverage in mobile information systems. This paper presents a comparison, wherein algorithms inspired by natural processes are applied to amplitude-only controlled beamforming techniques. Subsequently, a comprehensive assessment is undertaken to discern the merits and demerits of the weight control methodologies employed. Specifically, this study delves into the application of bat algorithms, multi-verse optimization, hybrid particle swarm optimization, and gray wolf optimization in various scenarios.

Keywords: Beamforming · ULA · Bat Algorithm · Multi-Verses Optimization · Hybrid Particle Swarm Optimizer and Gray Wolf Optimizer

1 Introduction

In wireless communication systems, highly directional antennas are often used to take advantage of their advantages. Combining a variety of radiating elements (an antenna array) creates highly directional antennas. Beamforming is the technique of combining radio signals from a set of separate antennas to create an equivalent directional antenna system. This directional antenna system (advanced antenna) has the ability to focus on radiating energy or receiving signals in a predetermined direction in space. In order to improve radio signal spectrum efficiency, reduce interference, and save energy, beamformers are frequently utilized in radar, sonar, and wireless communication systems. Additionally, adaptive beamformers have the ability to provide the correct weights for antenna arrays in order to produce desired patterns [1]. In addition, the growing proliferation of wireless devices has led to significant congestion within the electromagnetic propagation environment. Consequently, directional antenna systems emerge as a favorable approach for mitigating interference in radar, sonar, and wireless communication [10].

N. Thi Dieu Linh et al. (Eds.): ADHOCNETS 2023, LNICST 558, pp. 99–111, 2024.
https://doi.org/10.1007/978-3-031-55993-8_8

Amplitude-only controllers [4–6] change the excited amplitude at each array element. This method has been used and proven to work for adaptive beamformers using the metaheuristics algorithm to manage and turn off the ULA antenna in research [7]. A method of global search and optimization known as metaheuristics was created based on testing random solutions or searching in the search space of the problem. Specifically, the metaheuristic algorithms used and evaluated in this study are BA (Bat Algorithm), HPSOGWO (Hybrid Particle Swarm Optimizer and Gray Wolf Optimizer), and MVO (Multi-Verse Optimizer). Based on the behavior and hunting methods of bats, gray wolves, and particles in general, or based on multiverse theory to search for and optimize solutions through two processes of exploration and exploitation.

This study aims to evaluate the advantages and disadvantages of the recommendations in research [7–9] with consistent suggestions for each scenario while maintaining the highest and most stable level of performance. Specifically, five simulation scenarios, including convergence rate, optimized samples with single nulls, multiple nulls, and broad nulls, will be implemented through different excitation weight control techniques.

The rest of this paper is organized as follows: In Sect. 2, the problem is defined, in which the antenna array coefficients and the formation of the objective function are presented. Section 3 gives the general characteristics of nature-inspired algorithms. Section 4 describes in detail the three algorithms mentioned in the article. Simulation results with different scenarios for the amplitude-only beam generator are presented in Sect. 5. Section 6 is the conclusion.

2   Beamforming Approach Formulation

In advanced antenna systems, although there are different array geometries, the principle of signal processing techniques shares some common points. Therefore, for simplicity, only linear arrays will be analyzed in this section.

2.1   Array Factor of ULA Antenna

The 2N isotropic ULA antenna is utilized as an example and shown in Fig. 1. The array is symmetrically arranged along the x axis, and the array factor is [4]:

$$AF(\theta) = \sum_{n=-N}^{N} \omega_n e^{jndksin(\theta)} \tag{1}$$

where: $\omega_n = \omega_n^{re} + j\omega_n^{im} = a_n e^{j\delta_n}$ is the complex weight of nth array element; λ is wave length; $k = \frac{2\pi}{\lambda}$ is the wave number; d is the distance between adjacent elements.

In our study, the imaginary parts of weight $\omega_n^{im} = 0$ và $\omega_{-n}^{re} = \omega_n^{re}$; Therefore, the array factor in (1) can be rewritten as:

$$AF(\theta) = 2\sum_{n=1}^{N} \omega_n^{re} cos(ndksin(\theta)) \tag{2}$$

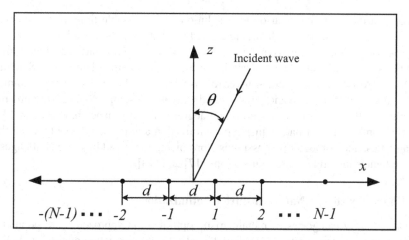

Fig. 1. The ULA antenna of 2N isotropic elements

The weights are real and symmetrical around the center of the array. As a result, the array layout is symmetrical around the major lobe at = 0 and the number of attenuators and calculation time are both cut in half. However, this approach still requires attenuators and amplitude controllers for practical phased array systems.

2.2 Objective Function

One of the ways to solve this optimization problem is to apply the penalty method [2]. Based on this method, a new objective function F is given as follows (3):

$$O = \begin{cases} \xi \sum_{i=1}^{I} \left[|AF_o(\theta_i)|^2\right], for\theta = \theta_i \\ \sum_{\theta=-90^0}^{90^0} \left[|AF_o(\theta) - AF_d(\theta)|^2\right], elsewhere \end{cases} \tag{3}$$

where: F_0 is used to reduce SLL and to keep beamwidth of main lobe within a maximum allowable change; F_d is for placing the null points; θ is angle of elevation.

However, choosing appropriate values for the penalty parameters can help solve the problem effectively. If the penalty parameters are too small, they can lead to under-leveling penalties for violations; conversely, when the penalty parameters are too large, they can lead to excessive penalties, thus the solution oversatisfies the condition. Constraint functions instead of minimizing the objective function [3]. This article chooses the penalty parameter $\xi = 10000$.

3 Nature Inspired Optimization

3.1 Inspiration of Optimization

A metaheuristic algorithm is a search and optimization method with the goal of finding the best solution in a large and complex search space [14, 16]. A common feature of metaheuristic algorithms is their ability to perform searches that may not be globally optimal, but they can find near-optimal solutions in reasonable time. Nature-inspired algorithms are a subset of metaheuristic algorithms that draw their inspiration from natural processes and mechanisms in nature. In order to solve optimization problems, these algorithms frequently simulate or draw inspiration from natural phenomena. Scientists have looked to a variety of natural sources for inspiration, including fish, birds, mammals, plants, ants, bees, bats, fish, and physical and chemical systems. As a result, numerous algorithms with varying functionalities and degrees of performance have emerged [17, 18]. The combination of nature-inspired optimization algorithms, computational electromagnetics, and computer processing is a promising tool to address the challenges of smart antennas in wireless communications [17] and [18].

3.2 Characteristics of Nature Inspired Optimization

The two primary categories of metaheuristic optimization approaches are population search optimization methods (PSOMs) and local search optimization methods (LSOMs) [19]. LSOMs start with a single solution and use neighborhood mechanisms to try to improve that single candidate agent [20]. Evolutionary computation and swarm intelligence are examples of PSOMs [21] and [22]. The nature-inspired optimization method uses this approach to manage the constrained exploration area: If an agent is far from the exploration area, it will adjust the values that disturbed the limits to its previous preferences in order to turn back toward the potential exploration area. The flowchart of the basic nature-inspired optimization algorithm is shown in Fig. 2.

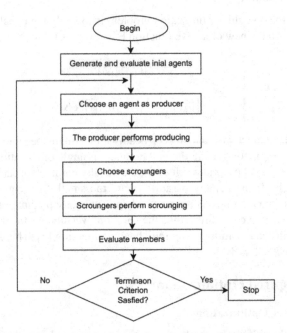

Fig. 2. Flowchart of the basic nature inspired optimizer algorithm

4 Evaluated Beamforming

Beamforming is based on the Nature-inspired optimization; specifically, in this paper, three algorithms (BA [11], HPSOGWO [12], MVO [13]) are used, taking advantage of amplitude-only control for interference suppression applications. They were constructed, and their flow diagram is shown in Figs. 3, 4 and 5.

Null-steering adaptive beamformers emerge as a promising solution for interference suppression in wireless communications and radar applications. We will develop algorithm-based adaptive beamformers for interference suppression applications in the following ways:

- Based on the idea that is introduced in Sects. 2 and 3;
- Applied for pattern nulling of ULAs, such as a single null, multiple nulls, and a broad null at directions of interference;
- Capable of maintaining the direction of the main lobe and the beamwidth while suppressing the sidelobes.

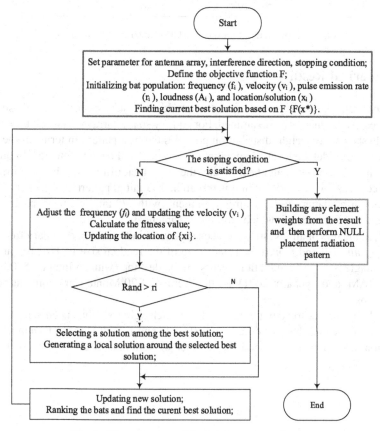

Fig. 3. Flow diagram of the BA-based beamformer

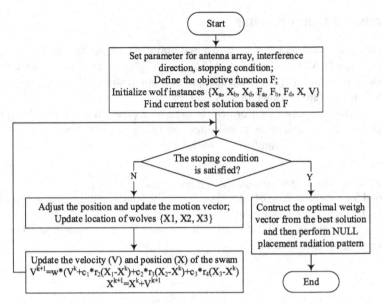

Fig. 4. Flow diagram of the HPSOGWO-based beamformer

5 Numerical Results

To demonstrate the variety and capability of sidelobe suppression and null steering techniques, five scenarios are examined. For equally spaced arrays, it is well known that the Chebyshev array weight distribution provides the best pattern in terms of the trade off between the sidelobe level and the main lobe's first-null beamwidth [15]. In order to manage the sidelobe level and beamwidth, the array factor of the Chebyshev array has been selected as the desired one in this research. The initial pattern has been a -30 dB Chebyshev array pattern for 20 isotropic elements with $\lambda/2$ inter-element spacing, with the exception of scenario 5, which employs 40 antennas.

The parameters of all investigation scenarios were initialized as boundary frequency values: $f\_min = 0$ and $f\_max = 1$; step size of the random size is 0.01; the jump of the theta angle is $1°$; All simulation results run on desktop (with an Intel i5–5300 CPU, 8GB of RAM, and Pycharm 2021) are the average of 20 Monte Carlo simulations for all scenarios.

Initial parameters for the algorithm: The search value x(i) has been set as: (i) the amplitude of the weights is limited from 0 to 1, and (ii) all stages of weight are 0; population size (pop) is 150; and the number of iterations is 20 except for the first scenario in Sect. 5.1.

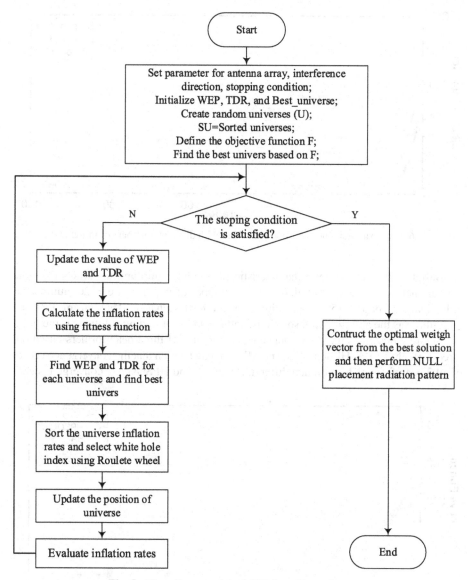

Fig. 5. Flow diagram of the MVO-based beamformer

5.1 Convergence Characteristic

In the first scenario, the convergence speed of the beamformer based on the proposed BA was studied. In order to do that, the −30 dB Chebyshev array pattern, the intended optimization pattern, was obtained by applying these beamformers. Furthermore, there are 100 repetitions and a random beginning bat population generation. In Fig. 6, their convergence rate is shown. It is evident that the BA-based beamformer with more bats has a faster rate of convergence.

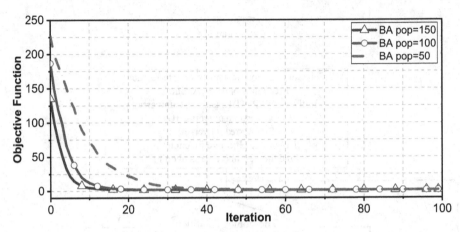

Fig. 6. Compare the objective function of BA with different numbers of individuals.

Based on the convergence characteristics of the bat algorithm, the article chooses the parameters for the BA bat algorithm as: number of iterations ite $= 20$, number of individual bats pop $= 150$ to investigate for the next scenarios. They ensure that the algorithm has the ability to find solutions, and the speed of finding solutions is the best.

Figure 7 describes the convergence characteristics of three beamformers based on three algorithms: BA, HPSOGWO, and MVO. It can be seen that the convergence speed of all 3 beamformers is not much different, with BA and HPSOGWO converge faster.

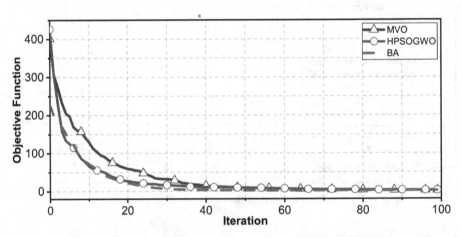

Fig. 7. Objective function comparisons of BA, HPSOGWO and MVO

5.2 Single Null

The second scenario illustrates the improved patterns with a single null. This null is arbitrary and set at any angle; in this test scenario, it is selected at the peak of the second sidelobe (14^0). Initialized with -30 dB Chebyshev array weights, the population. The majority of the properties of the original Chebyshev sample, such as almost half the power beam width (HPBW = 6.6^0) and the sidelobe level being nearly -30 dB, with the exception of the first sidelobe level, are maintained by the suggested beamformer-optimized sample, as shown in Fig. 8.

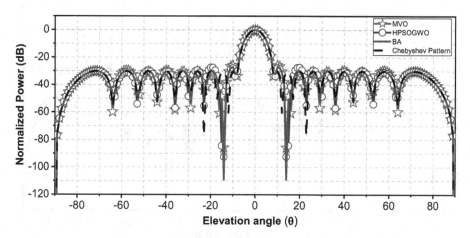

Fig. 8. Optimized pattern with a single null at $14°$

Figure 8 presents optimized patterns with single null obtained by BA, HPSOGWO and MVO. It indicates that the single null-pattern optimized by the BA is better than that of the HPSOGWO and MVO in terms of NDL at the desired null point. They are presented in detail in the following table:

	BA	HPSOGWO	MVO
Max SideLope	-27dB	-27.8dB	-25.8dB
Null Depth Level	-109dB	-92.5dB	-85.8dB

5.3 Multiple Null

Figure 9 shows the optimal patterns imposed in the third case with multiple nulls set at 14^0, 26^0, and 33^0. It is evident that the optimized pattern's nulls were precisely located in the designated direction. The BA pattern shows advantages over the HPSOGWO and MVO patterns in terms of NDL and SLL.

		BA	HPSOGWO	MVO
Max SideLope		-19.9dB	-14.3dB	-13.5dB
Null Depth Level	14^0	-85.8dB	-79.8dB	-63.4dB

(continued)

(*continued*)

		BA	HPSOGWO	MVO
	26^0	−72.7dB	−71.5dB	−89.5dB
	33^0	−74.5dB	−58.2dB	−64.7dB

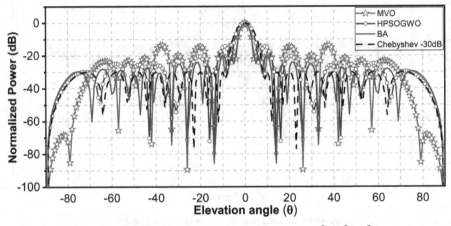

Fig. 9. Optimized pattern with a multiple null at 14^0, 26^0, 33^0.

5.4 A Broad Null

In interference suppression applications, a broad null is necessary if the directions of undesirable interferences' arrival vary significantly over time or are not precisely known, or if a null is continually guided to achieve the desired signal-to-noise ratio. In the fourth scenario, the pattern has an imposed broad null to show the capability of broad interference suppression $[20^0, 40^0]$. In terms of NDL and SLL, the BA pattern performs better than the HPSOGWO and MVO patterns. It is evident that a broad null on the BA pattern at the target broad has been obtained, with a minimum NDL of < -8.5 dB and a maximum NDL of -105 dB. There are no appreciable changes to the BA beamwidth, and the maximum SLL is -13.2 dB. Meanwhile, the NDL of MVO beamwidth is -68.5dB and that of HPSOGWO beamwidth is -75.5 dB but the SLL of them are -15.6 dB and -14 dB (Fig. 10).

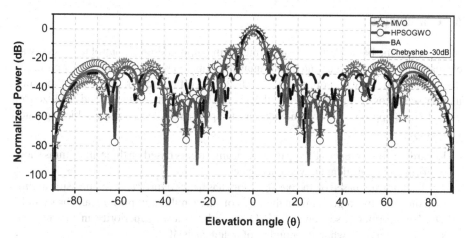

Fig. 10. Optimized pattern with a broad null from 20^0 to 40^0.

5.5 Change the Number of Antennas

In fact, changing the number of antennas can be done to achieve a number of different goals: increase service capacity, expand coverage, improve signal quality, etc. Figure 11 illustrates the optimized partern of all three algorithms when changing the number of antenna elements from 20 to 40. With a single null at 14^0, it is easy to see that in this case, the null suppression ability of the MVO algorithm (NDL = 121.9 dB) is much better than the other 2 algorithms ($NDL_{HPSOGWO} = -108.2$ dB and $NDL_{BA} = -97.7$ dB) while still ensuring SLL at < -28.3 dB.

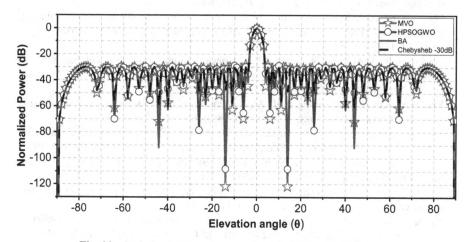

Fig. 11. Optimized pattern for a single null at $14°$ with 40 antennas

6 Conclusion

In this study, the bat algorithm beamformer with amplitude-only control technique was evaluated for its advantages and disadvantages compared with the multi-verse optimizer, the hybrid particle swarm optimizer, and the grey wolf optimizer. Through all the simulation scenarios mentioned above, the results have been evaluated and analyzed in detail to have appropriate recommendations to apply in each scenario to achieve greater efficiency.

- Regarding convergence ability, all three beamformers based on three algorithms show uniform and equivalent convergence speeds.
- The beamformer based on the bat algorithm has better interference suppression ability than the other two algorithms in the cases of single null, multiple null, and broad null.
- The beamformer based on the MVO algorithm shows superiority in interference suppression ability when the number of antennas is 40.
- The biggest advantage of the nature-inspired beamformers is their ability to adaptively suppress interference without losing the mainlobe.

References

1. Van Trees, H.L.: Optimum Array Processing: Part IV of Detection, Estimation, and Modulation Theory. John Wiley & Sons, Hoboken (2002)
2. Yeniay, Ö.: Penalty function methods for constrained optimization with genetic algorithms. Math. Comput. Appl. **10**(1), 45–56 (2005)
3. Yang, X.S.: Nature-Inspired Optimization Algorithms. Academic Press, Cambridge (2020)
4. Guney, K., Onay, M.: Amplitude-only pattern nulling of linear antenna arrays with the use of bees algorithm. Prog. Electromagn. Res. **70**, 21–36 (2007)
5. Mahto, S. K., et al.: Synthesizing broad null in linear array by amplitude-only control using wind driven optimization technique. In:2015 SAI Intelligent Systems Conference (IntelliSys), pp. 68-71. IEEE (2015)
6. Van Luyen, T., Van Cuong, N., Giang, T.V.B.: Convex optimization-based sidelobe control for planar arrays. In: 2023 IEEE Statistical Signal Processing Workshop (SSP), Hanoi, Vietnam, pp. 304-308 (2023)
7. Kha, H.M., Luyen, T.V., Cuong, N.V.: An efficient beamformer for interference suppression using rectangular antenna arrays. J. Commun. **18**(2), 116–122 (2023)
8. Tong, L., Nguyen, C., Le, D.: An Effective Beamformer for Interference Mitigation. In: Anh, N.L., Koh, S.J., Nguyen, T.D.L., Lloret, J., Nguyen, T.T. (eds.) Intelligent Systems and Networks. Lecture Notes in Networks and Systems, vol. 471, pp. 630–639. Springer, Singapore (2022). https://doi.org/10.1007/978-981-19-3394-3_73
9. Luyen, T.V., et al.: An efficient ULA pattern nulling approach in the presence of unknown interference. J. Electromagn. Waves Appl., 1–18 (2021)
10. Hoang, K. M., Van Tong, L., Van Nguyen, C.: A null synthesis technique-based beamformer for uniform rectangular arrays. In: 2022 International Conference on Advanced Technologies for Communications (ATC), pp. 13-17 (2022)
11. Yang, X.S.: A New Metaheuristic Bat-Inspired Algorithm. In: González, J.R., Pelta, D.A., Cruz, C., Terrazas, G., Krasnogor, N. (eds.) Nature Inspired Cooperative Strategies for Optimization (NICSO 2010). Studies in Computational Intelligence, vol. 284, pp. 65–74. Springer, Berlin (2010). https://doi.org/10.1007/978-3-642-12538-6_6

12. Singh, N., et al.: Hybrid algorithm of particle swarm optimization and grey wolf optimizer for improving convergence performance. J. Appl. Math. **2017** (2017)

13. Mirjalili, S., Mirjalili, S.M., Hatamlou, A.: Multi-verse optimizer: a nature-inspired algorithm for global optimization. Neural Comput. Appl. **27**, 495–513 (2016)

14. Thuc, K.X., Kha, H.M., Cuong, N.V., Luyen, T.V.: A metaheuristics-based hyperparameter optimization approach to beamforming design. IEEE Access **11**, 52250–52259 (2023)

15. Dolph, C.L.: A current distribution for broadside arrays which optimizes the relationship between beam width and side-lobe level. Proc. IRE **34**(6), 335–348 (1946)

16. Yang, X.-S.: Nature-Inspired Metaheuristic Algorithms. Luniver Press, Bristol (2010)

17. Yang, X.S.: Nature-inspired optimization algorithms: challenges and open problems. J. Comput. Sci. **46**, 101104 (2020)

18. Yang, X.S. (ed.): Nature-Inspired Algorithms and Applied Optimization, vol. 744. Springer, Cham (2018)

19. Fister Jr, I., et al.: A brief review of nature-inspired algorithms for optimization. arXiv preprint: arXiv:1307.4186 (2013)

20. Bolaji, A.L., Al-Betar, M.A., Awadallah, M.A., Khader, A.T., Abualigah, L.M.: A comprehensive review: krill herd algorithm (KH) and its applications. Appl. Soft Comput. **49**, 437–446 (2016)

21. Han, K.-H., Kim, J.-H.: Quantum-inspired evolutionary algorithm for a class of combinatorial optimization. IEEE Trans. Evolut. Comput. **6**, 580–593 (2002)

22. Abualigah, L., Diabat, A.: A novel hybrid Antlion optimization algorithm for multi-objective task scheduling problems in cloud computing environments. Cluster Comput., 1–19 (2020)

Investigation of Transmit Antenna Selection for MU-VASM Systems over Correlated Channels

Kieu Xuan Thuc[1], Tran Viet Vinh[2], Phu Liem Nguyen[3], Tong Van Luyen[1], Hoang Manh Kha[1], and Nguyen Thu Phuong[2(✉)] (iD)

[1] Hanoi University of Industry, No. 298, Cau Dien Street, Ha Noi, Viet Nam
{thuckx,luyentv,khahm}@haui.edu.vn
[2] Advanced Wireless Communications Group, Le Quy Don Technical University, No. 236, Hoang Quoc Viet, Ha Noi, Viet Nam
{tranvietvinhsqtt,phuong.nt}@lqdtu.edu.vn
[3] Le Quy Don Technical University, No. 236, Hoang Quoc Viet, Ha Noi, Viet Nam

Abstract. In a variable active antenna spatial modulation (VASM) system, the number of activated antennas adjusts dynamically according to the input spatial bitstream. Thus, it is a typical variation of spatial modulation techniques, known for its high flexibility and outstanding spectral efficiency. In this paper, the operation of the multi-user (MU) VASM system is investigated under correlated channel conditions. Furthermore, three transmit antenna selection (TAS) methods, including channel gain-based TAS (CG-TAS), Euclidean distance-based TAS (ED-TAS), and hierarchical combination-based TAS (HC-TAS), are applied to enhance the quality of the MU-VASM system. The effect of the correlated channel on the bit error rate (BER) performance of every user as well as the average BER (ABER) performance of the whole system is investigated for three TAS methods. The simulation results indicate that correlated channels degrade the system's performance. Nevertheless, the application of these TAS methods has noticeably improved the system's quality. In particular, HC-TAS with low computational complexity consistently delivers superior ABER improvement for the system compared to other TAS methods, even in scenarios with correlated channels.

Keywords: Transmit antenna selection · Variable active antenna spatial modulation · Correlated channel

1 Introduction

In the present day, telecommunications systems are increasingly developing, with increasing requirements for speed and transmission quality. In this context, multiple input multiple output (MIMO) systems [1,2], a combination of precoding and equalizer technologies [3,4], a non-orthogonal multiple access scheme [5,6], a radio frequency energy harvesting techniques [7,8] and multiple hops systems

N. Thi Dieu Linh et al. (Eds.): ADHOCNETS 2023, LNICST 558, pp. 112–124, 2024.
https://doi.org/10.1007/978-3-031-55993-8_9

[9,10] stand out as potent solutions for fifth-generation (5G) and beyond networks. However, the aforementioned systems and technologies utilize multiple radio frequency chains at the same time, leading to increased costs and requiring synchronization between antennas as well as inter-channel interference. To address these problems, the idea of using spatial modulation (SM) techniques in MIMO systems was first proposed in [11] and quickly became a prominent research trend in recent years [12].

The basic principle of the SM technique is to employ the index of only one activated antenna to carry additional bits of information in addition to the traditional amplitude and phase modulation (APM) symbols [11]. This approach aims to significantly increase spectral efficiency, reduce multi-antenna interference, and save on costs caused by RF chains. With such outstanding advantages, SM has been expanded into many different fields, and various variations of SM have been proposed to further improve the quality of this technique [12]. Among them, variable active antenna spatial modulation (VASM) emerges as a typical variant [13].

VASM operates on the principle of spatial modulation, that is, transmits information using both the APM symbol and the activated transmit antenna (TA) index. In contrast to SM, where a combination of some spatial bits represents the index of an activated TA, in VASM, each spatial bit represents the on/off state of a TA. Specifically, when the spatial bit is 1, the corresponding TA is activated, whereas if the spatial bit is 0, the corresponding TA is deactivated. This way, VASM activates from 1 to almost all of the system's antennas to carry additional information. It thus attains higher spectral efficiency when compared to SM and its renowned extensions, like generalized SM (GSM) [14] and quadrature SM (QSM) [15]. Additionally, VASM offers much greater flexibility than SM because it allows operation with an optional number of TAs instead of having to be a power of two like SM.

For systems operating on the SM principle in general and VASM in particular, the activated antennas are both a means of transmitting signals, but at the same time, their indices also carry a part of the information. For this reason, employing the VASM technique in MIMO systems requires careful transmit antenna selection (TAS) because it greatly affects the quality of the system [16].

The TAS algorithms for the downlink multi-user (MU) VASM system have been investigated in [17]. In this work, the authors proposed applying conventional antenna selection algorithms commonly used in SM systems, specifically channel gain-based TAS (CG-TAS) and Euclidean distance-based TAS (ED-TAS) [18,19], to the MU-VASM system. They also introduced a low-complexity but highly effective algorithm called hierarchical combination-based TAS (HC-TAS) to enhance the bit error rate (BER) performance of this system. However, it's important to note that this research is limited to the assumption of a completely uncorrelated transmission channel.

In another aspect, MIMO systems employ antenna arrays at both the transmitter and receiver can significantly enhance spectral efficiency and system performance. Nonetheless, spatial constraints often restrict scattering, resulting in a correlated channel, commonly referred to as spatial correlation [20].

The presence of correlation reduces the reliability of spatial bit detection [21]. Because of spatial correlation, it becomes challenging to differentiate between the channels connecting various transmit and receive antennas. Consequently, in such situations, uncertainties arise during the detection of spatial bits, which are utilized to choose active antennas. This, in turn, leads to a significant increase in BER. Previous studies [22] and [23] have evaluated the performance of SM and GSM under correlated Rayleigh and Rician channel conditions. The results show that the performance experiences a significant degradation as the correlation increases.

Inspired by these studies, this paper investigates the impact of spatial correlation on the performance of the downlink MU-VASM system. This work also evaluates the effectiveness of TAS algorithms in improving BER performance for the system in correlated channel scenarios.

The remaining sections of the paper are organized as follows: Sect. 2 provides an explanation of the system model for the MU-VASM transceiver over correlated channels. In Sect. 3, various TAS schemes for the MU-VASM system are presented. Section 4 contains the presentation of Monte Carlo simulation results and discussion. Finally, Sect. 5 concludes the paper.

Notations: Lowercase italic letters, lowercase bold letters, and uppercase bold letters represent variables, vectors, and matrices, respectively. $\mathbf{W} \in \mathbb{C}^{M \times N}$ denotes the size of the matrix $\mathbf{W}$, with M rows and N columns. $||.||$ and $||.||_F^2$ correspondingly describe the operations for calculating the norm and Frobenius norm of a vector or matrix. $(.)^T$ is the transpose operation of a vector or matrix. C_a^b is the symbol for the combination of b elements out of a total of a elements. $(.)^*$ denotes complex conjugate.

2   System Model Description

A typical downlink MU-VASM system model is depicted in Fig. 1 [17]. Equipped with a total of N_{total} TAs, the base station (BS) transmits K data bitstreams to K mobile users. Each data bitstreams is modulated utilising the VASM technique and emitted over a cluster consisting of N_t TAs. Precoders $\mathbf{W}_k$ are employed to mitigate multi-user interference. Each terminal user is equipped with N_r receiving antennas (RAs). We impose the constraint that, in this system, each TA is designated to transmit signals to only one user without being reused for transmitting multiple distinct signal streams, leading to the condition $N_{\text{total}} \geq KN_t$.

Prior to initiating the data transmission process, users send channel state information (CSI) back to the BS. Using the gathered CSI, the BS picks a subset of N_t TAs to perform signal modulation using VASM principle. Subsequently, these selected TAs are employed for transmission the signals to the users. Assuming that the transmission channel belongs to the slowly varying flat-fading Rayleigh and spatially correlated channel category, the channel state from the BS to the users remains stable within a certain duration of signal transmission. When channel conditions change, the antenna selection process is reinitiated from the beginning.

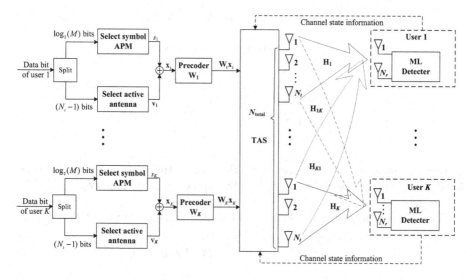

Fig. 1. Downlink MU-VASM system model

Without diminishing generality, we focus exclusively on the signal processing procedure for transmitting data bit streams from the BS to the k-th user's terminal device in this system, $1 \leq k \leq K$.

Firstly, we delve into the process of modulating the data bit sequence of the user k using the VASM technique. Specifically, within each signaling cycle, a sequence comprising $b = b_1 + b_2$ data bits is fed into the VASM mapping. In particular, $b_1 = \log_2(M)$ symbol bits are utilized for selecting an M-APM signal symbol. $b_2 = N_t - 1$ remaining spatial bits are employed for choosing the spatial vector $\mathbf{v}_k$, where non-zero positions correspond to activated antennas. The VASM signal vector, denoted as $\mathbf{x}_k$, is formed by mapping the symbol s_k into the spatial vector $\mathbf{v}_k$. Note that both the vector $\mathbf{x}_k$ and its elements must be normalized to ensure the transmit power constraint conditions, specifically, $E(\mathbf{x}_k{}^H \mathbf{x}_k) = 1$ and $x_k^i = 1/\sqrt{N_a}$, where $i \in [1; N_t - 1]$ and N_a is the number of activated TAs in a subset of TAs.

It should be noted that for the VASM technique, each element in the spatial bits b_2 corresponds to a state of one TA, meaning that if the bit is 1, the TA is activated; conversely, if the bit is 0, the TA is in a sleep mode. Notably, in the scenario where all bits of b_2 are zero, the last antenna in the antenna array is exclusively designated for transmitting the signal symbol. Under this operational principle, the quantity of activated TAs in the VASM may range from 1 to $N_t - 1$ TAs. As a result, the spectral efficiency achieved by VASM is $\log_2(M) + N_t - 1$ bit per channel user, which is significantly higher than that of other variants of SM [17]. The interrelation among spatial bits, spatial vector, and transmitted signal vector is elucidated in Table 1 below, where $N_t = 3$, i.e., $b_2 = 2$ bits.

At the transmitter, once N_t TAs are chosen and their indices used to modulate the signal using the VASM principle, the modulated signal is transmitted

Table 1. Antenna activation rule in the VASM technique with $N_t = 3$

Spatial bit b_2	Spatial vector $\mathbf{v}_k$	Transmit signal vector $\mathbf{x}_k$
00	$[0, 0, 1]^T$	$[0, 0, s_k]^T$
10	$[1, 0, 0]^T$	$[s_k, 0, 0]^T$
01	$[0, 1, 0]^T$	$[0, s_k, 0]^T$
11	$[1, 1, 0]^T$	$\frac{1}{\sqrt{2}}[s_k, s_k, 0]^T$

through these selected antennas. Note that, prior to transmission, the modulated signal vector has been multiplied by a precoding matrix, $\mathbf{W}_k \in \mathbb{C}^{N_t \times N_t}$, to mitigate multi-user interference, i.e., $\mathbf{W}_k\mathbf{x}_k$.

The received signal at the k-th terminal user is represented as follows:

$$\mathbf{y}_k = \mathbf{H}_k\mathbf{W}_k\mathbf{x}_k + \sum_{j=1, j \neq k}^{K} \mathbf{H}_{jk}\mathbf{W}_j\mathbf{x}_j + \mathbf{n}_i. \tag{1}$$

wherein $\mathbf{H}_k$ and $\mathbf{H}_{jk}$ are $N_r \times N_t$-sized matrices, representing the channels from the N_t selected TAs for users k and j at the BS to the N_r RAs at the terminal user k, respectively. $\mathbf{W}_k$ and $\mathbf{W}_j$ are precoder matrices, which are designed such that $\mathbf{H}_{jk}\mathbf{W}_j\mathbf{x}_j = 0$, if $j \neq k$, in order to eliminate multi-user interference. $\mathbf{n}_k$ represents the $N_r \times 1$ vector of independently and identically distributed (i.i.d.) $\mathcal{CN}(0, \sigma^2)$ additive white Gaussian noise.

In our MU-VASM system, we employ the well-established Kronecker [24] model to describe spatially correlated Rayleigh fading channel, which for the k-th user can be expressed as follows:

$$\mathbf{H}_k = \mathbf{L}_{r,k}^{1/2}\hat{\mathbf{H}}_k\mathbf{L}_{t,k}^{1/2}, \tag{2}$$

where $\hat{\mathbf{H}}_k \in \mathbb{C}^{N_r \times N_t}$ is a matrix with i.i.d. Gaussian entries having a zero mean and unit variance. $\mathbf{L}_{r,k}$ and $\mathbf{L}_{t,k}$ represent $N_r \times N_r$ receive and $N_t \times N_t$ transmit spatial correlation matrices of k-th user, respectively. The elements of $\mathbf{L}_{r,k}$ and $\mathbf{L}_{t,k}$ are given by [25]

$$l_{mn} = \begin{cases} l^{n-m}, & m \leq n \\ l_{nm}^*, & m > n \end{cases}, \quad |l| \leq 1, \tag{3}$$

where l is the correlation coefficient that characterizes the spatial correlation between the channel elements.

Due to $\mathbf{H}_{jk}\mathbf{W}_j\mathbf{x}_j = 0$, if $j \neq k$, the received signal at terminal user k can be expressed as follows:

$$\mathbf{y}_k = \mathbf{H}_k\mathbf{W}_k\mathbf{x}_k + \mathbf{n}_k. \tag{4}$$

Assuming that users have full CSI, both the conventional symbol s_k and the spatial vector $\mathbf{v}_k$ are jointly detected through an ML optimization problem that can be represented as follows:

$$\hat{\mathbf{x}}_k = [\hat{s}_k, \hat{\mathbf{v}}_k] = \arg\min_{s \in S, v \in \mathbf{V}} \|\mathbf{y}_k - \mathbf{H}_k\mathbf{W}_k\mathbf{x}_k\|_F^2. \tag{5}$$

3   Transmit Antenna Selection

TAS in the MU-VASM system is defined as the problem of selecting subsets of N_t TAs from the total number of N_{total} TAs in the BS to transmit each data stream independently to each user. This is aimed at improving the BER performance for each user and the average BER (ABER) performance for the system as a whole. In this section, the paper explores how TAS methods, including channel gain (CG) criteria, Euclidean distance (ED) criteria, and the hierarchical combination (HC) of CG and ED criteria, perform in the MU-VASM system under Rayleigh fading-correlated channel conditions. Without loss of generality, we consider the process of selecting N_t TAs at the BS to transmit data to the user k. Assuming the antennas are only used to transmit data to one user, that is, after a TA is selected to transmit data to a user, it is dropped from the antenna set to choice for the subsequent user. Thus the total number of antennas selected for the user k is $N_{\text{total}} - (k-1)N_t$ TAs.

3.1   Channel Gain Criteria

The MIMO channel from a total of $N_{\text{total}} - (k-1)N_t$ TAs located at the BS to N_r RAs at the k-th user is characterized as $\mathbf{H}_k^{\text{total}} \in \mathbb{C}^{N_r \times [N_{\text{total}} - (k-1)N_t]}$. Utilizing the CG criteria, the magnitudes of the column vectors within the $\mathbf{H}_k^{\text{total}}$ are quantified and subsequently arranged in descending order:

$$\underbrace{||\mathbf{h}_k^1||^2 \geq ||\mathbf{h}_k^2||^2 \geq \dots \geq ||\mathbf{h}_k^{N_t}||^2}_{N_t \text{ selected elements}} \geq \dots \geq ||\mathbf{h}_k^{N_{\text{total}} - (k-1)N_t}||^2. \qquad (6)$$

The N_t column vectors with the largest gain are chosen to form the transmission channel matrix from the BS to the k-th terminal user, which corresponds to the N_t selected TAs for signal modulation and delivery to user k.

In this approach, TAS relies solely on channel characteristics, making it simple and straightforward to implement. However, it does not yield a significant improvement in BER performance for the system.

3.2   Euclidean Distance Criteria

The ED criterion is an antenna selection algorithm in which a combination of TAs, $A_k^{\text{opt}} \in \mathcal{A}$, is selected to maximize the minimum Euclidean distance between all signal vectors as follows:

$$A_k^{\text{opt}} = \arg \max_{A_k \in \mathcal{A}} \{ \min_{\mathbf{x}_i \neq \mathbf{x}_j \in \mathbf{X}} ||\mathbf{H}_{A_k}(\mathbf{x}_i - \mathbf{x}_j)||_F^2 \}, \qquad (7)$$

where $\mathcal{A} = \{A_1, A_2, ..., A_c\}$, $c = C_{N_{\text{total}} - (k-1)N_t}^{N_t}$, is the set containing all possible combinations of TAs selecting N_t elements from $N_{\text{total}} - (k-1)N_t$ elements.

It can be seen that the ED criterion will be tested with all possible combinations of TAs, i.e., $C_{N_{\text{total}} - (k-1)N_t}^{N_t}$ combinations, to find the combination of TAs that satisfies 7. Obviously, an exhaustive search over all available combinations of TAs will optimize the system's performance, but on the contrary, it requires a huge amount of computation.

3.3　Hierarchical Combination Criteria

The HC criteria, proposed in [17], aims to achieve a balance between improving BER performance and reducing the computational burden of the system. In this approach, CG-TAS initially selects N_s temporary TAs, $N_t < N_s \ll N_{\text{total}}$, satisfying (6), followed by ED-TAS, which chooses N_t from the N_s selected by CG-TAS, satisfying (7).

HC-TAS performs a two-step sequential combination of CG-TAS and ED-TAS. This approach significantly reduces computational complexity while ensuring a high level of effectiveness in improving the BER performance of the system.

4　Simulation Results and Discussion

In this section, we simulate the MU-VASM system with the system configuration as follows: $N_{\text{total}} = 10$, $N_t = 3$, $K = 3$, $N_r = 4$, and QPSK modulation ($M = 4$). In the case of using HC-TAS, $N_s = 4$. In a sequential manner, TAS is conducted in the order of user 1, user 2, and user 3. No-TAS is the case where antennas are not selected but assigned randomly to users. The ABER performance is calculated as the average of the BER performance of the entirety of system users. Assume that the noise power at the users is the same, i.e., $\sigma_1^2 = \sigma_2^2 = ... = \sigma_K^2$.

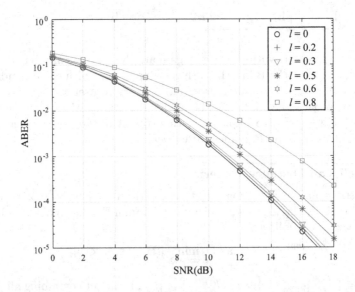

Fig. 2. ABER vs. signal-to-noise ratio (SNR) of the MU-VASM system with different channel correlation coefficients and without TAS

At the beginning, we study how the MU-VASM system works in correlated channel conditions. We vary the correlation coefficients and don't use antenna selection algorithms. Instead, TAs are randomly assigned to each user. The simulation results are depicted in Fig. 2. It is evident that as the correlation coefficient increases, the system's ABER performance deteriorates. This underscores the pronounced influence of channel correlation on the system's quality.

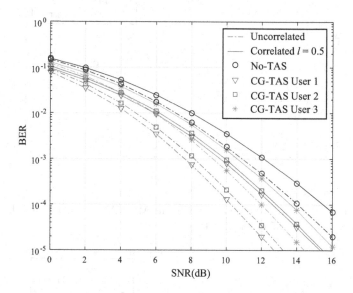

Fig. 3. BER vs. SNR for individual users in the MU-VASM system with channel correlation coefficient $l = 0.5$ employing CG-TAS

Subsequently, we selected a correlation coefficient of $l = 0.5$ due to its common usage to assess the potential enhancement in BER performance for the antenna selection methods CG-TAS, ED-TAS, and HC-TAS in the MU-VASM system. The BER performance of each user using these TAS methods is shown correspondingly in Fig. 3, 4, and 5. A common feature in these results is that users granted priority to select antennas initially attain superior BER performance compared to those who come after. More specifically, in this scenario, the BER performance decreases sequentially for user 1, user 2, and user 3.

Notably, with a relatively high channel correlation coefficient, i.e., $l = 0.5$, the BER quality of each user is significantly degraded compared to the uncorrelated channel scenario. However, thanks to the use of TAS methods, all users in the system achieve better BER performance than in the case of uncorrelated channels and without antenna selection. This confirms the role of TAS in enhancing the system's quality.

Figure 3 clearly illustrates that, when CG-TAS is employed under the influence of correlated channels, all three users (referred to as Users 1, 2, and 3) within the system achieve worse BER performance compared to all users in the case of uncorrelated channels. In addition, in the context of correlated channels, the disparity in BER performance among system users appears less pronounced when

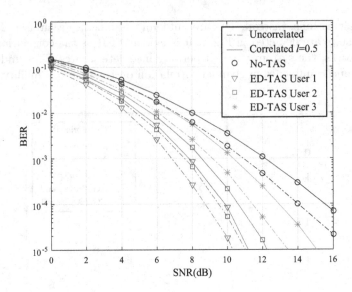

Fig. 4. BER vs. SNR for individual users in the MU-VASM system with channel correlation coefficient $l = 0.5$ employing ED-TAS

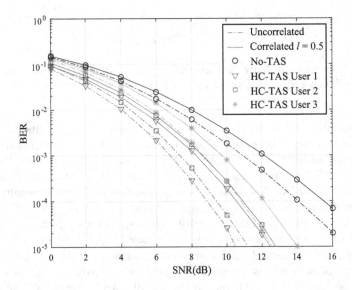

Fig. 5. BER vs. SNR for individual users in the MU-VASM system with channel correlation coefficient $l = 0.5$ employing HC-TAS

compared to the case of uncorrelated channels. This observation suggests that CG-TAS operates less effectively in improving BER performance for the system under correlated channels. This phenomenon can be attributed to the fact that

CG-TAS solely relies on the channel gain of each transmission path for antenna selection, and the channel gain is notably sensitive to channel correlation.

Figures 4 and 5 clearly depict that the variations in BER performance among individual users are not substantially pronounced in both scenarios of uncorrelated and correlated channels when the system employs ED-TAS and HC-TAS. This underscores the remarkable effectiveness of ED-TAS and HC-TAS in enhancing BER performance for users, even in the presence of channel correlation. This can be attributed to the fact that both ED-TAS and HC-TAS utilize channel characteristics as well as transmitted signals for antenna selection, thereby mitigating the impact of channel correlation. It is worth noting that the performance difference in BER among individual users of HC-TAS is moderate, in contrast to the significant discrepancy observed among users of ED-TAS. This is the reason behind HC-TAS achieving better overall system performance (ABER) compared to ED-TAS when averaged. This observation is further illustrated in Fig. 6 below.

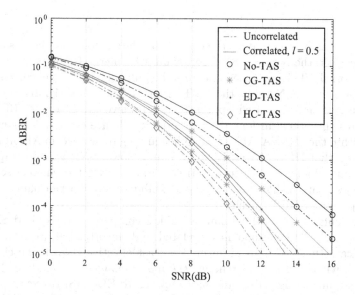

Fig. 6. Comparing ABER vs. SNR in the MU-VASM system using various TAS methods for both uncorrelated and correlated channels ($l = 0.5$)

In Fig. 6, we compare the extent of ABER performance improvement for the entire MU-VASM system utilising different TAS methods over uncorrelated channels and correlated channels ($l = 0.5$). The results show that, with the same channel correlation coefficient, all TAS algorithms achieve superior ABER performance compared to the No-TAS case. Even in the presence of channel correlation, using TAS still results in better system performance compared to the scenario of uncorrelated channels and without employing TAS. This result emphasizes the effectiveness of using TAS methods to improve the ABER performance of the system.

In a more specific analysis, we compare the required SNR (dB) to achieve ABER $= 10^{-4}$ among TAS methods in the MU-VASM system over uncorrelated and correlated channels. The results are presented in Table 2. It is implied that the lower the required SNR, the better the TAS method.

Table 2. Comparing the required SNR (dB) to achieve ABER $= 10^{-4}$ among TAS methods in the MU-VASM system over uncorrelated and correlated channels

TAS method	Uncorrelated (dB)	Correlated (dB)	SNR Difference (dB)
HC-TAS	10.10	11.41	1.31
ED-TAS	10.56	11.85	1.29
CG-TAS	11.22	13.06	1.84
No-TAS	14.00	15.45	1.45

It can be easily seen that, in the case of correlated channels, there is a noticeable increase in the required SNR across all TAS methods compared to uncorrelated channels. This increase highlights the influence of channel correlation on system performance. Notably, the No-TAS method demands significantly higher SNR values than TAS-based approaches to achieve an ABER of 10^{-4}. This underscores the potential for TAS methods to enhance communication performance within the MU-VASM system. When aiming to achieve an ABER of 10^{-4}, it is evident that HC-TAS and ED-TAS require lower SNR values compared to CG-TAS and No-TAS, both in uncorrelated and correlated channel scenarios. This implies that HC-TAS and ED-TAS exhibit superior performance in meeting the specified ABER threshold.

In particular, the third column in Table 2 compares the required SNR distances for each TAS method in correlated and uncorrelated scenarios. These data indicate that CG-TAS performs the least effectively when the channel is correlated, whereas ED-TAS remains the most reliable TAS method. HC-TAS experiences only a slight degradation compared to ED-TAS. However, HC-TAS still achieves better overall system ABER performance improvement than ED-TAS. It should be noted that HC-TAS has much lower complexity than ED-TAS. This demonstrates the superiority of HC-TAS as a simple yet highly effective antenna selection method for enhancing system ABER performance. This observation has been validated in [17], and it remains consistent even in the presence of correlated channel conditions.

5   Conclusion

In this paper, we have investigated the MU-VASM system in a correlated channel environment. Simulation results have demonstrated that as the channel correlation coefficient increases, the BER (or ABER) performance of the system deteriorates. Furthermore, the paper explored the application of well-known TAS algorithms, specifically CG-TAS, ED-TAS, and HC-TAS, to enhance the system's performance. Simulation results have clearly shown that, despite the detrimental impact of channel correlation on the BER (or ABER) performance, the employment of TAS methods has significantly improved the system's quality. In fact, even when channel correlation is present, the utilization of TAS continues to yield improved system performance compared to the scenario of uncorrelated channels without TAS implementation. ED-TAS and HC-TAS perform well even in correlated channels, with HC-TAS continuing to demonstrate superiority in enhancing ABER performance for the system.

References

1. Huong, T.T.T., Hiep, P.T.: Joint precoder and decoder for MIMO dual-hop relay systems in delay spread channels. Wireless Pers. Commun. **124**(2), 1247–1261 (2022)
2. Doanh, B.Q., Quan, D.T., Hieu, T.C., Hiep, P.T.: Combining designs of precoder and equalizer for MIMO FBMC-OQAM systems based on power allocation strategies. AEU-Int. J. Electron. C. **130**, 153572 (2021)
3. Phuong, N.T., Son, V.V., Hiep, P.T.: Combining precoding and equalization for interference cancellation in MU-MIMO systems with high density users. EURASIP J. Wirel. Commun. Netw. **2022**(1), 34 (2022)
4. Doanh, B.Q., Quan, D.T., Hiep, P.T., Hieu, T.C.: A combining design of precoder and equalizer based on shared redundancy to improve performance of ISI MIMO systems. Wireless Netw. **25**(5), 2741–2750 (2019)
5. Chi Hieu, T., Le Cuong, N., Manh Hoang, T., Thanh Quan, D., Thanh Hiep, P.: On outage probability and ergodic rate of downlink multi-user relay systems with combination of NOMA, SWIPT, and beamforming. Sensors **20**(17), 4737 (2020)
6. Cuong, N.L., Hoang, T.M., Phuong, N.T., Hiep, P.T.: Analysis of secrecy outage performance for full duplex NOMA relay systems with appearance of multiple eavesdroppers. Wireless Netw. **28**(7), 3157–3172 (2022)
7. Van Son, V., Trieu Duong, D., Manh Hoang, T., Thanh Quan, D., Thanh Hiep, P.: Analysing outage probability of linear and non-linear RF energy harvesting of cooperative communication networks. IET Signal Proc. **14**(8), 541–550 (2020)
8. Hiep, P.T., Hoang, T.M.: Non-orthogonal multiple access and beamforming for relay network with RF energy harvesting. ICT Express **6**(1), 11–15 (2020)
9. Hiep, P.T., Ono, F., Kohno, R.: Optimizing distance, transmit power, and allocation time for reliable multi-hop relay system. EURASIP J. Wirel. Commun. Netw. **2012**(1), 153 (2012)
10. Hiep, P.T., Hoang, N.H., Chika, S., Ryuji, K.: End-to-end channel capacity of MAC-PHY cross-layer multiple-hop MIMO relay system with outdated CSI. EURASIP J. Wireless Commun. Netw. **2013**(1), 144 (2013)
11. Mesleh, R., Haas, H., Ahn, C.W., Yun, S.: Spatial modulation - a new low complexity spectral efficiency enhancing technique. In: 2006 First International Conference on Communications and Networking in China, pp. 1–5 (2006)
12. Wen, M., et al.: A survey on spatial modulation in emerging wireless systems: Research progresses and applications. IEEE J. Sel. Areas Commun. **37**(9), 1949–1972 (2019)

13. Vinh, T.V., Hiep, P.T., Phuong, N.T.: Combined variable active antenna spatial modulation and NOMA to enhance spectral efficiency for multiple users MIMO systems. In: 2022 International Conference on Advanced Technologies for Communications (ATC), pp. 29–34 (2022)

14. Younis, A., Serafimovski, N., Mesleh, R., Haas, H.: Generalised spatial modulation. In: 2010 Conference Record of the Forty Fourth Asilomar Conference on Signals, Systems and Computers, pp. 1498–1502 (2010)

15. Mesleh, R., Ikki, S.S., Aggoune, H.M.: Quadrature spatial modulation. IEEE Trans. Veh. Technol. **64**(6), 2738–2742 (2015)

16. Rajashekar, R., Hari, K., Hanzo, L.: Antenna selection in spatial modulation systems. IEEE Commun. Lett. **17**(3), 521–524 (2013)

17. Vinh, T.V., Minh, N.H., Hiep, P.T., Phuong, N.T.: Transmit antenna selection for multi-user VASM systems: simplicity and fairness. AEU-Int. J. Electron. C. **170**, 154842 (2023)

18. Rajashekar, R., Hari, K., Hanzo, L.: Transmit antenna subset selection for single and multiuser spatial modulation systems operating in frequency selective channels. IEEE Trans. Veh. Technol. **67**(7), 6156–6169 (2018)

19. Aydın, E.: EDAS/COAS based antenna selection for code index modulation aided spatial modulation. Electrica **19**(2), 113–119 (2019)

20. Björnson, E., Jorswieck, E., Ottersten, B.: Impact of spatial correlation and precoding design in OSTBC MIMO systems. IEEE Trans. Wireless Commun. **9**(11), 3578–3589 (2010)

21. Özkoç, M.F., Koca, M., Sari, H.: Spatial modulation with signature constellations for increased robustness to antenna and channel correlations. Phys. Commun. **39**, 100984 (2020)

22. Simha, G.G., Koila, S., Neha, N., Raghavendra, M., Sripati, U.: Redesigned spatial modulation for spatially correlated fading channels. Wireless Pers. Commun. **97**, 5003–5030 (2017)

23. Jaiswal, G., Gudla, V.V., Kumaravelu, V.B., Reddy, G.R., Murugadass, A.: Modified spatial modulation and low complexity signal vector based minimum mean square error detection for MIMO systems under spatially correlated channels. Wireless Pers. Commun. **110**, 999–1020 (2019)

24. Oestges, C.: Validity of the Kronecker model for MIMO correlated channels. In: 2006 IEEE 63rd Vehicular Technology Conference, vol. 6, pp. 2818–2822 (2006)

25. Loyka, S.: Channel capacity of MIMO architecture using the exponential correlation matrix. IEEE Commun. Lett. **5**(9), 369–371 (2001)

Millimeter Wave Path Loss Modeling for UAV Communications Using Deep Learning

Pham Thi Quynh Trang[1,2(✉)], Duong Thi Hang[1], Ha Xuan Son[2],
Dinh Trieu Duong[2], and Trinh Anh Vu[2]

[1] University of Industry, Hanoi, Vietnam
{pham.trang,hangdt}@haui.edu.vn
[2] VNU University of Engineering and Technology, Hanoi, Vietnam
{duongdt,vuta}@vnu.edu.vn

Abstract. Unmanned Aerial Vehicles (UAVs) and millimeter waves are pivotal technologies in the sixth-generation (6G) mobile communication systems. Effective path loss modeling for UAV-based millimeter wave communications is critical for rapid and accurate data transmission. Traditional methods, such as deterministic, empirical, and machine learning-based approaches, are commonly used. This paper presents a groundbreaking approach that harnesses the power of deep learning, specifically the Long Short-Term Memory (LSTM) algorithm, to predict path loss in UAV-based millimeter wave communications, with a particular focus on UAV-to-UAV scenarios. Our experimental results demonstrate the exceptional performance of our deep learning model, achieving a remarkable term root-mean-square error (RMSE) of only 1.98 dB when compared to measurement results in test scenarios. This remarkable outcome underscores the profound significance of employing deep learning methodologies in predicting path loss, surpassing the capabilities of traditional methods. By leveraging deep learning, we advance the field of UAV-based millimeter wave communication modeling, enabling more precise and efficient data transmission in 6G networks.

Keywords: UAV · Deep Learning · path loss · LSTM algorithm

1 Introduction

The fifth-generation (5G) technology brings with it the significant promise of delivering ultra-fast data rates, extremely low latency, and vastly improved spectral efficiency. In the future, the emergence of data-intensive applications and the expansive wireless network will necessitate the development of sixth-generation (6G) communication technology. Both in the current 5G networks and in the forthcoming 6G networks, millimeter-wave technologies will assume a crucial role in achieving the envisioned network performance and communication objectives [1]. Because of their extensive bandwidth and elevated carrier frequencies, mmWave communications exhibit reduced scattering effects and more pronounced blocking effects in non-line-of-sight (NLoS) paths [2].

© ICST Institute for Computer Sciences, Social Informatics and Telecommunications Engineering 2024
Published by Springer Nature Switzerland AG 2024. All Rights Reserved
N. Thi Dieu Linh et al. (Eds.): ADHOCNETS 2023, LNICST 558, pp. 125–134, 2024.
https://doi.org/10.1007/978-3-031-55993-8_10

In addition, unmanned aerial systems have significant promise as technological enablers for wireless communication. They offer a cost-effective and efficient solution for temporarily connecting ground users in situations where ground infrastructure is unavailable. Within this field, establishing a high-capacity backhaul network with interconnectivity between unmanned aerial vehicles (UAVs) is a large challenge. Besides their capacity enhancement roles, UAV-BSs can serve vital functions during emergency situations such as earthquakes, floods, and similar events, when fixed infrastructure is either entirely or partially compromised and non-operational. Nevertheless, despite the advantages it offers, UAV-assisted networking also presents specific design challenges. These include issues related to energy efficiency (EE), trajectory planning, positioning, resource management, privacy, and more [3].

When multiple UAVs depend on one another to transmit data in an aerial multi-hop manner, conventional sub-6 GHz technologies are inadequate for handling high-load traffic aggregation. Therefore, the millimeter wave (mmWave) spectrum emerges as a comprehensive solution for completely wireless nodes, providing unparalleled bandwidth [3]. Combining millimeter wave communications with UAV networks can respond to the high throughput demands of the majority of UAV applications. Implementing mmWave communications within UAV networks offers two primary advantages:

1) The wide coverage of mmWave technology significantly increases the capacity of UAV networks, effectively meeting the demand for rapid response capabilities.
2) Through the utilization of mmWave technology, the data traffic of UAV network can be significantly augmented, as mmWave communications excel in providing high throughput for short-range transmissions [4].

For designing and developing wireless communication systems, it is essential to have a transmission channel model that describes the transmission of radio waves using channel parameters. Path loss is one of the most fundamental characteristics among the channel parameters, as it describes the power reduction of a signal traveling between the transmission device (Tx) and receiving device (Rx) in a propagation channel. Precise modeling of path loss is of utmost importance during the deployment of a system as it directly influences the received power of the intended signal and the levels of interference from unwanted signals in wireless communication systems. These parameters are indispensable for assessing wireless coverage and conducting interference analysis [5]. There are three conventional approaches for modeling path loss: empirical methods, deterministic methods, and machine learning-based (ML-based) methods [6]. Modeling the path loss of mmWave communications is a complex task due to their heightened susceptibility to transmission environments. Consequently, path loss modeling for mmWave propagation assumes a critical role in the design and analysis of communication systems.

In this paper, a path loss model is suggested, which employs a deep learning approach using Long Short-Term Memory networks (LSTM) for 60 GHz mmWave communication in UAV-to-UAV scenarios. The proposed model attains a satisfactory level of performance when predicting path loss in test scenarios with a public dataset. Experimental results demonstrate that the proposed LSTM path loss model in this study surpasses conventional empirical methods in accuracy.

The rest of the paper is structured in the following manner. In Sect. 2, we present the related works. Section 3 describes the data and proposed method in detail. Experimental results are discussed in Sect. 4. Lastly, Sect. 5 serves as the conclusion of the paper.

2 Related Works

2.1 The Free Space Reference Path Loss Models

The publications on transmission models have introduced various experimental path loss laws that depend on distance and frequency parameters. In free space reference (CI), the path loss models can be expressed in the following way [7]:

$$PL_{CI}(d, f) = PL_{FS,ref}(f) + 10n_{CI} \log_{10}(d) + \xi_{\sigma,CI} \qquad (1)$$

In this, $PL_{FS,ref}(f)$ represents the route loss determined at a reference distance of one meter using Friis' law for free space propagation.

$$PL_{FS,ref}(f) = 20log_{10}(\frac{4\pi f}{c}) \qquad (2)$$

In this:

  c: speed of light
  f: carrier frequency
  n_{CI}: the path loss exponent (PLE)
  $\xi_{\sigma,CI}$: the shadow fading obey Gaussian distribution with zero mean o and
  standard deviation of σ. The foundational equation provided in Eq. (1) applies
  for all most path loss models based on measurements.

2.2 Path Loss Modeling Method Based on Machine Learning

Machine learning-based methods acquire insights from statistical information derived from measurement data, empirical models, or preprocessed inputs generated from field simulations in the domain of radio propagation. These methods are then used to make predictions related to path loss values. Numerous studies in the field of path loss modeling with machine learning have been presented. They encompass a variety of approaches, such as neural networks, support vector regression, These methods encompass Convolutional Neural Networks (CNN) and decision tree-based approaches. The capacity to capture intricate relationships between inputs and outputs in machine learning-based methods makes them well-suited for path loss modeling. H. Cheng et al. introduced an attention-enhanced convolutional neural network (AE-CNN) path loss model for 5G communications in suburban settings. In order to overcome the constraints of local feature extraction and extract global information from input images, dilated convolution is utilized. The attention mechanism plays a key role in enabling the attention-enhanced convolutional neural network (AE-CNN) model to extract important properties relevant to propagation contexts by using global information from inputs. In test cases, the AE-CNN model demonstrates superior performance in terms of root mean square error compared to the most advanced deterministic and empirical approaches. [8]. Jo et al. present a machine-learning framework for path loss modeling that combines three key techniques: variance analysis based on Gaussian processes, principle component analysis (PCA)-assisted feature selection, and multi-dimensional regression based on artificial neural networks (ANNs). When compared to the traditional linear path loss plus log-normal shadowing mode, the combined path loss and shadowing model is more precise and adaptable [9]. Figure 1 shows our proposed procedure for predicting path loss based on deep learning. In this paper, our proposed procedure consists of three steps: preprocessing data, training, and evaluating results via test data.

3   Data and Path Loss Model

3.1   Data Collection and Preprocessing

The data used in this paper is sourced from a publicly available measurement dataset hosted on GitHub [10]. The dataset was collected from an actual measurement campaign using Facebook Terragraph channel sounders. The communication system was set between two UAVs at 60 GHz of carrier frequency [11].

The accuracy of a learning model depends on the training data introduced to it. To obtain an accurate model, it is necessary to have a well-distributed, large, and accurately measured dataset in addition to its computational and tuning parameters. Thus, preparing the data is a crucial step in creating an appropriate learning model. We divided the data preprocessing into two steps: The first step involves filtering out records with errors or missing fields. We address missing data by filling in the empty cells with the median values of the respective fields. In the second step, we also perform normalization to reduce processing time and mitigate bias. To prepare the training data, we partition all the measured data into two sets: the training set, which comprises 80% of the data, and the testing set, which constitutes 20%. Our method of achieving this division is uniform random sampling. During model optimization, the data for testing is specifically utilized to modify hyperparameters.

3.2   Feature Selection and Hyper-parameter

From the dataset, detailed features used in the training and testing model are shown in Table 1.

In this study, we used the LSTM model. Because path loss does not depend on time, the number of steps in the parameter is set $= 1$. The hyper-parameter, and optimization algorithms are shown in Table 2.

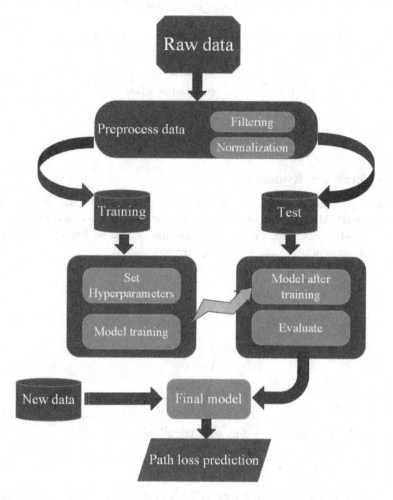

Fig. 1. Procedure of machine-learning-based path loss prediction.

Table 1. The features for training and testing.

Features name	Description
distance	The distance between 2 UAV (m)
altitude	The altitude of UAV compared to ground (m)
tx beam	Transmitter beam indices used for scanning
rx beam	Receiver beam indices used for scanning.
tx gain idx	Transmitter gain indices.
rx rf gain idx, rx if gain idx	The receiver gains indices from the Automatic Gain Control (AGC).
tx temp	Transmitter junction temperature
rx temp	The receiver node's junction temperature

Table 2. Hyper-parameter and optimization algorithm.

Hyper-parameter	Optimization algorithms
epochs = 50	LSTM layer: activation ='relu'
verbose = 0	Output layer: activation ='linear'
Dropout = 0.3	optimizer ='adam'
number of steps in =1	loss = 'mse'.
number of steps out = 1	

3.3 Performance Evaluation

The accuracy of the prediction findings is assessed using three statistical metrics: R2 (R-squared), MAE (mean absolute error, and RMSE (root mean square error [12]. These indicators, which are defined as follows, can be found by comparing the test dataset's actual values to the projected values:

$$MAE = \frac{1}{N} \sum_{i=1}^{N} |y_i - \hat{y}_i| \tag{3}$$

$$RMSE = \sqrt{\frac{1}{N} \sum_{i=1}^{N} (y_i - \hat{y}_i)^2} \tag{4}$$

$$R^2 = 1 - \frac{\sum_{i=1}^{N}(y_i - \hat{y}_i)^2}{\sum_{i=1}^{N}(y_i - avg(y))^2} \tag{5}$$

where $\hat{y}_i$ is the ith predicted value, y_i is the ith observed value.

3.4 Path Loss Model

A type of recurrent neural network (RNN) architecture in the deep learning space is called LSTM (Long Short-Term Memory). Because LSTM has feedback connections, as opposed to traditional neural networks, it can handle complete data sequences as opposed to simply individual data points. [13]. We applied the LSTM networks with hyperparameters and activation functions are described in Table 1. The proposed path loss prediction model for the mmWave Channel of UAV-to-UAV Communications scenario is shown in Fig. 2.

The Algorithm 1 returns a trained LSTM model. This trained LSTM model was then passed and used for the prediction phase of the path loss model as shown in Algorithm 2.

4   Results and Discussion

Figure 3 shows the path loss from the empirical models, the measured, and the predictions versus distance. Regarding the trend, the path loss values in the

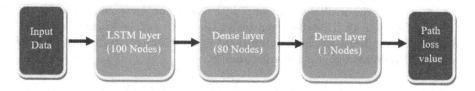

Fig. 2. LSTM path loss model based machine.

Algorithm 1. Training LSTM path loss model

1: Collect channel data from the public dataset.

2: Extract channel characteristic data for use as the training dataset.

3: Establish the prediction model of path loss based on the LSTM algorithm.

4: **for all** *epoch* = 1 to 50 **do**

5:     Train model

6:     Calculate RMSE, MAE and R2

7: **end for**

8: Return trained LSTM model

---

dataset are acquired through real measurements, and the predicted values generated by the proposed LSTM model align with the simulated loss graph based on Friis' law. According to Friis' law, the path loss value depends only on the carrier frequency and the distance between the transmitting device and the receiving device. However, from the results of the actual measurement campaign and analysis from [11], the path loss is also greatly influenced by the receive/transmit antenna beams, the height of the UAV as well and the environmental temperature. Observing Fig. 3, it is evident that our proposed model's predicted path loss closely aligns with the actual measured values. This result is obtained because, in addition to distance, the LSTM model considers input features such as the location vectors of Tx and Rx beam pairs, UAV altitude, and node junction temperature.

To provide a thorough evaluation of the LSTM model's performance, we calculated several key metrics, including the mean absolute error (MAE), root mean square error (RMSE), and R2 (R-squared), by comparing the predicted data with the true data. The results of this evaluation are presented in Table 2, where we examine the performance at different altitudes of the UAV. Notably, the results clearly demonstrate the LSTM model's effectiveness, as indicated by the RMSE values at each altitude being consistently smaller than those obtained through all-altitude calculations. According to the result from (1) with carrier frequency = 60GHz and Gaussian random variable with standard deviation σ

Algorithm 2. Predicting from the LSTM mode

1: Set input data.

2: Predict path loss from the LSTM model with given input data.

3: Return path loss value.

= 3.56 dB [11], the RMSE of the empirical model and measured values get at 7.66dB, MAE = 6.42. Table 3 demonstrates that the machine learning approach surpasses the empirical method, as indicated by all error metrics displaying lower values and yielding higher correlation results.

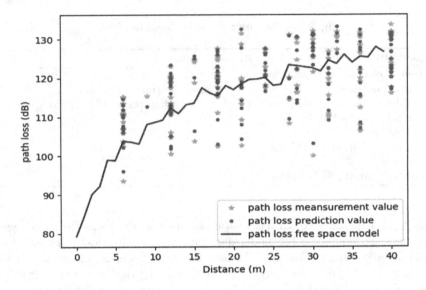

Fig. 3. Path loss prediction values based on LSTM model.

Table 3. MAE, RMSE, and R2 value of measurement path loss and predict path loss.

Altitude(m)	MAE (dB)	RMSE (dB)	R^2
All altitude(m)	1.48	1.98	0.95
H = 6 (m)	1.67	1.92	0.95
H = 12 (m)	1.58	1.95	0.95

Figure 4 illustrates a comparison of error rates using the MAE and RMSE indices with varying numbers of features applied to the identical training model. By examining Fig. 4, it becomes evident that the proposed features yield the lowest values for the MAE and RMSE indices, with MAE at 1.48 dB and RMSE at 1.98 dB. Meanwhile, if using only one feature which is a distance like the free space model, the highest error rates for MAE and RMSE are observed, reaching 5.45 dB and 6.66 dB, respectively. Even though considering the influence of each UAV's altitude, the error rate also reduces insignificantly.

In addition, Fig. 4 also shows the R2 value for different cases, including scenarios with only one feature (distance between two UAVs), two features (distance and altitude of UAVs), and multiple features as outlined in Table 1. The R2 value

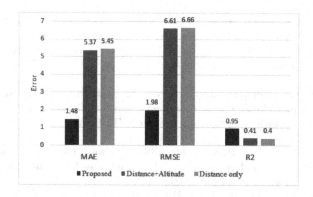

Fig. 4. The MAE, RMSE, and R2 vs number of feature

reaches its peak at 0.95 when the model's input aligns with the recommendations in Table 1, while the input data includes both the distance and altitude of the UAVs, the R2 value only reaches 0.41. This result shows the suitability of the selection of input parameters with the proposed LSTM model.

5   Conclusion

In this paper, we proposed an LSTM model designed to predict path loss in UAV-to-UAV transmission scenarios, operating at a carrier frequency of 60 GHz, based on publicly available measurement data. Our proposed LSTM model exhibited its superiority over the traditional empirical Free Space path loss method. Notably, machine learning-based path loss methods offer the advantage of incorporating a wider range of parameters compared to empirical techniques. In our proposed model, we harnessed parameters such as distance, Tx and Rx beam pairs, UAV altitude, and node junction temperature as input variables, showcasing the flexibility and effectiveness of machine learning in addressing the complex challenges of path loss modeling in UAV-based millimeter wave communications.

References

1. Hong, W., et al.: The role of millimeter-wave technologies in 5G/6G wireless communications. IEEE J. Microwaves. **1**(1), 101–122 (2021)
2. Al-Ogaili, F., Shubair, R.M.: Millimeter-wave mobile communications for 5G: challenges and opportunities. In: IEEE International Symposium on Antennas and Propagation, pp. 1003–1004 (2016)
3. Abubakar, A.I., et al.: A survey on energy optimization techniques in UAV-based cellular networks: from conventional to machine learning approaches. MDPI J. Drones **7**, 214 (2023)
4. Abubakar, W., Yi, Y., Liu, Y., Deng, Y., Nallanathan, A.: Clustered UAV networks with millimeter wave communications: a stochastic geometry view. IEEE Trans. Commun. (2020)

5. Polese, M., et al.: Integrated access and backhaul in 5G mmWave networks: potential and challenges. IEEE Commun. **58**, 62–68 (2020)
6. Jang, K.J., et al.: Path loss model based on machine learning using multidimensional Gaussian process regression. IEEE Open Access J. **10**, 115061–115073 (2022)
7. Rappaport, T.S., Xing, Y., MacCartney, G.R., Molisch, A.F., Mellios, E., Zhang, J.: Overview of millimeter wave communications for fifth-generation (5G) wireless networks-with a focus on propagation models. IEEE Trans. Antennas Propag. **65**, 6213–6230 (2017)
8. Cheng, H., Ma, S., Lee, H., Cho, M.: Millimeter wave path loss modeling for 5G communications using deep learning with dilated convolution and attention. IEEE Open Access J. **9**, 62867–62879 (2021)
9. Jo, H.S., Park, C., Lee, E., Choi, H.K., Park, J.: Path loss prediction based on machine learning techniques: principal component analysis, artificial neural network, and gaussian process. MPDI J. **20**, 1927 (2020)
10. GitHub. https://github.com/wineslab/uav-to-uav-60-ghz-channel-model
11. Polese, M., Bertizzolo, L., Bonati, L., Gosain, A., Melodia, T.: An experimental mmWave channel model for UAV-to-UAV communications. In: 4th ACM Workshop on Millimeter-wave Networks and Sensing Systems (2020)
12. Isabona, J., Srivastava, V.M.: Hybrid neural network approach for predicting signal propagation loss in urban microcells. In: Proceedings of IEEE Region 10 Humanitarian Technology CONFERENCE R10-HTC 2016, pp. 1–5 India (2016)
13. Bengio, Y., Simard, P., Frasconi, P.: Learning long-term dependencies with gradient descent is difficult. IEEE Transactions on Neural Networks. **5**(2), 157–166 (1994)

Network Solutions

Enhance Secrecy Performance of the Cooperative NOMA/UAV Network Applying NSGA-II Algorithm

Anh Le-Thi[1]([✉]), Thuc Kieu-Xuan[1], Hong Nguyen-Thi[2], and Nhung Tran-Phuong[1]

[1] Hanoi University of Industry, Hanoi, Vietnam
{leanh,thuckx,nhungtp}@haui.edu.vn
[2] Posts and Telecommunications Institute of Technology, Hanoi, Vietnam

Abstract. In this paper, we propose and analyze the security performance of cooperative power-domain non-orthogonal multiple access systems (NOMA) for multiple users with the assistance of UAV over Rice fading channels. In the proposed system, multi-destination users are allocated various powers and communicate with the transmitter (Tx) via the UAV relaying node. UAV acts as an intermediate node that transmits the signal to the user through the amplification and forward (AF) protocol. A friendly jammer node interferes with the received signals at eavesdroppers to enhance the system's security. In addition, in order to increase the security quality of the system through both secrecy capacity, in this paper, a multi-objective optimization technique NSGA-II is applied to maximize the secrecy capacity at the valid users and minimize the received signal's quality at the eavesdropping node. Finally, we analyze the influence of critical system parameters on secrecy performance, such as transmit power, distance of UAV from the ground, and distance between friendly jammer and base station.

Keywords: Power-domain NOMA · rice fading · multi-objective optimization · NSGA-II

1 Introduction

With the rapid development of wireless techniques, communication with the assistance of drones or unmanned aerial vehicles (UAVs) has been seen as a promising solution for current and future network infrastructure deployments [1,2]. With high mobility, flexible deployment, and low cost, UAVs can be deployed as relaying stations or aerial base stations to help establish temporary communication infrastructure in emergencies. For example, UAV communication can be set up for disaster-affected areas, reducing the load on areas with dense

Supported by Hanoi University of Industry.

N. Thi Dieu Linh et al. (Eds.): ADHOCNETS 2023, LNICST 558, pp. 137–149, 2024.
https://doi.org/10.1007/978-3-031-55993-8_11

equipment density. Besides, the NOMA technique is also considered a potential candidate for future mobile networks because of its high spectrum efficiency, low latency, and serving many users [3,4]. Recently, due to the benefits of the NOMA technique and UAV communication, the combination of NOMA-UAV has been an interesting topic. Some publications [5–7] have studied the NOMA cooperative communication network with the help of UAVs.

Security is a critical aspect of future wireless networks that the research community focuses on now. Developing techniques for enhancing secure transmission in the wireless medium is an intricate problem that needs to be focused on research. Because of the principle of broadcasting radio communication, signals on wireless channels can be overheard by eavesdroppers. One of the methods against eavesdropping attract is exploiting jamming signals [8,9]. Some publications investigated the secrecy performance of NOMA and UAV communication [10–12]. However, no studies have been published on improving the security of NOMA/UAV systems using multi-objective optimization techniques, applying variations of genetic algorithms such as the Non-dominated Sorting Genetic Algorithm (NSGA-II) [13]. Thus, in this paper, we propose a new power-domain NOMA network with the help of a UAV relaying station and apply NSGA-II to improve the secrecy capacity and reduce the effect of the eavesdropper.

2   Communication Model and Phases

2.1   Communication Model

Figure 1 presents our proposed communication scheme of multi-NOMA users and a base station with the assistance of an intermediate node as a UAV applying AF protocol in the presence of an eavesdropper and a friendly jammer. Because of the working principle of PD-NOMA, the node operating on the poor channel is allocated higher power; conversely, the node undergoing the better link is assigned lower power. In our model, the first user (U_1) is assumed to be furthest from the base station, followed by the second user (U_2), and the user closest to the source node is the Lth user (U_L). Thus, (U_1) is allocated the highest level of transmitted power, and a second power level is assigned to (U_2), and the lowest power is assigned to (U_L). The source signal (x_s) is a superimposed signal of L users x_1, x_2,..., and x_L. Moreover, the UAV relaying node forwards the received signal from the ground source node to NOMA users. The ground-air link is a BS-UAV connection, and air-ground links are UAV-user connections that undergo Rice fading channels. NOMA-user applies the successive interference cancellation (SIC) to detect the desired user signal.

In this design, we denote h_0, h_l with $l = 1, 2, ..., L$, h_E, and $h_{UAV,Jl,JE}$ are the channel coefficients of the ground-air link BS-UAV, the air-ground links UAV-U_l, the air-ground link UAV-Eavesdropper, and friendly jammer - UAV, jammer-users, jammer-eavesdropper links respectively. The distances of BS-UAV, UAV-U_l, UAV-Jammer, UAV-E and Jammer-U_l, Jammer-E links are d_0, d_l, d_J, d_E, and d_{Jl} respectively.

The ground-air links are communications connections from the BS and friendly jammer to the UAV, and air-ground links are from the UAV to the users and eavesdroppers. These links are Rician fading channels which include two components that are line-of-sight propagation (direct path) and non-line-of-sight propagation (NLoS), and can be expressed as $h = \sqrt{\frac{K_h}{K_h+1}} h^{LoS} + \sqrt{\frac{1}{K_h+1}} h^{NLoS}$.

With $h \in H = \{g_{km}, g_{mj}\}, j = \{1,2\}$ where K_h, h^{LoS}, and h^{NLoS} are the Rician factor, Los components, and NLoS components of channel h, respectively. The NLoS parts hNLoS are i.i.d. complex Gaussian distributed with zero mean and unit variance.

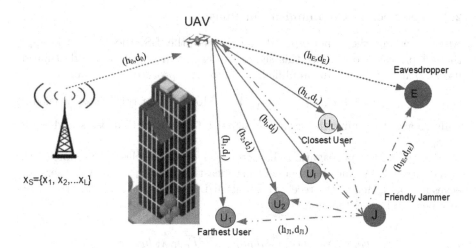

Fig. 1. The proposed network model

In addition, we assume that (1) the ground-air and air-ground connections of BS-UAV, J-UAV, and UAV-users, UAV-E suffer Rician fading channels; (2) there is no direct path between BS and NOMA users, BS and Eavesdropper, BS and jammer; (3) the local channel state information (CSI) is assumed at the relay, and the global CSI is presumed at BS and the users.

2.2   The First Communication Phase

BS transmits the source signal of multiple NOMA-users to the intermediate node UAV. This signal is represented mathematically as follows:

$$x_S = \sum_{l=1}^{L} \sqrt{P_l \alpha_l} s_l, \qquad (1)$$

where x_l (l=1,2,..., L) is denoted as the signal to user l, and P_l is denoted as the power allocation level corresponding to the lth user which satisfies the condition $\sum_{l=1}^{L} P_l = P_S$ and $P_1 \geq P_2 \geq ... \geq P_l \geq ... \geq P_L$.

Then, the received signal at UAV relaying node is composed of the signal from BS and the friendly Jammer. Thus, the received signal at UAV can be expressed ass

$$y_{UAV} = \sum_{l=1}^{L} \sqrt{P_l}s_l h_0 + \sqrt{P_J}s_J h_J + n_{UAV}^{[a]} \tag{2}$$

Here, the channel coefficients of the link BS - UAV, friendly jammer-UAV are denoted by h_0, and h_J respectively; and $n_{UAV}^{[a]} \sim CN\left(0, \sigma_{aR}^2\right)$ is antenna white Gaussian noise (AWGN).

2.3   The Second Communication Phase

After receiving the superimposed signal from the BS, the UAV will apply the AF protocol to amplify this signal before forwarding it to the destination users. Denoting G as an amplified factor of AF protocol, G is calculated as $G = \left(\sum_{l=1}^{L}\sqrt{P_l}|h_0|^2 + P_J|h_J|^2 + \sigma_{UAV}^2\right)^{-1}$. Moreover, in this phase, a friendly jammer also transmits the jamming signal to all destination users and eavesdroppers.

Because of the propagation characteristics of the wireless environment, the signals from UAV and Jammer will broadcast to legitimate NOMA users and eavesdroppers. Hence, the received signals at L destinations users and the eavesdropper can be written as follows:

$$
\begin{aligned}
y_{U_l} = \sum_{l=1}^{L} & \sqrt{GP_rP_l}s_l h_0 h_l + \sqrt{GP_r}n_{UAV}h_l + n_{U_l} \\
& + \underbrace{\sqrt{GP_rP_J}s_J h_l h_J + \sqrt{P_J}s_J h_{Jl}}_{Total jamming signals}.
\end{aligned}
\tag{3}
$$

and,

$$
\begin{aligned}
y_E = \sum_{l=1}^{L} & \sqrt{GP_rP_l}s_l h_0 h_E + \sqrt{GP_r}n_{UAV}h_E + n_E \\
& + \underbrace{\sqrt{GP_rP_J}s_J h_E h_J + \sqrt{P_J}s_J h_{JE}}_{Total jamming signals}
\end{aligned}
\tag{4}
$$

Here, n_{U_l} and n_E are the AWGN at U_l and E respectively; P_r is transmitted power at UAV relaying node.

Because the legitimate users can eliminate the jamming signals from the Friendly Jammer and due to the SIC at the NOMA receiver of each user, the SINRs at any user (User l) can be expressed as,

$$
\gamma_{1l} = \frac{|h_0|^2|h_l|^2}{\frac{\sum_{l=2}^{L} P_l}{P_1}|h_0|^2|h_l|^2 + \frac{\sigma_{UAV}^2}{P_1}|h_l|^2 + \frac{\sigma_{U_l}^2 \sum_{l=1}^{L} P_l}{P_r P_1}|h_0|^2 + \frac{P_J\sigma_{U_l}^2}{P_r P_1}|h_J|^2 + \frac{\sigma_{U_l}^2 \sigma_{UAV}^2}{P_r P_1}}
\tag{5}
$$

We can see that $\sigma_{U_l}^2 \sigma_{UAV}^2 << P_r P_1$, thus $\frac{\sigma_{U_l}^2 \sigma_{UAV}^2}{P_r P_1} \to 0$, then Eq.(5) can be rewritten as

$$\gamma_{1l} = \frac{|h_0|^2 |h_l|^2}{\frac{\sum_{l=2}^{L} P_l}{P_1}|h_0|^2|h_l|^2 + \frac{\sigma_{UAV}^2}{P_1}|h_l|^2 + \frac{\sigma_{U_l}^2 \sum_{l=1}^{L} P_l}{P_r P_1}|h_0|^2 + \frac{P_J \sigma_{U_l}^2}{P_r P_1}|h_J|^2} \tag{6}$$

Similarly, we have:

$$\gamma_{2l} = \frac{|h_0|^2 |h_l|^2}{\frac{\sum_{l=3}^{L} P_l}{P_2}|h_0|^2|h_l|^2 + \frac{1}{P_2}\sigma_{UAV}^2|h_l|^2 + \frac{\sum_{l=1}^{L} P_l}{P_r P_2}|h_0|^2\sigma_{U_l}^2 + \frac{P_J}{P_r P_2}|h_J|^2\sigma_{U_l}^2} \tag{7}$$

...
...
...

$$\gamma_{ll} = \frac{|h_0|^2 |h_l|^2}{\frac{\sum_{j=l+1}^{L} P_l}{P_l}|h_0|^2|h_l|^2 + \frac{1}{P_l}\sigma_{UAV}^2|h_l|^2 + \frac{\sum_{l=1}^{L} P_l}{P_r P_l}|h_0|^2\sigma_{U_l}^2 + \frac{P_J}{P_r P_l}|h_J|^2\sigma_{U_l}^2} \tag{8}$$

...
...
...

$$\gamma_{Ll} = \frac{|h_0|^2 |h_l|^2}{\frac{\sigma_{UAV}^2}{P_L}|h_l|^2 + \frac{\sigma_{U_l}^2 \sum_{l=1}^{L} P_l}{P_r P_L}|h_0|^2 + \frac{P_J \sigma_{U_l}^2}{P_r P_L}|h_J|^2} \tag{9}$$

At Eavesdropper, in this paper, we consider the worst-case scenario: applying the parallel interference cancellation to guarantee the capacity of best decoding [14]. This means E can eliminate the interference of $x_2,..., x_L$ when decoding x_1, similar to other cases. Moreover, E cannot eliminate the jamming signal from the friendly jammer. Thus, the SINRs of user signals at E can be expressed as follows:

$$\gamma_{1E} = \frac{|h_0|^2 |h_E|^2}{\left(\begin{array}{l} \frac{P_J}{P_1}|h_E|^2|h_J|^2 + \frac{\sigma_{UAV}^2}{P_1}|h_E|^2 + \frac{P_J \sum_{l=1}^{L} \sqrt{P_l}}{P_r P_1}|h_0|^2|h_{JE}|^2 + \\ \frac{P_J^2}{P_r P_1}|h_J|^2|h_{JE}|^2 + \frac{P_J \sigma_{UAV}^2}{P_r P_1}|h_{JE}|^2 + \frac{\sum_{l=1}^{L} \sqrt{P_l}\sigma_E^2}{P_r P_1}|h_0|^2 + \frac{P_J \sigma_E^2}{P_r P_1}|h_J|^2 \end{array} \right)} \tag{10}$$

...
...

$$\gamma_{lE} = \frac{|h_0|^2|h_E|^2}{\left(\begin{array}{l} \frac{P_J}{P_l}|h_E|^2|h_J|^2 + \frac{\sigma_{UAV}^2}{P_l}|h_E|^2 + \frac{P_J\sum\limits_{l=1}^{L}\sqrt{P_l}}{P_rP_l}|h_0|^2|h_{JE}|^2 \\ + \frac{P_J^2}{P_rP_l}|h_J|^2|h_{JE}|^2 + \frac{P_J\sigma_{UAV}^2}{P_rP_l}|h_{JE}|^2 + \frac{\sum\limits_{l=1}^{L}\sqrt{P_l}\sigma_E^2}{P_rP_l}|h_0|^2 + \frac{P_J\sigma_E^2}{P_rP_l}|h_J|^2 \end{array}\right)} \tag{11}$$

$$\cdots$$
$$\cdots$$

$$\gamma_{LE} = \frac{|h_0|^2|h_E|^2}{\left(\begin{array}{l} \frac{P_J}{P_L}|h_E|^2|h_J|^2 + \frac{\sigma_{UAV}^2}{P_L}|h_E|^2 + \frac{P_J\sum\limits_{l=1}^{L}\sqrt{P_l}}{P_rP_L}|h_0|^2|h_{JE}|^2 \\ + \frac{P_J^2}{P_rP_L}|h_J|^2|h_{JE}|^2 + \frac{P_J\sigma_{UAV}^2}{P_rP_L}|h_{JE}|^2 + \frac{\sum\limits_{l=1}^{L}\sqrt{P_l}\sigma_E^2}{P_rP_L}|h_0|^2 + \frac{P_J\sigma_E^2}{P_rP_L}|h_J|^2 \end{array}\right)} \tag{12}$$

3   Secrecy Performance Analysis

In this part, we investigate the secrecy performance of our PD-NOMA/UAV model. To enhance the secrecy capacity of this system and interference with the eavesdropping links, we apply the multi-objective optimization technique as NSGA-II. Remarkably, the problem is the maximization of the sum of the secrecy capacity of NOMA users and the minimization of the capacity of the eavesdropper.

The secrecy capacity at any node is defined as follows

$$C_{\text{sec}}^l = \left[R_{s_l}^{U_l} - R_{s_l}^{E}\right]^+. \tag{13}$$

Here, according to Shannon capacity, $R_{s_l}^{U_l} = \log_2(1 + \gamma_{ll})$ as data rate at user l^{th}, with $l = 1, 2, ..., L$, and $R_{s_l}^{E} = \log_2(1 + \gamma_{lE})$ as data rate at the eavesdropper.

Due to the NOMA principle, user l^{th} has to decode the successfully stronger signals and then detect its desired signal. The data rate at user l^{th} can be expressed as $R_{s_l}^{U_l} = \log_2\left(1 + \min\limits_{l=1,..,L}\{\gamma_{ll}\}\right)$. Thus, secrecy capacity at user l^{th} can be formulated as follows

$$C_{\text{sec}}^l = \left[\log_2\left(1 + \min\limits_{l=1,..,L}\{\gamma_{ll}\}\right) - \log_2(1 + \gamma_{lE})\right]^+ \tag{14}$$

The sum of the secrecy capacity (SSC) of our proposed system can be expressed as

$$C_{\text{sec}} = \sum_{l=1}^{L} C_{\text{sec}}^l \tag{15}$$

The problem is defined as how to maximize the SSC and minimize the capacity at Eavesdropper. And this problem can be formulated as follows

$$\max_{P_1,..,P_l,..,P_L} C_{sec} = \sum_{l=1}^{L} \left[\log_2 \left(1 + \min_{l=1,..,L} \{\gamma_{ll}\} \right) - \log_2 \left(1 + \gamma_{lE} \right) \right]^+ \text{ and}$$

$$\min_{P_1,..,P_l,..,P_L} R_l^E = \log_2 \left(1 + \gamma_{lE} \right) \quad (16)$$

$$\text{subject to}: \quad \gamma_{jl} \underset{j,l=\{1,2,...,L\}}{} \geq \gamma_0 \quad (16.1)$$

$$\sum_{l=1}^{L} P_l \leq P_S^{max} \quad (16.2)$$

$$P_1 \geq P_2 \geq ... \geq P_l \geq ... \geq P_L investigates the influence P_r \geq e_0 \quad (16.3)$$

Here γ_0 is a threshold at which the user signal can be decoded, and e_0 is the threshold power, which means the minimum power to transmit the signal from the relaying UAV node.

To solve the problem of two objectives in Eq. 16 under multiple constraint conditions (16.1), (16.2), (16.3) and (16.4), we apply Non-Dominated Sorting Genetic Algorithm II (NSGA-II). NSGA II is a well-known application to solve multi-objective optimization problems [15]. It is an elitist non-dominated sorting genetic algorithm. To put it another way, the best solutions of the previous iteration are kept unchanged in the current one. In addition, it adopts an elite preservation strategy and uses an explicit diversity preservation technique. Firstly, the offspring population is created from the parent population, which is initialized. Before using non-dominated to classify, both populations are combined. Then, the assignment of rank 1 for the best non-dominated font is to obtain a new filled population. This continues for successive fronts with the assignment of ranks. The crowding distance sorting is also utilized to obtain the greater diversity of the Pareto front. The crowding distance sorting is also utilized to obtain the greater diversity of the Pareto front. Crowding distance implies the closeness of a solution to its neighbors, so the greater the distance, the better the diversity of the Pareto front. It means a more suitable solution for the problem. The offspring population is created from the parent population using crowded tournament selection, crossover, and mutation operators. This whole operation iterates until it meets a termination criterion. Fig. 2 show the flow-chart of NSGA-II procedure.

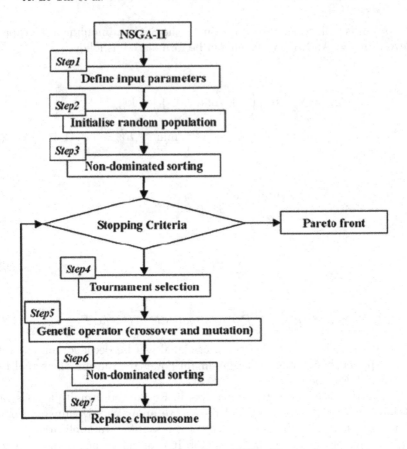

Fig. 2. The flow-chart of the NGSA-II procedure

4   Simulation Results and Discussions

In this section, we present simulation results for problems in Eq.(16) to investigate the secrecy capacity sum of our proposed PD-NOMA/UAV network in the presence of an eavesdropper. Without loss of general, we do experiments for two NOMA users. All of the simulation results are performed in Python language.

To be more detail, the parameters used in this model are the UAV's coverage radius $r = 30m$, height from ground to UAV as $h_{uav} = 50m$, the transmitted power from the UAV as $P_r = 30dBm$, the target secrecy rate R_1 and R_2 in range $[0, 3.5]$ (bits/s/Hz), the signal-decoded threshold at users γ_0 belongs to $[0, 4]$ (dB), path-loss exponent $m = 3$, and Rice coefficient $K = 13$. By applying NSGA-II to address the problem (16), we set up the NSGA-II multi-objective Python program, including maximizing the function of the secrecy capacity sum of the system and minimizing the function of the user's data rate at the eavesdropper.

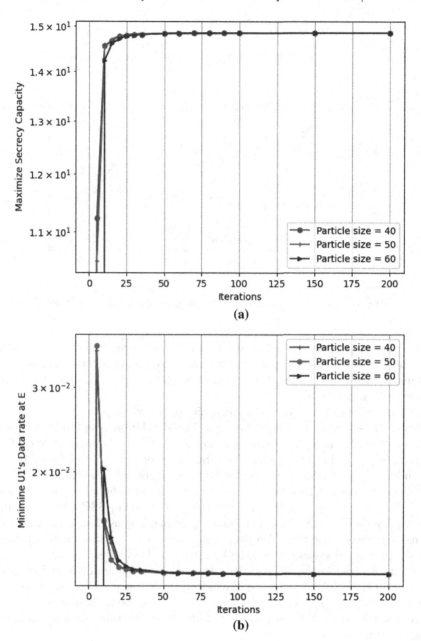

Fig. 3. NSGA-II Convergence behavior

Figure 3 shows the NSGA-II algorithm's convergence behavior of our proposed system model for two objectives: maximization of the secrecy capacity (Fig. 3a) and minimization of user signal at E (Fig. 3b). These figures illustrate

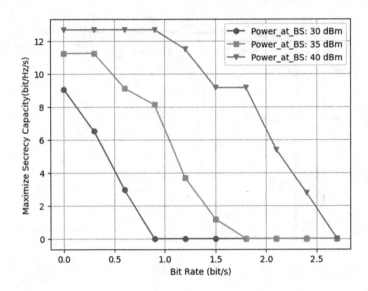

Fig. 4. Sum Secrecy Capacity with different BS's Transmit Powers

three cases of particle size (40,50,60) and two considered-functions for NSGA-II in which all the cases of particle size, the convergence algorithm is archived around iteration 30th. Thus, the convergence of the NSGA-II algorithm in this model system is satisfied.

Then, we investigate the secrecy capacity of the whole proposed system with different BS's transmit power levels and the simulation result in Fig. 4. It is detailed that the increasing value of power level at BS enhances the SSC of the system. In particular, at $P_S = 40dBm$ SSC is better than that of $P_S = 30dBm$.

In Fig. 5, the SSCs are examined with the changes of the heights of UAV (40, 50, 60) m versus the threshold value of users' decoded-signal (γ_0 in the range [0,4] dB). It can be seen that from Fig. 5, the trends of SSC curves are alike in that SSC descends to zero at around $\gamma_0 = 4dB$ means that if the data rate at users increases the SSC also decreases. Moreover, the SSC of the proposed system model is decreased when the height of the UAV rises.

Figure 6 presents the effect of the strength of the jamming signal from the jammer on the user's data rate at Eavesdropper. Three power levels of Jammer are $P_J = (0, 0.5 *P_S, P_S)$ and $P_S = 40dBm$. As shown in Fig. 6, when P_J increases, the user's data rate at E declines. It means that the information of legal users is more secure.

Finally, Fig. 7 investigates the influence of weights of making decisions with data rate minima function at illegal users. The parameters in these simulations are set up as data rate is in the range [0,3.5] bit/s, the transmit power at BS $P_S = 40dBm$, weights for data rate minima function (0.2, 0.6, 0.8). Overall,

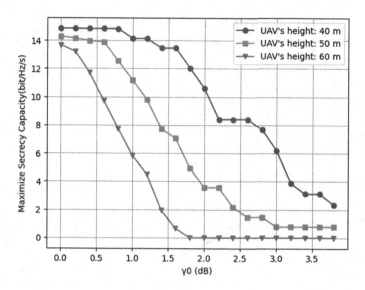

Fig. 5. The height of UAV effect on Sum Secrecy capacity

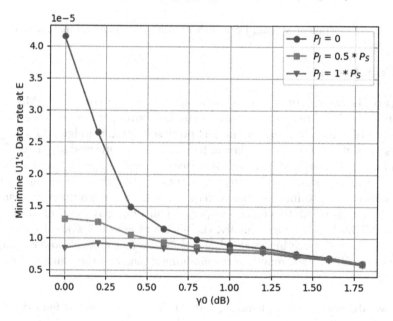

Fig. 6. Effect of Power levels at Jammer on data rate minima function at E

Fig. 6 shows that the trends of SSC lines for all cases are similar. Specifically, It can be seen that the weights of that function slightly increase users' data rate at eavesdroppers.

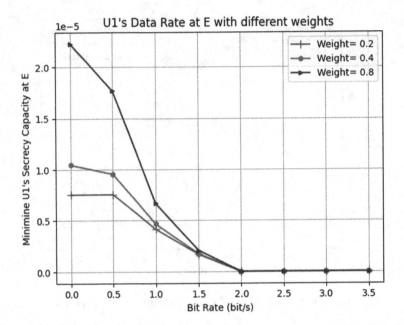

Fig. 7. Weights of Making Decision with data rate minima function at E

5   Conclusion

In this paper, we examined the secrecy capacity sum of the PD-NOMA model system in the UAV-relaying network in the Eavesdropper's occurrence and the assistance of a friendly jammer. In this proposed system design, BTS communicates to multi-NOMA users via the help of a UAV intermediate node. Then, ground-air and air-ground links undergo Rice channels. A friendly jammer broadcasts the jamming signals to interfere with transmitting the Eavesdropper - UAV link. Additionally, to increase the secrecy capacity of our proposed system and decrease the signal at the Eavesdropper, a multi-objective optimization technique - NSGA-II is applied. Finally, the effects of essential system parameters on secrecy capacity are investigated including the transmitted power level, the height of the UAV, the strength of the jamming signal, and the weights of making decisions.

Acknowledgment. This work was supported by Hanoi University of Industry, Hanoi.

References

1. Merwaday, A., Guvenc, I.: UAV-assisted heterogeneous networks for public safety communications. In: 2015 IEEE Wireless Communications and Networking Conference Workshops (WCNCW), pp. 329–334 (2015)
2. Li, T., Sheng, M., Lyu, R., Liu, J., Li, J.: UAV assisted heterogeneous wireless networks: potentials and challenges. ZTE Commun. **16** (2018)

3. Ghafoor, U., Ali, M., Khan, H.Z., Siddiqui, A.M., Naeem, M.: NOMA and future 5G and B5G wireless networks: a paradigm. J. Netw. Comput. Appl. 103413 (2022)
4. Le, T.A., Kong, H.Y.: Evaluating the performance of cooperative NOMA with energy harvesting under physical layer security. Wirel. Pers. Commun. **108**, 1037–1054 (2019)
5. Chaudhary, B.P., Shankar, R., Mishra, R.K.: A tutorial on cooperative non-orthogonal multiple access networks. J. Defense Model. Simul. **19**(4), 563–573 (2022)
6. Azam, I., Shahab, M.B., Shin, S.Y.: Energy-efficient pairing and power allocation for NOMA UAV network under QoS constraints. IEEE Internet Things J. **9**(24), 25011–25026 (2022)
7. Huang, Q., Wang, W., Weidang, L., Zhao, N., Nallanathan, A., Wang, X.: Resource allocation for multi-cluster NOMA-UAV networks. IEEE Trans. Commun. **70**(12), 8448–8459 (2022)
8. Li, Y., Wang, W., Liu, M., Nan Zhao, X., Jiang, Y.C., Wang, X.: Joint trajectory and power optimization for jamming-aided NOMA-UAV secure networks. IEEE Syst. J. **17**(1), 732–743 (2022)
9. Chen, B., Li, R., Ning, Q., Lin, K., Han, C., Leung, V.C.: Security at physical layer in NOMA relaying networks with cooperative jamming. IEEE Trans. Veh. Technol. **71**(4), 3883–3888 (2022)
10. Le, T.A., Kong, H.Y.: Secrecy analysis of a cooperative NOMA network using an EH untrusted relay. Int. J. Electron. **106**(6), 799–815 (2019)
11. Wang, J., Zhang, J., Han, M., Pan, G.: Secrecy outage analysis for UAV assisted satellite-terrestrial SWIPT systems with NOMA. Digit. Sign. Process. **123** (2022)
12. Diao, D., Wang, B., Cao, K., Dong, R., Cheng, T.: Enhancing reliability and security of UAV-enabled NOMA communications with power allocation and aerial jamming. IEEE Trans. Veh. Technol. **71**(8), 8662–8674 (2022)
13. Diao, D., Wang, B., Cao, K., Weng, J., Dong, R., Cheng, T.: Secure wireless-powered NOMA communications in multi-UAV systems. IEEE Trans. Green Commun. Networking (2023)
14. Ma, H., Zhang, Y., Sun, S., Liu, T., Shan, Y.: A comprehensive survey on NSGA-II for multi-objective optimization and applications. Artif. Intell. Rev. 1–54 (2023)
15. Deb, K., Pratap, A., Agarwal, S., Meyarivan, T.: A fast and elitist multiobjective genetic algorithm: NSGA-II. IEEE Trans. Evol. Comput. **6**(2), 182–197 (2002). https://doi.org/10.1109/4235.996017

Fake News Detection Based on Multi-view Fuzzy Clustering Algorithm

Hoang Thi Canh[1,2], Pham Huy Thong[3(✉)], Le Truong Giang[3],
and Phan Dang Hung[3]

[1] Graduate University of Science and Technology, Vietnam Academy of Science
and Technology, Hanoi, Vietnam
[2] Thai Nguyen University of Information and Communication Technology,
Thai Nguyen, Vietnam
htcanh@ictu.edu.vn
[3] Hanoi University of Industry, Hanoi, Vietnam
{thongph,letruonggiang,phanhung}@haui.edu.vn

Abstract. The rapid development of technology and the internet has
enabled users to access and share a large amount of information from
various sources. This brings many benefits, but also the emergence of
false and inaccurate information, also known as fake news. Fake news
can lead to misunderstandings and significant impacts on the economy
and society. Therefore, detecting and minimizing fake news is necessary.
Machine learning algorithms and artificial intelligence technology can
be used to detect and eliminate fake news. In this paper, we propose a
new method for detecting fake news using multi-view fuzzy clustering on
multi-view data collected from multiple sources. Our proposed method
first extracts features from multi-view data, such as the title, content,
and social media engagement of news articles. It then uses multi-view
fuzzy clustering to group the news articles into clusters. Finally, it uses a
semi-supervised learning algorithm to classify the clusters as either real
or fake news. Additionally, the paper provides experimental results to
evaluate the effectiveness and accuracy of the proposed algorithm.

Keywords: Multi-view data · multi-view clustering · fuzzy clustering

1 Introduction

In the contemporary era, the rapid evolution of technology and the internet has
ushered in a plethora of opportunities for individuals to access and disseminate
information from a myriad of sources. This accessibility has ushered in a multitude of advantages, including the ability to acquire knowledge, facilitate work,
and provide entertainment. Nonetheless, this ease of access has also precipitated

N. Thi Dieu Linh et al. (Eds.): ADHOCNETS 2023, LNICST 558, pp. 150–166, 2024.
https://doi.org/10.1007/978-3-031-55993-8_12

certain challenges, most notably the proliferation of false and inaccurate information, leading to misunderstandings and exerting a detrimental influence on the decisions of individuals and communities. Consequently, in recent years, the detection and mitigation of false information have emerged as focal points of interest among researchers. A pivotal solution to tackle this issue involves the employment of machine learning algorithms and artificial intelligence technology to identify and eradicate counterfeit information, ensuring that users can harness information accurately and efficiently.

The term "multi-view data" refers to information collected from diverse sources, methodologies, or viewpoints regarding a particular entity [1]. This data is characterized by multiple perspectives, with each viewpoint furnishing distinct attributes for the purposes of knowledge discovery, offering varied insights about the same subject with varying degrees of precision and reliability. However, these different views often encompass complementary information that can be harnessed. Through the amalgamation of insights from multiple viewpoints, a more comprehensive and accurate representation of entities can be obtained, thus enriching the processes of data analysis and decision-making.

Data clustering stands as a pivotal challenge in the realm of data mining, with the objective of identifying and unveiling significant data clusters within extensive datasets, thereby furnishing information to support the decision-making process [2]. This process entails segregating an initial dataset into clusters, where the elements within each cluster exhibit similarity to one another, while those in different clusters demonstrate dissimilarity [3]. This clustering approach facilitates data mining, especially within the context of substantial datasets, by effectively organizing data based on their inherent characteristics [4,5]. However, the majority of existing clustering algorithms are tailored for single-view data, while contemporary practical challenges often involve multi-view data. Consequently, there is an imperative need to devise advanced clustering methodologies that can adeptly unearth knowledge from these multi-view datasets, propelling multi-view clustering into the forefront of research interest in recent times.

Multi-view Clustering (MvC) represents a data clustering methodology that harnesses numerous independent viewpoints to uncover groups of similar data within these perspectives [6]. The amalgamation of information from diverse viewpoints and the revelation of shared implicit knowledge across these perspectives deliver substantial benefits to data clustering. Applying multi-view clustering to identify fake news clusters through datasets collected from multiple sources emerges as an innovative and efficacious approach.

In contrast to single-view clustering methods, multi-view clustering boasts a plethora of advantages, including enhanced clustering quality, diminished reliance on individual viewpoints, and more efficient processing of intricate data [7]. Nevertheless, multi-view clustering is not devoid of challenges, encompassing the necessity for independent viewpoints, the complexity of merging distinct clustering methodologies, and the management of a multitude of viewpoints, entailing costs associated with data collection, processing, and storage [7].

The issue of fake news detection is besieged by its own set of complexities and difficulties. Fake news continues to evolve and proliferate, employing sophisticated forgery techniques and artificial intelligence to generate highly convincing counterfeit content. The dearth of annotated data compounds the problem, allowing fake news to disseminate rapidly across social media and other digital platforms, thereby rendering detection and control arduous tasks. To surmount these challenges, a multifaceted approach, drawing upon advanced methodologies and techniques, including machine learning, natural language processing, social network analysis, and community contributions, is indispensable to combat and identify fake news.

Researchers worldwide have diligently sought solutions to the aforementioned challenges. Seminal research on multi-view clustering methods by Bickel and Scheffer [8] in 2004 laid the foundation for subsequent developments. Their work extended K-means and Expectation Maximization (EM) clustering methods to accommodate multi-view environments, specifically handling text data featuring two conditionally independent perspectives. Subsequently, numerous multi-view clustering methodologies have been proposed [9–11].

The efficacy of the MvC algorithm hinges on two pivotal principles: the complementary principle and the consensus principle [7]. The complementary principle underscores the importance of leveraging multiple distinct viewpoints to comprehensively and accurately depict data entities. Although individual viewpoints provide adequate information for specific knowledge discovery tasks, disparate perspectives often encompass supplementary data that can be leveraged. In contrast, the consensus principle aims to maximize consistency across multiple viewpoints.

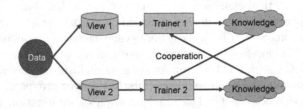

Fig. 1. General process of the co-training algorithm [7]

The co-training algorithm, introduced by Blum and Mitchell in 1998 [12], has emerged as a pioneering technology, firmly establishing itself as one of the most prominent methodologies within the realm of multi-view learning. The primary objective of this algorithm is to maximize consensus across viewpoints, thereby achieving the broadest consensus and enhancing clustering performance. The general procedure of the conventional co-training algorithms is shown in Fig. 1. According to the procedure, the algorithm is trained alternately in order to maximize the consistency of the two distinct views by using prior information or by learning knowledge from each other.

The prevailing body of research in fake news detection predominantly relies on supervised methods, which necessitate the construction of a classification model using diverse feature sets encompassing news content [13], message propagation [14], and social contexts [15]. While these techniques exhibit promising results, they are burdened by a significant drawback: they require a meticulously annotated dataset for training the classification model. The accumulation of a substantial number of annotations is a labor-intensive and time-consuming endeavor, involving in-depth analysis of news content and the inclusion of supplementary corroborative evidence, such as authoritative reports. While crowdsourcing for annotation collection may alleviate the burden of expert review, it carries the potential risk of compromising annotation quality [16].

Despite the multitude of previous research endeavors aimed at addressing the challenge of fake news detection, none have employed multi-view fuzzy clustering as a means to analyze and detect counterfeit news. Consequently, the primary objective of this paper is to bridge this research gap by introducing a fuzzy clustering methodology leveraging the co-training algorithm on a multi-view dataset for the identification of fake news clusters characterized by distinct attributes. This dataset is sourced from diverse origins, and this methodology is denominated as MCFC (Multi-View Co-trained Fuzzy Clustering). The efficacy of this proposed approach is rigorously evaluated through experiments conducted on datasets obtained from a range of sources, with the overarching goal of fake news detection.

The remaining sections of this paper are structured as follows: Sect. 2 delineates the approach to hard and fuzzy clustering on single-view data. Section 3 provides an overview of the proposed methodology. Section 4 presents experimental results and analysis, alongside comparative assessments. Finally, the conclusion section furnishes key takeaways and outlines prospective avenues for future research in subsequent publications.

2   Related Work

The detection of fake news has become a prominent focus in recent research within the realm of social media studies. Current strategies for identifying fake news can be broadly categorized into two principal groups: those centered on the analysis of news content and those oriented towards scrutinizing social contexts [17].

Approaches grounded in news content typically involve the extraction of linguistic and visual attributes. Linguistic elements, encompassing lexical and syntactic features, are harnessed to capture the distinctive writing styles and sensational headlines frequently associated with counterfeit news items [18]. Conversely, visual attributes are employed to unveil manipulated images or unique characteristics of visuals used in fake news dissemination. Models reliant on news content-based features can be further classified into two categories: (1) knowledge-based methods, which rely on external sources to validate the accuracy of claims within news content, and (2) style-based techniques, which detect stylistic manipulations like deceit and subjectivity [19].

In contrast, social context-driven approaches incorporate features derived from user profiles, post content, and social networks. User profiles are utilized to assess user characteristics and credibility, while features extracted from user-generated posts reflect social responses such as stances [20]. Network features are acquired by constructing specific social networks, including diffusion networks or co-occurrence networks [21]. Social context models can be categorized as either stance-based, which leverage user opinions to infer news veracity, or propagation-based, which employ propagation techniques to model unique information dissemination patterns [20–22]. It is worth noting that these approaches primarily fall under the category of supervised methods, focusing on feature extraction and their utilization within supervised learning frameworks [19].

In addition, this paper introduces a novel fuzzy clustering methodology applied to multi-view datasets for the purpose of detecting fake news clusters. This approach leverages established research platforms such as the K-means and FCM algorithms to achieve its objectives.

2.1   K-Means

The K-means algorithm stands as a prominent clustering technique within the realms of data analysis and machine learning. Its primary objective revolves around dividing a given dataset into K separate clusters. Within this partitioning process, each cluster finds its representation through a centroid. This methodological approach is instrumental in unearthing concealed patterns within the data while effectively grouping data points that share similarities together [23]. This algorithm's fundamental principle hinges on an objective function, which plays a pivotal role in driving the clustering process. The mathematical formulation for this objective function is depicted as follows:

$$J_m(u,v) = \sum_{k=1}^{N} \sum_{j=1}^{c} u_{kj} . \|x_k - v_j\|^2 \rightarrow Min \tag{1}$$

With constraint conditions:

$$\begin{cases} \sum_{j=1}^{c} u_{kj} = 1 \\ u_{kj} \in \{0, 1\} \end{cases}$$

In which: X is the source dataset $X = \{x_1, x_2, ..., x_N\}$ with N data points, c is the number of clusters, v is the set of cluster centers, u_{kj} is the membership degree of element k in cluster j.

By solving the objective function (1), we obtain the formulas for cluster centroids (2) as follows:

$$v = \frac{\sum_{k=1}^{N} u_{kj} x_k}{\sum_{k=1}^{N} u_{kj}} \tag{2}$$

The K-means algorithm is a robust clustering technique renowned for its proficiency in data segmentation through centroid-based partitioning. It boasts several merits, including simplicity, speed, and scalability. However, it is not without limitations. Notably, K-means exhibits sensitivity to the initial positions of cluster centers and demands the predefined number of clusters. These constraints have the potential to impact its overall performance.

2.2 Fuzzy C-Means

Fuzzy C-Means (FCM), proposed by Bezdek and colleagues in 1984 [24], is a widely recognized fuzzy clustering algorithm rooted in Zadeh's theory of fuzzy sets [25]. FCM serves the purpose of data partitioning into clusters by considering the similarity among data points. In the FCM approach, each data point is associated with all clusters, represented by values between 0 and 1, denoting the degree of similarity between the data point and each cluster. The central focus of the FCM fuzzy clustering algorithm revolves around optimizing the distances between data points and cluster centroids [26]. This optimization is achieved through the objective function defined by formula (3).

$$J_m(u,v) = \sum_{k=1}^{N} \sum_{j=1}^{c} (u_{kj})^m . ||x_k - v_j||^2 \rightarrow Min \qquad (3)$$

With constraint conditions:

$$\begin{cases} \sum_{j=1}^{c} u_{kj} = 1 \\ u_{kj} \in [0,1] \end{cases}$$

In which: X is the source dataset $X = \{x_1, x_2, ..., x_N\}$ with N data points, c is the number of clusters, v is the set of cluster centers, u_{kj} is the membership degree of element k in cluster i, m is the fuzzy parameter.

By solving the objective function (3), we obtain the formulas for cluster centroids (4) and membership degrees (5) as follows:

$$v = \frac{\sum_{k=1}^{N} (u_{kj})^m x_k}{\sum_{k=1}^{N} (u_{kj})^m} \qquad (4)$$

$$u_{kj} = \left(\sum_{j=1}^{c} \left(\frac{d_{ik}}{d_{jk}} \right)^{2/(m-1)} \right)^{-1} \qquad (5)$$

The FCM (Fuzzy C-Means) method allows a data point to have membership degrees in multiple clusters, leading to enhanced clustering performance when compared to traditional methods like K-means. This flexibility in membership assignment enables FCM to capture complex patterns and relationships in the data, making it a valuable technique for various clustering tasks.

3   The Proposed Method

In this study, we introduce a novel approach to fuzzy multi-view clustering by employing a co-training algorithm. Our method is applied to a diverse multi-view dataset gathered from multiple sources, featuring distinctive characteristics, including variations in the number of records within each view, discrepancies in the number of attributes across different views, and a complex many-to-many relationship between the views.

3.1   Algorithm Idea

The MCFC algorithm consists of three steps as follows:

Step 1: Fuzzy clustering for unlabeled data in each view. In this step, the Fuzzy C-Means (FCM) algorithm is independently applied to each view (viewA and viewB) to partition data points into clusters. The result of this step includes cluster centroids and corresponding membership degrees for each view. The membership degrees are denoted as: $\bar{u}^A$ (membership degree of a data point on viewA with respect to the centroids) and $\bar{u}^B$ (membership degree of a data point on viewB with respect to the centroids).

Step 2: Calculate the dependency degrees of data points in viewA on the cluster center in viewB (and vice versa).

Step 3: Multi-view co-training fuzzy semi-supervised clustering. In this step, the results from viewA are used as training data for viewB, and vice versa. The goal is to maximize cross-consensus across all views and achieve the broadest consensus.

3.2   Algorithm Details

Building on the ideas presented in the previous section, this part will elaborate on the modeling of the proposed approach. The objective function of the method is represented by three components, as follows:

$$J(u^A, u^B, v^A, v^B) = \sum_{k_A=1}^{N_A} \sum_{j=1}^{c} u_{k_A j}^{A}{}^2 ||x_{k_A}^A - v_j^A||^2$$

$$+ \sum_{k_B=1}^{N_B} \sum_{j=1}^{c} u_{k_B j}^{B}{}^2 ||x_{k_B}^B - v_j^B||^2$$

$$+ \sum_{k_A=1}^{N_A} \sum_{j=1}^{c} (u_{k_A j}^{A} - u_{k_A j}^{AB})^2 ||x_{k_A}^A - v_j^A||^2$$

$$+ \sum_{k_B=1}^{N_B} \sum_{j=1}^{c} (u_{k_B j}^{B} - u_{k_B j}^{BA})^2 ||x_{k_B}^B - v_j^B||^2 \qquad (6)$$

$$+ \sum_{k_A=1}^{N_A} \sum_{j=1}^{c} (u_{k_A j}^{A} - \overline{u}_{k_A j}^{A})^2 ||x_{k_A}^A - v_j^A||^2$$

$$+ \sum_{k_B=1}^{N_B} \sum_{j=1}^{c} (u_{k_B j}^{B} - \overline{u}_{k_B j}^{B})^2 ||x_{k_B}^B - v_j^B||^2 \rightarrow Min$$

With constraint conditions:

$$\begin{cases} \sum_{j=1}^{c} u_{kj}^A = \sum_{j=1}^{c} u_{kj}^B = 1 \\ u_{kj} \in [0, 1] \end{cases}$$

Explanation: $x_{k_A}^A, x_{k_B}^B$ are the data points on viewA and viewB respectively. v_j^A, v_j^B are the cluster centers in viewA and viewB. $u_{k_A j}^A, u_{k_B j}^B$ represent the dependency degree of data point k to cluster j in viewA and viewB respectively. $\overline{u}_{k_A j}^A, \overline{u}_{k_B j}^B$ represent the dependency degree of data point k_A, k_B to cluster j after using the FCM algorithm on viewA and viewB respectively.

The objective function (6) is represented by three components, as follows:

– The component represents fuzzy clustering:

$$\sum_{k_A=1}^{N_A} \sum_{j=1}^{c} u_{k_A j}^{A}{}^2 ||x_{k_A}^A - v_j^A||^2$$

and

$$\sum_{k_B=1}^{N_B} \sum_{j=1}^{c} u_{k_B j}^{B}{}^2 ||x_{k_B}^B - v_j^B||^2$$

– The component represents co-training:

$$\sum_{k_A=1}^{N_A} \sum_{j=1}^{c} (u_{k_A j}^{A} - u_{k_A j}^{AB})^2 ||x_{k_A}^A - v_j^A||^2$$

and

$$\sum_{k_B=1}^{N_B} \sum_{j=1}^{c} \left(u_{k_Bj}^{B} - u_{k_Bj}^{BA} \right)^2 ||x_{k_B}^{B} - v_j^{B}||^2$$

- The component represents semi-supervised:

$$\sum_{k_A=1}^{N_A} \sum_{j=1}^{c} \left(u_{k_Aj}^{A} - \overline{u}_{k_Aj}^{A} \right)^2 ||x_{k_A}^{A} - v_j^{A}||^2$$

and

$$\sum_{k_B=1}^{N_B} \sum_{j=1}^{c} \left(u_{k_Bj}^{B} - \overline{u}_{k_Bj}^{B} \right)^2 ||x_{k_B}^{B} - v_j^{B}||^2$$

The cluster centers are calculated according to the following formula:

$$v_j^{A} = \frac{\sum_{k_A=1}^{N_A} \left[u_{k_Aj}^{A}{}^2 + (u_{k_Aj}^{A} - u_{k_Aj}^{AB})^2 + (u_{k_Aj}^{A} - \overline{u^A}_{k_Aj})^2 \right].x_{k_A}^{A}}{\sum_{k_A=1}^{N_A} \left[u_{k_Aj}^{A}{}^2 + (u_{k_Aj}^{A} - u_{k_Aj}^{AB})^2 + (u_{k_Aj}^{A} - \overline{u^A}_{k_Aj})^2 \right]} \tag{7}$$

$$v_j^{B} = \frac{\sum_{k_B=1}^{N_B} \left[u_{k_Bj}^{B}{}^2 + (u_{k_Bj}^{B} - u_{k_Bj}^{BA})^2 + (u_{k_Bj}^{B} - \overline{u^B}_{k_Bj})^2 \right].x_{k_B}^{B}}{\sum_{k_B=1}^{N_B} \left[u_{k_Bj}^{B}{}^2 + (u_{k_Bj}^{B} - u_{k_Bj}^{BA})^2 + (u_{k_Bj}^{B} - \overline{u^B}_{k_Bj})^2 \right]} \tag{8}$$

The Lagrange multiplier method is used to determine the degree of u_{kj}^{A} and u_{kj}^{B} :

$$u_{k_Aj}^{A} = \frac{1 - \sum_{i_A=1}^{N_A} \Delta_{i_Aj}}{\sum_{i_A=1}^{N_A} \frac{d_{k_Aj}^{A}{}^2}{d_{i_Aj}^{A}{}^2}} + \Delta_{k_Aj} \tag{9}$$

Explanation:

$$\Delta_{k_Aj} = \frac{u_{k_Aj}^{AB} + \overline{u}_{k_Aj}^{A}}{3}$$

$$u_{k_Bj}^{B} = \frac{1 - \sum_{i_B=1}^{N_B} \Delta_{i_Bj}}{\sum_{i_B=1}^{N_B} \frac{d_{k_Bj}^{A}{}^2}{d_{i_Bj}^{B}{}^2}} + \Delta_{k_Bj} \tag{10}$$

Explanation:

$$\Delta_{k_Bj} = \frac{u_{k_Bj}^{BA} + \overline{u}_{k_Bj}^{B}}{3}$$

The algorithm diagram is depicted in Fig. 2.

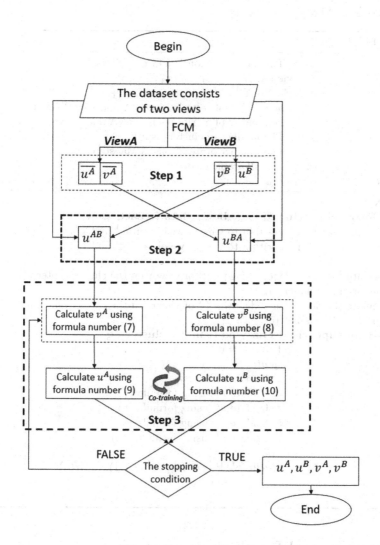

Fig. 2. Algorithm diagram

3.3 MCFC Algorithm Table

Algorithm 1: MCFC

Input	- The dataset X consists of two views:
	viewA: $X^A = \{x_1^A, x_2^A, x_3^A, \ldots, x_n^A\}$
	viewB: $X^A = \{x_1^A, x_2^A, x_3^A, \ldots, x_n^A\}$
	The number of records in viewA and viewB is equal.
	The number of attributes in viewA and viewB may differ.
	- The number of clusters is c
	- The number of iterations is Maxstep
	- The allowable error ϵ
Output	u^A, u^B, v^A, v^B

BEGIN

Step1: Fuzzy clustering for unlabeled data in each view

1.1. Applying the FCM algorithm to viewA, we obtain $\overline{u}^A$ and $\overline{v}^A$.

1.2. Applying the FCM algorithm to viewB, we obtain $\overline{u}^B$ and $\overline{v}^B$.

Step2:

2.1. Calculate the dependency degree u^{AB} of viewA on the cluster center v^B using the formula number (5).

2.2. Calculate the dependency degree u^{BA} of viewB on the cluster center v^A using the formula number (5).

Step3: Semi-supervised Fuzzy co-training clustering

        3.1. Init t = 0

        Repeat:

        3.2. $t = t + 1$

        3.3. Update v^A using formula (7)

        3.4. Update v^B using formula (8)

        3.5. Update u^A using formula (9)

        3.6. Update u^B using formula (10)

        Until:

        $Max\{||u^{A(t+1)} - u^A(t||, ||u^B(t+1) - u^B(t||\} \leq \epsilon$

        or $t \geq$ Maxstep

END

---

4 Experimental Results

4.1 Environmental Configuration

To validate the performance of the proposed method, the research team conducted simulations using datasets collected from two sources. The datasets include: **Fake and real news dataset** https://www.kaggle.com/datasets/clmentbisaillon/fake-and-real-news-dataset (It's called viewA), **Fake News** https://www.kaggle.com/competitions/fake-news/data (It's called viewB).

The detailed information about the dataset presented in Table 1.

Table 1. Summary of the multi-view data sets

	No. of clusters	No. of objects	No. of variables
ViewA	2	4	44898
ViewB	2	4	5070

The experimental setup was performed on an Apple MacBook Air M1 2020 with a configuration of 8GB/256GB/7-core GPU, using Python programming language version 3.10. To assess performance, we use the following criteria: ACC (accuracy score), DB (Davies-Bouldin index), NMI(Normalized Mutual Information) and ARI (Adjusted Rand Index).

i) Clustering accuracy [27]: Cluster accuracy measures the level of accuracy in labeling data points within each cluster. A higher ACC value indicates better clustering performance.

$$\text{ACC} = \frac{\text{Number of correctly classified points}}{\text{Total number of points}}$$

in which: Number of correctly classified points refers to the total number of points in the clustering that are assigned the correct label. Total number of points represents the total number of points in the clustering.

ACC is used to evaluate the quality of a clustering. It measures the ratio of correctly classified instances by the model. A higher ACC indicates a higher proportion of correct classifications, suggesting a better clustering model. In the case of binary clustering, ACC can also be understood as the accuracy of correctly predicting classifications.

ii) Clustering quality: We use the DB measure (Davies-Bouldin index) [28]. Cluster quality measures the separation and cohesion among clusters. A smaller DB value indicates better cluster quality. To compute the DB index, several quantities are involved. Let us denote by δ_k the mean distance of the points belonging to cluster C_k to their barycenter $G^{\{k\}}$:

$$\delta_k = \frac{1}{n_k} \sum_{i \in I_k} \|M_i^{\{k\}} - G^{\{k\}}\| \tag{11}$$

Let us also denote by

$$\Delta_{kk'} = d(G^{\{k\}}, G^{\{k'\}}) = \|G^{\{k'\}} - G^{\{k\}}\|$$

the distance between the barycenters $G^{\{k\}}$ and $G^{\{k'\}}$ of clusters C_k and C'_k.

One computes, for each cluster k, the maximum M_k of the quotients $\frac{\delta_k + \delta_{k'}}{\Delta_{kk'}}$ for all indices $k' \neq k$. The Davies-Bouldin index is the mean value, among all the clusters, of the quantities M_k:

$$C = \frac{1}{K} \sum_{k=1}^{K} M_k = \frac{1}{K} \sum_{k=1}^{K} \max_{k' \neq k} \left(\frac{\delta_k + \delta_{k'}}{\Delta_{kk'}} \right) \tag{12}$$

The DB index serves as a criterion to compare different clustering algorithms or evaluate the performance of a single algorithm. A lower DB index indicates better clustering quality, where clusters are more compact and well-separated. Conversely, a higher DB index suggests poorer clustering performance, with clusters being less cohesive and more overlapping.

iii) ARI(Adjusted Rand Index) [27]: The Adjusted Rand Index is a measure used to assess the similarity between two clusters or between a cluster and the ground truth, for the purpose of evaluating the quality of data clustering.

The formula to calculate ARI for a single view can be expressed as follows:

$$\text{ARI} = \frac{\text{RI} - \text{Expected\_RI}}{\max(\text{RI}_{\max} - \text{Expected\_RI}, 0)} \tag{13}$$

in which: ARI represents the Adjusted Rand Index. RI denotes the Rand Index, which measures the agreement between the predicted clusters and the true labels. Expected_RI represents the expected Rand Index under the assumption of random label assignments. RI_max is the maximum possible Rand Index, calculated as the expected Rand Index when the predicted cluster assignments perfectly match the true labels.

The ARI is computed by subtracting the expected Rand Index from the actual Rand Index and dividing it by the maximum possible difference between the Rand Index and the expected Rand Index. The ARI ranges between -1 and 1:

- A value close to 1 indicates a high agreement between the predicted clusters and the true labels, beyond what would be expected by chance. It suggests that the clustering algorithm has accurately captured the underlying structure of the data.
- A value close to 0 suggests random agreement, meaning that the clustering results are not significantly better than random chance.
- A negative value implies a disagreement that is worse than random, indicating that the clustering results are worse than random chance.

Therefore, a higher ARI value is desirable, indicating a better agreement between the predicted clusters and the true labels. A value of 1 indicates a perfect clustering solution, while values close to 0 or negative values indicate poor or random clustering results.

iv) NMI(Normalized Mutual Information) [27]: The Normalized Mutual Information is a clustering metric that quantifies the degree of information shared between two clusterings, providing a normalized measure of their similarity. The formula to calculate NMI for a single view can be expressed as follows:

$$\text{NMI} = \frac{2 \times \text{MI}(V, L)}{\text{H}(V) + \text{H}(L)} \tag{14}$$

in which: NMI represents the Normalized Mutual Information. $\text{MI}(V, L)$ denotes the Mutual Information between the predicted clusters in view V and the true labels L. It measures the shared information or agreement between the two sets. $\text{H}(V)$ is the entropy of the predicted clusters in view V. It quantifies the uncertainty or disorder within the predicted clusters. $H(L)$ represents the entropy of the true labels. It measures the uncertainty or disorder within the true labels.

The NMI is calculated by dividing the twice the Mutual Information by the sum of the entropies of the predicted clusters and the true labels. This normalization accounts for the differences in the sizes of the clusters and the number of unique labels. By using the NMI for a single view, we can evaluate how well the clustering algorithm captures the structure and patterns within that particular view. It provides insights into the quality of clustering within that view and helps in assessing the performance of different algorithms or parameter settings for that specific view.

4.2 Results and Discussion

The MCFC method is compared with two other methods, K-means [23] and FCM [24]. We installed the K-means and FCM algorithms on the viewA and viewB datasets. Afterward, we merged the two datasets from two views: viewA (title, text) and viewB (title, text) to validate the proposed algorithm. The comparison results are shown in Table 2.

In Table 2 , MCFC achieved better values according to the criteria of ACC, ARI, and NMI. Therefore, the MCFC method outperformed the K-means and FCM methods in achieving cluster accuracy.

In Fig. 3, a chart presents the results of three algorithms (K-means, FCM, and MCFC) based on metrics such as ACC, DB, ARI, and NMI. According to the chart, the MCFC algorithm demonstrates identical clustering results across both views. Thus, the proposed algorithm can distinguish between real and fake news equally on both views.

Table 2. Table of experimental results comparing three algorithms (Bold values indicate the best results)

Algorithms	Kmeans			FCM			MCFC		
Data	ViewA	ViewB	Average	ViewA	ViewB	Average	ViewA	ViewB	Average
ACC	0.6588	0.4724	0.5656	0.6588	0.4724	0.5656	**0.8722**	**0.8722**	**0.8722**
DB	0.5102	0.4997	0.5050	**0.5100**	**0.4994**	**0.5047**	0.8702	0.8702	0.8702
ARI	0.1009	0.0028	0.0518	0.1016	0.0027	0.0521	**0.5541**	**0.5541**	**0.5541**
NMI	0.0742	0.0022	0.0382	0.0748	0.0021	0.0384	**0.4529**	**0.4529**	**0.4529**

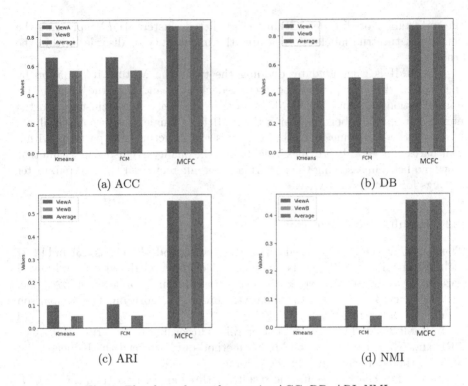

(a) ACC   (b) DB

(c) ARI   (d) NMI

Fig. 3. The chart shows the metrics ACC, DB, ARI, NMI

5   Conclusions and Future Works

This study presents MCFC, a novel co-training fuzzy multi-view clustering model. MCFC is specifically designed to analyze multi-view data originating from diverse sources, effectively capturing the inherent characteristics of such data. Empirical investigations carried out as part of this study reveal that the MCFC method surpasses both K-means and FCM methods in terms of clustering accuracy. Furthermore, this method excels in accurately classifying genuine and fake news, offering users a reliable means of accessing and utilizing information with precision and efficiency. These promising findings serve as a catalyst for future research endeavors within the realm of multi-view clustering.

Despite its evident effectiveness when dealing with multi-source data, the MCFC model exhibits certain limitations. Notably, it involves a substantial number of parameters, and the repetitive co-training process contributes to prolonged computational time and inefficiency. These challenges become particularly pronounced when handling multi-source data with more than two distinct perspectives. Addressing the intricacies of multi-view data, especially when derived from divergent sources with varying perspectives, necessitates the continuous development of innovative algorithms in forthcoming research initiatives.

Acknowledgments. This work has been supported by Vietnam National University, Hanoi under the Project, code: QG.23.66.

References

1. Li, X., et al.: A multi-view model for visual tracking via correlation filters. Knowl. Based Syst. **113**, 88–99 (2016)
2. Tuan, T.M., et al.: A new approach for semi-supervised fuzzy clustering with multiple fuzzifiers. Int. J. Fuzzy Syst. **24**(8), 3688–3701 (2022)
3. Al-Amri, S.S., Kalyankar, N.V.: Image segmentation by using threshold techniques. arXiv preprint arXiv:1005.4020 (2010)
4. Thong, P.H., et al.: Picture-neutrosophic trusted safe semi-supervised fuzzy clustering for noisy data. Comput. Syst. Sci. Eng. **46**(2) (2023)
5. Huan, P.T., et al.: TS3FCM: trusted safe semi-supervised fuzzy clustering method for data partition with high confidence. Multimed. Tools Appl. **81**(9), 12567–12598 (2022)
6. Zhu, Z., et al.: Shared Subspace Learning for Latent Representation of Multi-View Data. J. Inf. Hiding Multim. Signal Process. **5**(3), 546–554 (2014)
7. Yang, Y., Wang, H.: Multi-view clustering: a survey. Big Data Min. Anal. **1**(2), 83–107 (2018)
8. Bickel, S., Scheffer, T.: Multi-view clustering. ICDM **4**, 2004 (2004)
9. Ye, F., et al.: New approaches in multi-view clustering. Recent Appl. Data Cluster. **195** (2018)
10. Xu, C., Tao, D., Xu, C.: A survey on multi-view learning. arXiv preprint arXiv,1304.5634 (2013)
11. Sun, S.: A survey of multi-view machine learning. Neural Comput. Appl. **23**, 2031–2038 (2013)
12. Blum, A., Mitchell, T.: Combining labeled and unlabeled data with co-training. In: Proceedings of the Eleventh Annual Conference on Computational Learning Theory (1998)
13. Wang, W.Y.: "liar, liar pants on fire": a new benchmark dataset for fake news detection. arXiv preprint arXiv:1705.00648 (2017)
14. Wu, L., Huan, L.: Tracing fake-news footprints: characterizing social media messages by how they propagate. In: Proceedings of the Eleventh ACM International Conference on Web Search and Data Mining (2018)
15. Ma, J., et al.: Detect rumors using time series of social context information on microblogging websites. In: Proceedings of the 24th ACM International on Conference on Information and Knowledge Management (2015)
16. Kim, J., et al.: Leveraging the crowd to detect and reduce the spread of fake news and misinformation. In: Proceedings of the Eleventh ACM International Conference on Web Search and Data Mining (2018)
17. Shu, K., et al.: Fake news detection on social media: a data mining perspective. ACM SIGKDD Explor. Newsl. **19**(1), 22–36 (2017)
18. Potthast, M., et al.: A stylometric inquiry into hyperpartisan and fake news. arXiv preprint arXiv:1702.05638 (2017)
19. Yang, S., et al.: Unsupervised fake news detection on social media: a generative approach. In: Proceedings of the AAAI Conference on Artificial Intelligence, vol. 33(01) (2019)

20. Jin, Z., et al.: News verification by exploiting conflicting social viewpoints in microblogs. In: Proceedings of the AAAI Conference on Artificial Intelligence, vol. 30(1), pp. 2972–2978 (2016)
21. Ruchansky, N., Seo, S., Liu, Y.: CSI: a hybrid deep model for fake news detection. In: Proceedings of the 2017 ACM on Conference on Information and Knowledge Management (2017)
22. Wu, K., Yang, S., Zhu, K.Q.: False rumors detection on Sina Weibo by propagation structures. In: 2015 IEEE 31st International Conference on Data Engineering, pp. 651–662. IEEE (2015)
23. Ikotun, A.M., et al.: K-means clustering algorithms: a comprehensive review, variants analysis, and advances in the era of big data. Inf. Sci. (2022)
24. Bezdek, J.C., Ehrlich, R., Full, W.: FCM: the fuzzy c-means clustering algorithm. Comput. Geosci. **10**(2–3), 191–203 (1984)
25. Zadeh, L.A.: Fuzzy sets. Inf. Control **8**(3), 338–353 (1965)
26. Tuan, T.M., Thong, P.H., Ngan, T.T.: An improvement of trusted safe semi-supervised fuzzy clustering method with multiple fuzzifiers. J. Comput. Sci. Cybernet. **38**(1), 47–61 (2022)
27. Wang, J., Liu, Y., Ye, W.: FMvC: fast multi-view clustering. IEEE Access **11**, 12808–12820 (2023)
28. Davies, D.L., Bouldin, D.W.: A cluster separation measure. IEEE Trans. Pattern Anal. Mach. Intell. **2**, 224–227 (1979)

An Efficient Approach to the k-Strong Barrier Coverage Problem Under the Probabilistic Sensing Model in Wireless Multimedia Sensor Networks

Nguyen Thi My Binh[1(✉)], Nguyen Van Thien[1], Ho Viet Duc Luong[2],
and Dang The Ngoc[3]

[1] Hanoi University of Industry, Hanoi, Vietnam
{binhntm,thiennv}@haui.edu.vn
[2] Hanoi University of Science and Technology, Hanoi, Vietnam
[3] Posts and Telecommunications Institute of Technology, Hanoi, Vietnam
ngocdt@ptit.edu.vn

Abstract. Barrier coverage (BC) is a potential coverage model in wireless multimedia sensor networks (WMSNs) for applications such as intrusion detection and border surveillance. This model necessitates a chain of sensors positioned across the deployment region with overlapping sensing fields. However, achieving k-strong barrier coverage following the initial random sensor deployment poses significant challenges. BC holes frequently emerge within the sensing fields, even in high-density sensor. Previous research primarily focused on addressing the problem of constructing k-strong barrier coverage under a Boolean disk or a sector coverage model. This approach leads to inaccurate assessments of barrier coverage quality. To address the limitation, this paper presents an efficient scheme for achieving k-strong barrier coverage in heterogeneous WMSNs (HeWMSNs) using the minimum number of mobile sensors, while employing a probabilistic sector coverage model. By leveraging the proposed probabilistic sector sensing coverage model, we formulate the problem of attaining k-strong barrier coverage in HeWMSNs as a combinatorial optimization problem called KSB-HeWMSN. Subsequently, an efficient evolutionary algorithm is developed to tackle this problem. Through both analytical analysis and experimental evaluations conducted on multiple instances, the proposed algorithm demonstrates its suitability for the KSB-HeWMSN problem and its superior solution quality compared to previous approaches.

Keywords: Heterogeneous wireless multimedia sensor networks · barrier coverage · k-strong barrier coverage · evolutionary algorithm

1 Introduction

Barrier coverage (BC) in wireless Internet of Things sensor networks is garnering more and more attention from academia to industry all over the world [9,21]. BC is a well-known appropriate coverage model in wireless sensor networks (WSNs) for intrusion

© ICST Institute for Computer Sciences, Social Informatics and Telecommunications Engineering 2024
Published by Springer Nature Switzerland AG 2024. All Rights Reserved
N. Thi Dieu Linh et al. (Eds.): ADHOCNETS 2023, LNICST 558, pp. 167–180, 2024.
https://doi.org/10.1007/978-3-031-55993-8_13

detection and border surveillance applications that aim to detect intruders attempting to penetrate protected areas [1, 11]. BC is a sensing region made up of nodes or sensor clusters connected over the entire deployment zone, creating one or more sensor barriers that act as a "virtual fence" to detect intrusions. In contrast to full coverage, barrier coverage can effectively detect intruders with fewer sensor nodes since it does not have to detect a moving intruder along every point of his trajectory in the monitored area. BC can be sufficient if the object can be detected by at least k distinct sensors before it penetrates through the sensor field. This requires a WSN providing k strong barrier coverage over a region of interest (ROI) such that any crossing path intersects with the sensing areas of k distinct sensors [18]. Sensor nodes, however, can typically be dispersed or dropped randomly in large numbers over a vast inaccessible, or hostile territory. It is challenging to achieve strong barrier coverage after an initial random deployment of sensors since their locations cannot be predicted or controlled. Therefore, optimizing WSNs deployment costs or the minimization of sensor count while guaranteeing robust barrier coverage in extensive geographical areas assumes paramount significance.

Today, heterogeneous wireless multimedia sensor networks (HeWMSNs) have drawn tremendous attention due to their potential impacts on scientific research and numerous attractive applications. Heterogeneous networks consist of sensors with different capabilities and therefore can bring benefits such as improving network performance, reliability of data transmission, prolonging network lifetime, decreasing the latency of data transportation, reducing the cost of developing network, etc. [12]. Wireless multimedia sensor networks (WMSNs) can significantly improve the sensing ability on environments and description ability of environmental events [16], with the development of various types of multimedia sensors, such as camera sensors, video sensors, etc. These sensors comply with the directional sensing model and can collect much richer information (images or video) than others with omni-directional sensing models. However, WMSNs have unique features of the directional sensing model, such as angle of view, working direction, and line of sight. These features have brought in new challenges such as the requirement for using more parameters to model the directional sensors and the increasing complexities of solving the k strong barrier coverage problem in WMSNs. Although prior research has extensively examined the challenge of achieving k strong barrier coverage in the directional sensing coverage model, a majority of these investigations have been predicated on several assumptions. Firstly, their prevalent utilization of Boolean sectors as the sensing coverage models for the sensors [8, 10, 13] has introduced inaccuracies in assessing the coverage quality along the barrier since every point within the sensor's sensing range is equally considered. Secondly, homogeneous sensor networks have been assumed in these studies. Lastly, the solutions proposed in the literature have ample room for quality enhancement.

As previously highlighted, it is of utmost importance to address the k strong barrier coverage problem in HWMSNs while simultaneously minimizing the sensor count. Furthermore, the introduction of a novel sensing coverage model that surpasses the constraints of the Boolean model assumes great significance. Consequently, in this study, we propose an efficient heuristic algorithm that aims to minimize the required quantity of mobile sensors while attaining k-strong barriers within HeWMSN, achieved by utilizing a probabilistic sector sensing model.

The main contributions of this paper are as follows:

- Formulate the k-strong barrier coverage problem in HeWMSNs under the proposed probabilistic sector sensing model into a combinatorial optimization problem known as KSB-HeWMSN.
- Proffer an elite evolutionary algorithm called KSB-EA with a new individual representation, suitable crossover and mutation operators for solving KSB-HeWMSN.
- Conduct various experimental scenarios to examine the proposed algorithms and compare the proposed method to state-of-the-art.

The rest of the paper is organized as follows. Section 2 presents Related works. Preliminaries and formulation for the KSB-HeWMSN problem are discussed in Sect. 3. Section 4 introduces the proposed algorithms. Experimental results are given and analyzed in Sect. 5. Finally, the conclusions of the paper are presented in Sect. 6.

2   Related Works

BC problems in WSNs can be classified into weak barrier coverage and strong barrier coverage [21]. Regarding weak barrier coverage, the minimal exposed path is thought to be the worst-case coverage, which is a weak barrier coverage. Recently, Binh et al. have investigated this field such as [3,4,14,19]. The minimal exposure path (MEP) is a typical path of the worst coverage in WSNs. The MEP problem aims to find a path where an intruder can penetrate through a region with the lowest probability of being detected and was proven an NP-Hard problem [7], and Binh et al. have proposed efficient heuristic algorithms for solving it with different scenarios.

With reference to strong barrier coverage, algorithms for building barriers have been researched in various respects. Saipulla et al. in [15] studied how to deploy efficiently for barrier coverage in WSNs and established a tight lower bound for the existence of barrier coverage under line-based deployments. Recently, Ma et al. in [13] suggested precise algorithms for rotatable line-based deployed directional sensors to cover barriers. To determine the best sensor orientations for BC with the least amount of sensor deployment, the study offered two optimization models for the problem, one based on integer linear programming and the other based on mixed-integer linear programming. The suggested algorithms can achieve better coverage and use fewer sensors than existing techniques, according to simulation data.

Furthermore, Zhang et al. [22] also focused on the k-barrier coverage problem in omni-directional WSNs, which is then transformed into a global optimization problem. The authors proposed a heuristic algorithm, which was combined with particle swarm optimization and artificial immunity for solving the problem. The research of [17] focused the ways to improve barrier coverage by combining mobile sensors with a probabilistic sensing model. Most recently, Chen et al. in [8] described how to effectively leverage the rotational capabilities of fixed sensors and the mobility capabilities of mobile sensors to achieve k-barrier coverage in a randomly deployed hybrid visual sensor network. The study focused on three issues: minimizing the number of mobile sensors needed, reducing the overall moving distance, and solving the maximum number of strong barriers with deployed stationary and mobile sensors. To solve these issues, they developed a robust k-barrier coverage enhancing scheme (KCES) and a virtual barrier curve (VBC) model to translate the k-barrier construction issues into issues with repairing barrier gaps in k turns. These studies are the most relevant to ours. However, their proposed algorithms are not efficient because the quality of solutions and the computation time are still room for improvement.

In short, after delving into the related works to the problem of constructing k-strong barrier coverage in HeWMSNs while minimizing the requirement of mobile sensor nodes (referred to as the KSB-HeWMSN problem), we find out that this problem holds significant importance in both theoretical studies and practical applications, but it presents several intrinsic challenges that need to be addressed.

3   Preliminaries and Problem Formulation

3.1   Preliminaries

The Probabilistic Sector Coverage Model

A multimedia sensor s can be characterized by an 8-tuple $\langle\, x, y, r_1, r_2, \alpha, \beta, \gamma_1, \gamma_2 \rangle$, where (x, y) is the position P of the sensor node; r_1 and r_2 respectively denotes an uncertain and a maximum sensing radius of the sensor; α is half of the sensing angle; $\beta = \angle(\overrightarrow{Wd}, \overrightarrow{Px})$ is the orientation angle, where $\overrightarrow{Px}$ is the horizontal axis and $\overrightarrow{Wd}$ is the unit vector whose direction coincides with the bisector of the sensing angle; and γ_1, γ_2 are parameters set according to the physical properties of the sensor. The coverage function of the probabilistic sector model is given as

$$f(s, O) = \begin{cases} 1 & \text{if } d \leq r_1 \text{ and } d \cdot \cos(\alpha) \leq \overrightarrow{PO} \cdot \overrightarrow{Wd}, \\ \exp(-\gamma_1 \cdot \delta^{\gamma_2}) & \text{if } r_1 < d \leq r_2 \text{ and } d \cdot \cos(\alpha) \leq \overrightarrow{PO} \cdot \overrightarrow{Wd}, \\ 0 & \text{otherwise} \end{cases} \quad (1)$$

demonstrating the probability of object O detected by sensor s, where $\overrightarrow{PO}$ is the vector from sensor's position P to object O, $d = \left|\overrightarrow{PO}\right|, \delta = d - r_1$.

Strong Barrier with Desired Probability $\mathcal{P}$

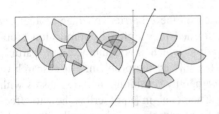
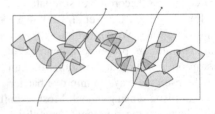

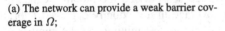

(a) The network can provide a weak barrier coverage in Ω;

(b) The network can provide a strong barrier coverage in Ω

Fig. 1. Illustration of the two types of barrier coverage on the region of interest Ω

A strong barrier with desired probability $\mathcal{P}$ is a set of sensors ensuring that every intruder's path is detected by that set with a probability greater than or equal to $\mathcal{P}$. A HeWMSN deployed over a RoI is said to achieve k-strong barrier if there exists a set of k disjoint strong barriers with desired probability $\mathcal{P}$ (Fig. 1).

Weighted Barrier Graph

Based on the above definitions, a weight barrier graph (WBG) is defined as a set $\langle \mathcal{V}, \mathcal{E}, \mathcal{W} \rangle$, where $\mathcal{V} = \{\mathsf{lb}, v_1, v_2, ..., v_n, \mathsf{rb}\}$ is the set of vertices representing n sensor nodes and two boundaries of the RoI, i.e. the left boundary $\mathsf{lb} \equiv v_0$ and the right boundary $\mathsf{rb} \equiv v_{n+1}$; $\mathcal{E} = \{(v_i, v_j) | i = \overline{0, n}; j = \overline{1, n+1}\}$ is the set of edges; and $\mathcal{W}$ is the weight mapping, where the edge $e(v_i, v_j)$ is associated with a weight denoted as $\mathbf{w}(v_i, v_j)$, representing the minimum number of mobile sensors required to connect vertices v_i and v_j. Figure 2a depicts a HeWMSN including 6 sensors deployed randomly in a ROI and Fig. 2b illustrates the WBG constructed from that network.

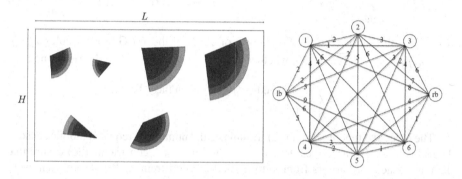

(a) A HeWMSN deployed in the RoI.   (b) The WBG built from the network.

Fig. 2. Illustration of transforming from HeWMSN to WBG

3.2 Problem Formulation

Given a region of interest Ω with the width W and the height H, where n heterogeneous multimedia sensors are randomly deployed. The objective of the KSB-HeWMSN problem is to construct k-strong barrier coverage while minimizing the number of required mobile sensors to fill the gap among initial static sensors. The KSB-HeWMSN's input and output can be formulated more precisely as follows:

Input:

- L, H: the length and the height of the RoI Ω
- n: the number of multimedia sensors
- $\mathcal{S} = \{s_i = (x_i, y_i, r_{1i}, r_{2i}, \alpha_i, \beta_i, \gamma_{1i}, \gamma_{2i}) | i \in 1...n\}$: set of multimedia sensors deployed in the RoI Ω.
- $r_{1m}, r_{2m}, \alpha_m, \gamma_{1m}, \gamma_{2m}$: the properties of mobile multimedia sensors

- k: the number of strong barriers, $k \leq n$
- $\mathcal{P}$: the desired probability, $0 < \mathcal{P} \leq 1$

Output: The minimum number of required mobile multimedia sensors.

Objective:

$$\underset{x_{p_i p_j l} | p_i, p_j \in \mathcal{V}, l = \overline{1,k}}{\text{minimize}} \quad N_m = \sum_{l=1}^{k} \sum_{(p_i, p_j) \in \mathcal{E}} \mathbf{w}(p_i, p_j) x_{p_i p_j l} \tag{2a}$$

subject to

$$x_{p_i p_j l} \in \{0, 1\} \quad \forall p_i, p_j \in \mathcal{V}, l \in \{1, 2, \ldots, k\}, \tag{2b}$$

$$\sum_{p_j \in \mathcal{V}; l = \overline{1,k}} x_{p_0 p_j l} = \sum_{p_i \in \mathcal{V}; l = \overline{1,k}} x_{p_i p_{n+1} l} = k, \tag{2c}$$

$$\sum_{p_i \in \mathcal{V}; l = \overline{1,k}} x_{p_i p_j l} = \sum_{p_m \in \mathcal{V}; l = \overline{1,k}} x_{p_j p_m l} \leq 1 \quad \forall p_j \in \mathcal{V} \backslash \{\mathsf{lb}, \mathsf{rb}\} \tag{2d}$$

where $\mathcal{V}$ is the set of vertices, $\mathcal{E}$ is the set of edges of the WBG; the variables $x_{p_i p_j l}$, with $p_i, p_j \in \mathcal{V}, l = \overline{1,k}$ decide whether the edge (p_i, p_j) is on the j-barrier or not:

$$x_{p_i p_j l} = \begin{cases} 1, & \text{if the edge } (p_i, p_j) \text{ is on the } j\text{-barrier}, \\ 0, & \text{otherwise} \end{cases} \tag{3}$$

The objective function N_m in (2) formulates the number of required mobile sensors. The constraint (2b) describes the value domain of $x_{p_i p_j l}$, constraints (2c) ensure that there are exactly k barriers from lb to rb, and last constraint (2d) indicates that every sensor p_j appear in at most one barrier.

4   Proposed Algorithm

Evolutionary algorithms are a class of optimization algorithms inspired by the process of natural selection, which can surmount many optimization problems in various areas such as [2,4–6,14,19]. They iteratively evolve a population of candidate solutions through processes such as mutation, crossover, and selection to find optimal or near-optimal solutions to complex problems. This section describes an improved efficient evolution algorithm named KSB-EA to solve the KSB-HeWMSN problem with a flowchart demonstrated in Fig. 3. The pseudocode of the proposed algorithm is described in Algorithm 1.

4.1   Solution Representation and Population Initialization

In KSB-EA, an individual, which represents a feasible solution, is a permutation sequence including $n + k$ integer items, where n items assigned values from 1 to n represent n sensors, and k items assigned values as $n + 1$ represent k-strong barrier. Assume that these k items' indices are $a_1, \ldots, a_k$ and $a_0 = 0$, then each individual can be extracted to gain k strong barriers, with the i-th barrier formatted as

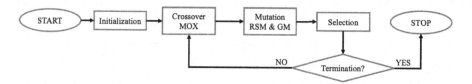

Fig. 3. Basic steps of the proposed algorithm KSB-EA.

Algorithm 1: KSB-EA

Input: The list of sensors S, number of strong barriers k, the desired probability $\mathcal{P}$.
Parameters: Population size Pop_{size}; crossover and mutation rates p_c, p_m; maximum number of generations $G_{\max}$
Output: The sub-optimal solution for the KSB-HeWMSN problem.

1 **begin**
2   **Initialization:** Apply Algorithm 2
3   **Main loop: while** *terminate condition not met* **do**
4   Crossover and Mutation:
5   **foreach** *individual* **ind** *in the population* **do**
6   **if** $\mathcal{U}(0,1) < p_c$ **then**
7   **ind**$' \leftarrow$ a random individual in the population
8   Add MOX(**ind**, **ind**$'$) to the population (Algorithm 3).
9   **end**
10   **if** $\mathcal{U}(0,1) < p_m$ **then**
11   Add RSM(**ind**) and GM(**ind**) to the population (Algorithm 4 and 5).
12   **end**
13   **end**
14   Evaluate and select individuals. (described in Section 4.3).
15   **end**
16   **return** the best individual of the population.
17 **end**

$(\text{lb}, x_{a_{i-1}+1}, ..., x_{a_i-1}, \text{rb})$. Figure 4 demonstrates an individual corresponding to a solution of the problem in Fig. 2a with 6 sensors ($n = 6$) and 3 barriers ($k = 3$). To ensure the diversity of the population, we use a random method to initialize which provides validity guarantees for the generated individuals described in Algorithm 2. The number of individuals is limited by the population size Pop_{size}.

4.2 Crossover and Mutation Operators

The crossover and mutation operators in evolutionary algorithms are pivotal components that significantly contribute to enhancing the diversity present within the population. In this paper, a new crossover operator referred to as MOX, which is a modified version of the traditional order crossover [20], is proposed and described in Algorithm 3. We also incorporate two types of mutation operators: Reverse Sequence Mutation (RSM) and Greedy Mutation (GM), whose details are shown in Algorithm 4 and 5 respectively. The GM draws inspiration from the note that when k is equal to 1, the

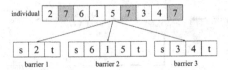

Fig. 4. An individual for the problem in Fig. 2a and the 3-strong barrier solution.

Algorithm 2: Initialization

---

1 **for** $idx \leftarrow 1$ **to** Pop_{size} **do**
2     $c \leftarrow$ an array of $n + k$ elements; $x \leftarrow$ an array of $n + 1$ zeros
3   **for** $l \leftarrow 1$ **to** $n + k$ **do**
4   **do**
5           $c[l] \leftarrow \text{random}(1, n)$
6   **while** $x[c[l]] \geq \max(c[l])$
7        $x[c[l]]++$
8   **end**
9   Add c to population
10 **end**

Algorithm 3: MOX Crossover operator

Input: The parents individuals $p_1 = \{x_1, x_2, ..., x_{n+k}\}$ and $p_2 = \{y_1, y_2, ..., y_{n+k}\}$
Output: The offspring individual $c = \{c_1, c_2, ..., c_{n+k}\}$

---

1 $t \leftarrow \text{random}(1, k)$; Copy t random consecutive barriers from p_1 to c.
2 **for** $i \leftarrow 1$ **to** $n + k$ **do**
3   **if** $t < k$ *and* $y_i = n + 1$ **then**
4        $c_i \leftarrow y_i; t \leftarrow t + 1$
5   **else if** $t < k$ *and* $y_i \notin p_1$ **then**
6        $c_i \leftarrow y_i$
7   **end**
8 **end**
9 **return** c

---

solution to this problem is simply the shortest path from lb to rb in the WBG. However, considering a barrier as a subgraph of the WBG, it is possible to achieve an improved barrier by finding the shortest path within it. The vertices that are not part of the barrier can be reused in subsequent barriers to construct more optimal barriers. The GM operates by utilizing a set called *list* to store the vertices, and it employs the Dijkstra algorithm to find the shortest path on the WBG using the vertices in *list* from lb to rb.

Algorithm 4: RSM operator

Input: The individual $c = \{c_1, c_2, ..., c_{n+k}\}$
Output: The mutated individual $c' = \{c'_1, c'_2, ..., c'_{n+k}\}$

1 $point1, point2 \leftarrow$ two random integers in $\overline{1, n+k}$ that $point2 > point1$; $c' \leftarrow c$
2 **for** $i \leftarrow point1$ **to** $point2$ **do**
3 $\quad | \quad c'_i \leftarrow c_{point2-i+1}$
4 **end**
5 **return** c

Algorithm 5: GM Operator

---

1 **Input:** The individual $c = \{c_1, c_2, ..., c_{n+k}\}$
2 **Output:** The mutated individual $c' = \{c'_1, c'_2, ..., c'_{n+k}\}$
3 $C' \leftarrow$ an empty set of barriers; $list \leftarrow \{lb, rb\}$;
4 **for** $l \leftarrow 1$ **to** $n+k$ **do**
5 $\quad$ **if** $c[l] \neq n+1$ **then**
6 $\quad | \quad$ Add $c[l]$ to $list$
7 $\quad$ **else**
8 $\quad | \quad b \leftarrow$ the shortest path from lb to rb through $list$'s nodes;
9 $\quad | \quad$ Add b to C'. Remove nodes in b from $list$ (except for lb, rb)
10 $\quad$ **end**
11 **end**
12 Encode C' to an individual c';
13 **return** c'.

4.3 Population Selection, Termination Condition and Computational Complexity Analysis

Following the crossover and mutation operators, each individual **ind** is assigned a fitness value denoted as $f(\textbf{ind})$ calculated using the objective function N_m as detailed in the previous section. The population is subsequently organized in ascending order based on the fitness values of individuals, then the top Pop_{size} individuals with the least fitness are selected to persist and evolve in the succeeding generations. The evolution process continues until the fixed number of generation G_{max} is reached, which is the termination condition mentioned in line 3, Algorithm 1.

The computational complexity of computing the fitness function f for each individual is $\mathcal{O}(n)$. The computational complexity of crossover and mutation operators for each individual is also $\mathcal{O}(n)$. Hence, the computational complexity of KSB-EA is $\mathcal{O}(Pop_{size}G_{max}n^2(p_c + p_m))$.

5 Experiments

To prove the effectiveness of the proposed algorithm, we have conducted various experiments with different experimental scenarios to compare KSB-EA with prior algorithms in [22] and [8]. Thorough evaluations and analyses were performed to give deep sights into the experimental results. All experiments were conducted on a server with Intel core i5 v4@2.20 GHz, 16 GB RAM, and Windows 10 OS. The code was written in Java.

5.1 Experimental Settings

We considered two network scales, which are the small-scale one with a RoI of size 100[m] ×20[m], and the large-scale one with a RoI of size 500[m] ×100[m]. Based on the network scale, we set different values for parameters, as shown in Table 1. Here, $\mathcal{U}(a, b)$ denotes the uniform distribution over the interval $[a, b]$.

Table 1. Parameter settings for networks

Parameter	Small-scale networks	Large-scale networks
Number of static sensors n	$50, 80, 110, 140, 170, 200$	$1000, 1250, 1500, 1750, 2000$
Sensing radiuses r_1, r_2	$r_1 = 2, r_2 = 10$	$r_1 \sim \mathcal{U}[4, 6], r_2 \sim \mathcal{U}[10, 20]$
Half of sensing angle α	$60°, 180°$	$\alpha \sim \mathcal{U}[30°, 90°]$
Sensor distribution	Uniform, Gauss, Exponential	
Number of barriers k	$3, 4, 5, 6, 7$	$9, 11, 13, 15, 17$
Desired probability $\mathcal{P}$	60%, 80%	60%, 80%
Physical properties	$\gamma_1 = \gamma_2 = 0.1$	$\gamma_1 = \gamma_2 = 0.1$

We defined an experimental instance as a combination of the **N**umber of **S**tatic sensors (NS), half of the sensing **A**ngle (A), the sensing **R**adius (R) and the sensor distribution (we use these abbreviations to name our experimental instances). We also named each experimental instance using the parameters. For example, in small-scale networks, NS200-A60-UNI describes an experimental instance with 200 static sensors, each sensor has half of the sensing angle of 60°C and sensor distribution is uniform. In large-scale networks, NS1000-GAU describes an experimental instance with 1000 static sensors and the sensor distribution is Gauss.

The number of barriers k, the desired probability $\mathcal{P}$, and the physical properties of sensors γ_1, γ_2 are not considered as parts of an experimental instance, since we run our experiments on the same experimental instance with different values of those. Facing direction β is the same for all experimental instances (always uniformly distributed in $[0, 360]$), thus not included in the experimental instance. Here, we called an input for the KSB-EA algorithm a data point, which combines an experimental instance and a specific value of $k, \mathcal{P}, \gamma_1, \gamma_2$. In total, we have 36 experimental instances of small-scale networks and 15 experimental instances of large-scale networks. In combination with different values of k and $\mathcal{P}$, we get 360 data points for small-scale networks and 150 data points for large-scale networks. Through various experiments, we have chosen the most suitable parameters for the proposed algorithm, which are population size $Pop_{size} = 2000$, the maximum number of generations $G_{max} = 500$, crossover rate $p_c = 0.5$ and mutation rate $p_m = 0.1$. Each data point was run 10 times and the average results are reported.

5.2   Experimental Results

In this part, we compare our proposed algorithm KSB-EA with the state-of-the-art algorithms which are AIPSO of [22] and KCES of [8]. AIPSO and KCES algorithms are replicated to compare with our proposed KSB-EA. The datasets of KSB-EA include datasets based on parameters from KCES in [8] and AIPSO in [22] to guarantee that comparisons between algorithms are fair. The parameters are chosen so that these algorithms share a number of fitness functions and calculations in common.

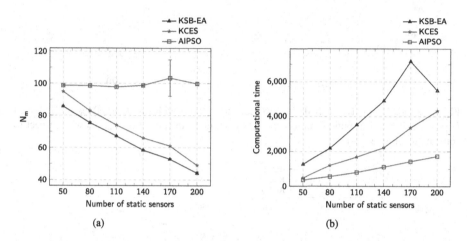

Fig. 5. Comparison between our proposed KSB-EA, KCES [8], and AIPSO [22] with different values of NS, fixed $k = 5, \alpha = 60$, uniform distribution (small-scale networks): (a) with respect to the number of required mobile sensors N_m; (b) with respect to computational time (ms).

Figure 5a shows that KSB-EA obtains much better results than KCES and AIPSO with respect to the solution quality, i.e. the number of mobile sensors N_m. Especially, our KBS-EA is 40% better than AIPSO and 11% better than KCES on average respectively. The reason behind this is the effectiveness of different aspects of KSB-EA such as the individual representation, population initialization method, as well as our proposed evolutionary operators.

Figure 6 shows an even more significant difference between KSB-EA, KCES, and AIPSO. From Fig. 6a, we can see that N_m for AIPSO varies in the range [640, 880], while N_m for KSB-EA and KCES almost approach zero. Actually, on average, KSB-EA found the solution with $\overline{N_m} = 207.4$ for $n = 1000$ and $\overline{N_m} = 9.8$ for $n = 2000$ while KCES found the solution with $\overline{N_m} = 276.9$ for $n = 1000$ and $\overline{N_m} = 14.3$ for $n = 2000$. For standard deviation, it is obvious that AIPSO is highly unstable while KSB-EA and KCES give almost the same results for all runs. The computational time observed in Fig. 6b is not much different from that in Fig. 5b: in general, the computational time of KSB-EA is longer than that of AIPSO and KCES. This is reasonable because KSB-EA has more sophisticated operators than AIPSO and KCES, which is also a trade-off between the solution quality and computational time of the two algorithms.

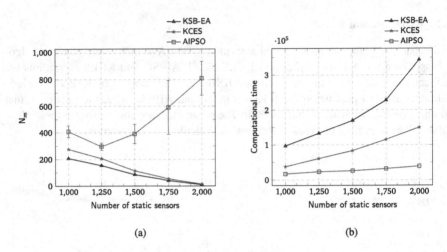

Fig. 6. Comparison between KSB-EA, KCES, and AIPSO with different values of NS, fixed $k = 13$, uniform distribution (large-scale network): (a) with respect to N_m; (b) with respect to computational time (ms).

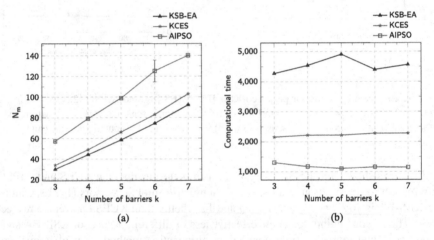

Fig. 7. Comparison between KSB-EA, KCES, and AIPSO with different values of k, fixed NS $=$ 140, uniform distribution (small-scale network): (a) with respect to the number of required mobile sensors N_m; (b) with respect to computational time (ms).

Comparison results between KSB-EA, KCES, and AIPSO when varying the number of barriers k are shown in Fig. 7. The results give the same insights as what we have analyzed so far, i.e. KSB-EA is much better than KCES and AIPSO with respect to N_m and standard deviation while the opposite holds for computational time.

6   Conclusion

The k-strong barrier coverage problem in heterogeneous multimedia sensor networks by minimizing the addition of mobile sensors called KSB-HeWMSN, which is the subject of investigation in this paper, has significant meaning for evaluating the quality of surveillance of wireless sensor networks. The KSB-HeWMSN problem is formulated as a combinatorial optimization problem, and then an elite evolutionary algorithm is proposed to solve it. To evaluate the performance of our algorithm, various experimental scenarios are designed, including small-scale and large-scale networks with different numbers and types of sensors, dimensions of ROIs, and deployment methods. The simulation results demonstrate the efficacy of the proposed algorithm in tackling the KSB-HeWMSN problem, surpassing the efficiency of previous algorithms.

Acknowledgement. This research is funded by Hanoi University of Industry under grant number $25 - 2022 - RD/HD - DHCN$ for Nguyen Thi My Binh.

References

1. Al-Qurabat, A.K.M., Abdulzahra, S.A.: An overview of periodic wireless sensor networks to the internet of things. In: IOP Conference Series: Materials Science and Engineering, vol. 928, p. 032055. IOP Publishing (2020)
2. Binh, H.T.T., Binh, N.T.M., Hoang, N.H., Tu, P.A.: Heuristic algorithm for finding maximal breach path in wireless sensor network with omnidirectional sensors. In: 2016 IEEE Region 10 Humanitarian Technology Conference (R10-HTC), pp. 1–6. IEEE (2016)
3. Binh, H.T.T., Binh, N.T.M., Ngoc, N.H., Ly, D.T.H., Nghia, N.D.: Efficient approximation approaches to minimal exposure path problem in probabilistic coverage model for wireless sensor networks. Appl. Soft Comput. **76**, 726–743 (2019)
4. Binh, N.T.M., Binh, H.T.T., Van Linh, N., Yu, S.: Efficient meta-heuristic approaches in solving minimal exposure path problem for heterogeneous wireless multimedia sensor networks in internet of things. Appl. Intell. **50**(6), 1889–1907 (2020)
5. Binh, N.T.M., Hoang Long, D., Ngoc, N., Thanh Binh, H.T., Phuong, N.K.: Investigate evolutionary strategies for black-box attacks to deepfake forensic systems. In: Proceedings of the 11th International Symposium on Information and Communication Technology, pp. 126–133 (2022)
6. Binh, N.T.M., Ngoc, N.H., Binh, H.T.T., Van, N.K., Yu, S.: A family system based evolutionary algorithm for obstacle-evasion minimal exposure path problem in internet of things. Expert Syst. Appl. **200**, 116943 (2022)
7. Chechik, S., Johnson, M.P., Parter, M., Peleg, D.: Secluded connectivity problems. Algorithmica **79**(3), 708–741 (2017)
8. Chen, G., Xiong, Y., She, J.: A k-barrier coverage enhancing scheme based on gaps repairing in visual sensor network. IEEE Sens. J. **23**(3), 2865–2877 (2023). https://doi.org/10.1109/JSEN.2022.3227601
9. Das, S., Debbarma, M.K.: A survey on coverage problems in wireless sensor network based on monitored region. In: Kolhe, M.L., Trivedi, M.C., Tiwari, S., Singh, V.K. (eds.) Advances in Data and Information Sciences. LNNS, vol. 39, pp. 349–359. Springer, Singapore (2019). https://doi.org/10.1007/978-981-13-0277-0_29
10. Fan, X., Wang, S., Wang, Y., Xu, J., Chi, K.: Energy-efficient barrier lifetime prolonging scheme based on repairing in directional sensor networks. IEEE Syst. J. **14**(4), 4943–4954 (2020)

11. Kocakulak, M., Butun, I.: An overview of wireless sensor networks towards internet of things. In: 2017 IEEE 7th Annual Computing and Communication Workshop and Conference (CCWC), pp. 1–6. IEEE (2017)
12. Lu, K., Qian, Y., Guizani, M., Chen, H.H.: A framework for a distributed key management scheme in heterogeneous wireless sensor networks. IEEE Trans. Wirel. Commun. **7**(2), 639–647 (2008)
13. Ma, Z., Li, S., Huang, D.: Exact algorithms for barrier coverage with line-based deployed rotatable directional sensors. In: 2020 IEEE Wireless Communications and Networking Conference (WCNC), pp. 1–7. IEEE (2020)
14. Nguyen, T.M.B., Thang, C.M., Nguyen, D.N., Huynh, T.T.B.: Genetic algorithm for solving minimal exposure path in mobile sensor networks. In: 2017 IEEE Symposium Series on Computational Intelligence (SSCI), pp. 1–8. IEEE (2017)
15. Saipulla, A., Westphal, C., Liu, B., Wang, J.: Barrier coverage of line-based deployed wireless sensor networks. In: IEEE INFOCOM 2009, pp. 127–135. IEEE (2009)
16. Shen, H., Bai, G.: Routing in wireless multimedia sensor networks: a survey and challenges ahead. J. Netw. Comput. Appl. **71**, 30–49 (2016)
17. Si, P., Ma, J., Tao, F., Fu, Z., Shu, L.: Energy-efficient barrier coverage with probabilistic sensors in wireless sensor networks. IEEE Sens. J. **20**(10), 5624–5633 (2020)
18. Tao, D., Wu, T.Y.: A survey on barrier coverage problem in directional sensor networks. IEEE Sens. J. **15**(2), 876–885 (2014)
19. Thi My Binh, N., et al.: An elite hybrid particle swarm optimization for solving minimal exposure path problem in mobile wireless sensor networks. Sensors **20**(9), 2586 (2020)
20. Umbarkar, A.J., Sheth, P.D.: Crossover operators in genetic algorithms: a review. ICTACT J. Soft Comput. **6**(1) (2015)
21. Wu, F., Gui, Y., Wang, Z., Gao, X., Chen, G.: A survey on barrier coverage with sensors. Front. Comput. Sci. **10**(6), 968–984 (2016)
22. Zhang, Y., Sun, X., Yu, Z.: K-barrier coverage in wireless sensor networks based on immune particle swarm optimisation. Int. J. Sens. Netw. **27**(4), 250–258 (2018)

An Efficient Method for Solving the Best Coverage Path Problem in Homogeneous Wireless Ad-Hoc Sensor Networks

Nguyen Van Thien, Nguyen Thi My Binh[✉], and Dang Trong Hop

Faculty of Information and Technology, Hanoi University of Industry, Hanoi, Vietnam
binhntm@haui.edu.vn

Abstract. Barrier coverage is a well-established model within the domain of Wireless Ad-hoc Sensor Networks (WASNs), which finds substantial utility in numerous military and security applications within the Internet of Things (IoT). It is particularly pertinent for monitoring and detecting objects in motion across the sensing field. This research paper delves into the central aspect of barrier coverage within WASNs, with a specific focus on the maximal exposure path (MaEP) problem, a problem proven to be NP-Hard. The MaEP problem entails the pursuit of an optimal coverage path that either conserves energy or minimizes energy consumption while maintaining a short traversal distance. Prior studies in this domain predominantly relied on problem formulations based solely on Euclidean distance metrics, often addressed through computational geometry methodologies. However, this approach encounters significant challenges in scenarios characterized by large-scale, intricate, and highly sophisticated WASNs. To surmount this limitation, our research first casts the MaEP problem within the framework of the integral of sensing field intensity. Subsequently, we introduce a modified particle-swarm-optimization-based algorithm denoted as MaEP-PSO, meticulously designed to efficiently address the MaEP problem. To gauge the efficacy of this proposed algorithm, we conduct an extensive series of experiments and present comprehensive experimental results.

Keywords: Wireless Ad-hoc Sensor Networks · barrier coverage · Best coverage path · Maximal exposure path

1 Introduction

Coverage within wireless Ad-hoc sensor networks (WASNs) or Wireless Sensor Networks (WSNs) represents a fundamental and integral aspect that characterizes the network's capability and effectiveness in monitoring its designated sensing field. Generally, coverage is widely regarded as a critical metric for assessing the quality of service provided by WSNs. The choice of specific coverage metrics may vary across different ad-hoc network scenarios, contingent upon the intended objectives of the network model. Within the realm of WSNs, barrier coverage (BC) holds a prominent position as a well-established model, primarily applied in the domains of surveillance and intrusion

© ICST Institute for Computer Sciences, Social Informatics and Telecommunications Engineering 2024
Published by Springer Nature Switzerland AG 2024. All Rights Reserved
N. Thi Dieu Linh et al. (Eds.): ADHOCNETS 2023, LNICST 558, pp. 181–195, 2024.
https://doi.org/10.1007/978-3-031-55993-8_14

detection. The central goal of BC is to efficiently monitor and detect the movement of objects traversing through the WSN. This essentially necessitates that the WSN maintains a high quality of service, as indicated by the degree of coverage it provides.

Recently, the academic community has extensively explored various methodologies aimed at assessing the quality of coverage of WSNs. Among these metrics, exposure has emerged as a particularly efficient and effective measurement for evaluating the level of coverage or the overall quality of service provided by WSNs [2,5,9,10,13]. Exposure exhibits a direct proportionality to the degree of coverage, signifying that higher exposure corresponds to improved coverage. This metric, exposure, occupies a central role in the domain of WASNs [7,11,12]. This research specifically concentrates on the exploration of penetration paths, a significant subdomain within the broader context of barrier coverage. More precisely, it delves into the quest for an optimal coverage path known as the Best-Case Coverage Path (BCCP) within WSNs. The BCCP framework pertains to the analysis of coverage concerning the trajectories traversed by mobile agents, including entities such as robots or human operators. In the pursuit of collecting information as they traverse the defined area, these mobile agents possess the capability to interact with sensor nodes. This interaction serves various purposes, encompassing data transmission and the reception of new tasks. Consequently, it becomes highly desirable for these mobile agents to maintain close spatial proximity to the sensor nodes during their movement within the field. This strategic proximity optimization plays a pivotal role in enhancing operational efficiency, primarily by minimizing factors such as power consumption.

The BCCP can be formulated in various ways, such as through a Maximal Support Path (MSP) or a Maximal Exposure Path (MaEP) [6]. While an MSP was defined as a path that minimizes the maximum distance between any point on the path and the sensor nodes, the MaEP between a source position and a destination position was a path in the sensor connecting the two points such that the exposure received from traveling the path is maximal [14]. The work in [6] had proved that MaEP belongs to NP-Hard problem. We are the first defining a MaEP as the integral of an intensity function. Efficient resolution of the BCCP problem can yield substantial advantages, as it finds applicability in several intrinsic applications. These applications often address queries related to optimizing data harvesting and deriving maximum benefits from WSNs while traversing the sensing field. For instance, consider the scenario of a light-detecting network. In this context, imagine a solar-powered autonomous robot navigating the network with the goal of accumulating the most light within a specified time frame. By utilizing the BCCP of the light-detecting network, the solar-powered robot can maximize its light intake during the allotted time. Consequently, the BCCP holds considerable importance for a user aiming to maximize the benefits or detection capabilities of the network.

In light of these considerations, this paper directs its attention to the MaEP problem in homogeneous wireless sensor networks known as MaEP-HWSN. Notably, the MaEP is a NP-Hard problem, and must incorporate a maximum length constraint or a delay constraint to specify the duration for which an object can remain within the sensor field. Without such constraints, an object could potentially perpetually travel without reaching its destination or indefinitely linger at a point with positive exposure, thereby accumulating infinite coverage. Therefore, we propose an efficient nature inspired meta-heuristic algorithm for solving the MaEP, called MaEP-PSO (MaEP- Particle Swarm Optimization). The nature inspired meta-heuristic algorithms can surmount a lot of optimization problems in various fields such as [1–5, 10, 13].

The main contributions of this paper are as follows:

- Formulate the maximal exposure path problem in homogenous wireless sensor networks under the Boolean sensing and the attenuated sensing model.
- Proffer an efficient strategy named MaEP-PSO for solving the considered problem.
- Conduct various experimental scenarios to examine the proposed algorithms and compare the proposed method to state-of-the-art. Analyze the results and give some insights into the performance obtained by the proposed algorithm.

The rest of the paper is organized as follows. Section 2 presents Related works. Preliminaries and formulation for the MaEP problem are discussed in Sect. 3. Section 4 introduces the proposed algorithms. Experimental results are given and analyzed in Sect. 5. Finally, the conclusions of the paper are presented in Sect. 6.

2   Related Works

This section provides a succinct overview of pertinent research concerning the barrier coverage problem in WSNs, with particular emphasis on the MaEP problem, which holds significant relevance in numerous practical applications. Barrier coverage problems within Wireless Ad-hoc Sensor Networks (WASN) can be broadly categorized into two distinct domains: constructing intrusion barriers and identifying penetration paths [15]. Notably, the exploration of penetration paths represents a highly dynamic and captivating research area within this field [1–3, 5, 8–10, 14].

Veltri et al. were the pioneers in introducing the MaEP concept in their work [14]. Notably, they established the NP-Hard nature of the MaEP problem. Subsequently, the authors proposed a localized approximation algorithm to address this challenge, leading to the generation of approximate solutions. In the study conducted by Megerian et al. [8], attention was directed towards both the worst and best-case coverage problems within sensor networks. In the context of the best-case coverage problem, the authors introduced the notion of a support concept to formalize the Best-Case Support-Based Coverage Problem. They then devised a computational approach, employing techniques from computational geometry and graph theory, particularly the Delaunay triangulation and graph search algorithms, to address this problem. Furthermore, in a separate study by Binh et al. [1], the focus was placed on the Maximal Breach Path, specifically catering to the safety considerations related to intruders attempting to penetrate the network, corresponding to the worst-case coverage scenario. In response to this challenge, the authors developed a heuristic algorithm aimed at effectively resolving the Maximal Breach Path problem.

The literature presented in [2, 3, 5, 9, 10] has extensively explored the domain of the worst-case coverage path, which is inherently associated with the concept of the Minimal Exposure Path (MEP). These studies have approached this problem from various angles, incorporating different sensing models, varying environmental assumptions, and other relevant factors. Subsequently, they have introduced efficient algorithms designed to address these challenges effectively. The authors in [10, 13] specifically directed their attention toward the Minimal Exposure Path problem within wireless mobile sensor networks, denoted as MMEP. Initially, they formalized the MMEP problem, subsequently transforming it into a high-dimensional numerical-functional optimization problem characterized by non-differentiation and non-linearity. To contend with these inherent characteristics, the authors proposed the HPSO-MMEP algorithm. This algorithm draws inspiration from natural evolutionary processes, blending principles from genetic algorithms and particle swarm optimization techniques.

In the research conducted by Binh et al. [2], the authors embarked upon the formulation of the MEP problem within the framework of the Probabilistic Coverage Model, incorporating noise considerations. In this context, they introduced a novel definition for the exposure measurement specific to this model. Subsequently, they transformed this problem into a numerical functional optimization challenge. To effectively address these characteristics, the authors devised two approximation methods tailored to solving the modified problem. In their work presented in [5], the research focus shifted towards a systematic and comprehensive investigation of the MEP problem under real-world network environments, taking into account the presence of obstacles. The authors introduced an algorithm designed to construct arbitrary-shaped obstacles within the deployment area of WSNs. They proposed an elite algorithm, namely the Family System-based Evolutionary Algorithm, which incorporates innovative concepts related to the Family System. This algorithm was specifically developed to efficiently tackle the challenges posed by their problem domain. Furthermore, they extended the capabilities of a custom-made simulation environment to incorporate a diverse range of network topologies and obstacle configurations.

After conducting an exhaustive review of references pertaining to the BCCP problem, it becomes evident that a significant portion of prior research has primarily concentrated on addressing the MSP problem. These approaches typically leverage computational geometry methodologies such as the Voronoi Diagram and Delaunay Triangulation to convert the continuous geometric search space of the problem into a discrete graph problem. Nevertheless, it is noteworthy that computational geometry-based algorithms tend to centralize their computations, whereas MSP problems inherently involve distributed elements. Moreover, it is imperative to recognize that the BCCP problem has been formally classified within the category of NP-Hard problems. Consequently, there exists an opportunity to enhance the quality of solutions generated through previous research endeavors. Consequently, the primary focus of this paper shifts towards addressing the MaEP within homogeneous WSNs.

3   Preliminaries and Problem Formulation

3.1   Preliminaries on the Sensing Model and Exposure of a Crossing Path

The Attenuated Disk Sensing Model.
The sensing model characterizes the sensing or coverage capability of a sensor node concerning points or objects. There exist several types of sensing models, and a common feature among most of them is that the sensing quality or intensity of a sensor diminishes as the distance from the sensor node increases. In such instances, it becomes

feasible to disregard the coverage measure and practical approximations can be derived by truncating the coverage measure for greater distances. One of the most elementary models introduced in this context is the Boolean disk sensing model, which defines its sensing function as follows:

$$f(s_i, l) = \begin{cases} 1 & \text{if } d(s_i, l) \leq r \\ 0 & \text{otherwise} \end{cases} \tag{1}$$

where s_i represents the position of the sensor, l denotes the location under consideration, and $d(s_i, l)$ signifies the Euclidean distance between them. Additionally, r is used to denote the sensing range of the sensor. Figure 1a visually illustrates the Boolean disk coverage model.

This paper, however, delves into a more precise and extensively employed sensing model recognized as the "attenuated disk sensing model". The mathematical expression characterizing the sensing function $f(s_i, l)$ for the attenuated disk model is as follows:

$$f(s_i, l) = \min\left\{1, \frac{C}{d^\lambda(s_i, l)}\right\} \tag{2}$$

where C is a constant depending on the essence of a sensor, λ is the attenuation exponent, which depends both on the sensor and the environment. An illustration of this sensing model can be found in Fig. 1b.

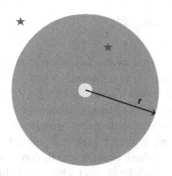
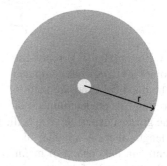

(a) The Boolean disk sensing model.   (b) The attenuated disk sensing model.

Fig. 1. Illustration of sensing models

We will now examine the capability to concurrently sense or cover multiple sensor nodes at a specific point within their sensing field, a concept commonly referred to as "the sensing intensity model". Within a WASN, each sensor node is endowed with a maximum transmission power, enabling it to communicate with all nodes residing within its transmission range. Consequently, in a WASN comprising a set of sensor nodes $S = \{s_1, \ldots, s_N\}$, the cumulative exposure of an object within the sensing field, or at any given point within the sensor field, can be defined as the summation of all individual exposure values, expressed as follows:

$$I(S, l) = \sum_{i=1}^{N} f(d(s_i, l)) \tag{3}$$

Exposure of a Crossing Path and the Maximal Exposure Path

Exposure refers to the sensor network's capability to detect an object as it traverses the sensing field. It can be informally described as the anticipated, mean capability to observe a target within the sensor field. To provide a more formal definition, exposure can be expressed as the integral of a sensing function, typically contingent on the distance from sensors along a path originating from a beginning point denoted as B and extending to a destination point designated as D.

Consider two points, denoted as $B = (x_B, y_B)$ and $D = (x_D, y_D)$, situated within a two-dimensional sensor field. A path connecting these points is conceptualized as a continuous function, represented as $P(t) = (x(t), y(t))$, subject to the boundary conditions $x(0) = x_B$, $x(T) = x_D$, $y(0) = y_B$, and $y(T) = y_D$. The exposure along this path can be defined as the cumulative exposure experienced by the sensor network as an object traverses this path. This cumulative exposure can be expressed as follows:

$$E(f(S, (x(t), y(t)))) = \int_0^T I(S, (x(t), y(t))) \sqrt{\left(\frac{dx(t)}{dt}\right)^2 + \left(\frac{dy(t)}{dt}\right)^2} \, dt \tag{4}$$

$$\approx \sum_{k=0}^{\lfloor T/\Delta t \rfloor} \sum_{i=1}^{N} f(s_i, P(k \cdot \Delta t)) \, \Delta t \tag{5}$$

where $I(S, (x(t), y(t)))$ represents the exposure incurred by the sensor network S at the point $(x(t), y(t))$, as computed through Eq. (3) and Δt is sufficiently small.

The maximal exposure path is formally defined within a sensor network as a path connecting two predetermined points within the sensor field, distinguished by exhibiting the greatest exposure, as specified in Eq. (4). It is worth noting that, with increasing path length, there is a higher likelihood of achieving a greater exposure value. Consequently, in the context of maximal exposure paths, there exists a length constraint, wherein the length of these paths must not surpass a predefined acceptable threshold.

3.2 Problem Formulation

In the context of a WASN comprising N homogeneous sensors deployed randomly, denoted as $S = s_1, s_2, ..., s_N$, situated within a region of interest Ω with dimensions $W \times H$ and governed by an exposure model, we consider an intruder's trajectory within this monitored region. The intruder commences its journey at a starting point $B(x_B = 0, y_B)$ and concludes it at an ending point $D(x_D = H, y_D)$, characterized by a constant velocity V_I. The concept of the "maximal exposure path" between the starting location B and the ending location D refers to a specific path within the sensor network that connects these two points. Importantly, this path is selected to maximize the exposure received as the target traverses it. This problem of finding the above-mentioned path is named MaEP (Maximal Exposure Path in Homogeneous Wireless Ad-hoc Sensor Networks). More precisely, this problem is formulated as follows.

Input

- W, H: the width and the length of the sensing field Ω.
- N: the number of homogeneous sensors
- $S = \{s_i = \langle(x_i, y_i)\rangle\}_{i=1}^{N}$: the set of sensors in the field.
- V_I: the speed of intruder.
- $(x_B, y_B); (x_D, y_D)$: the coordinates of the source point B and destination point D.
- ℓ: the maximum length of the crossing path.

Output: A path $\mathcal{P} : [0, T] \rightarrow [0, H] \times [0, W]$ in region Ω connecting B and D.
Objective: The exposure of path $\mathcal{P}$ is maximized, which means:

$$\sum_{k=0}^{\lfloor T/\Delta t \rfloor - 1} \sum_{i=1}^{N} \min\left\{1, \frac{C}{d^\lambda(s_i, \mathcal{P}(k \cdot \Delta t))}\right\} \Delta t \rightarrow \max \qquad (6)$$

Constrains: There is a maximum length ℓ constraint on the maximal exposure path so the object cannot keep on moving in the sensor field to accumulate infinite exposure.

4 Proposed Algorithm

PSO Algorithm is an intelligent way of solving tricky problems by mimicking how creatures work together. This section describes an efficient particle-swarm-optimization-based algorithm named MaEP-PSO to solve the considered MaEP problem with a flowchart demonstrated in Fig. 2. In MaEP-PSO, a particle (individual) represents a feasible solution for the MaEP problem and can be depicted as an ordered sequence of contiguous points, commencing at the source point denoted as B and concluding at the destination point denoted as D. These points are commonly referred to as the genes of the individual. The number of genes within an individual in MaEP-PSO is predetermined and set by a parameter denoted as m. Figure 3 illustrates the path derived from an individual, which includes a sequence of six points, namely $P_1, \ldots, P_6$, connected in the specified order. According to the problem, the individual must also satisfy the constraint of maximum length.

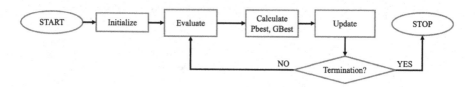

Fig. 2. The flowchart of the proposed algorithm MaEP-PSO.

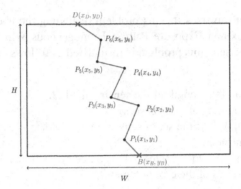

Fig. 3. Illustration of individual.

To initialize individuals in MaEP-PSO, first, the field is partitioned equally into m segments, each having a height of H/m. Then, $m-1$ points $P_1, P_2, .., P_{m-1}$ is randomly generated where the point P_i has its x-coordinate is $i * H/m$ and its y-coordinate is a random real number in range $[0, W]$. An individual is created with each of its genes are the intersecting points of the line $(0, y_B), P_1, P_2, .., P_{m-1}, (0, y_D)$ and the line $x = j\Delta x$ where $j = 0...n$. The number of individuals in the population is limited by the population size P_s. The pseudo-code of the above initialization method is described in Algorithm 1.

The update of velocity and location vectors, which have m dimensions corresponding to m points, in MaEP-PSO are described as follows:

The velocity of the i-th particle at the time $t+1$ is calculated by:

$$v_i(t+1) = \omega v_i(t) + c_1 r_1(Pbest(t) - u_i(t)) + c_2 r_2(Gbest(t) - u_i(t)) \qquad (7)$$

where, $v_i(t)$ is the velocity vector of the i-th individual at the time i; $u_i(t)$ is the location vector of the i-th particle in the search space at the time i; $Pbest_i(t)$ is the best position that the particle had achieved until the time i; $Gbest(t)$ is the best position that the particle in the swarm system that had achieved until the time i; r_1, r_2 are random numbers between $(0, 1)$ and generated at each iteration randomly for each particle; ω, c_1, c_2 are constants, in which ω is consider as inertial, and c_1, c_2 called acceleration coefficient.

Algorithm 1: MaEP-PSO individual initialization

Input:
- The size of Ω: W, H, the beginning and destination point B, D
- The scale unit: Δx
- The number of segments: m

Output:
An individual $indi = (y_B, y_1, ..., y_{m-1}, y_E)$,

1 **begin**
2      $y \leftarrow y_B$; $k \leftarrow (H/m)$;
3   **for** $i := 1$ **to** $m - 1$ **do**
4          $ys \leftarrow random(0, W)$; $yi \leftarrow (ys - y)/k$;
5   **for** $j := 1$ **to** $k - 1$ **do**
6              $indi \leftarrow indi \cup y$;
7              $y \leftarrow y + yi$;
8   **end**
9   **end**
10      $indi \leftarrow indi \cup y_E$
11 **end**

The pseudo-code for MaEP-PSO is described as follows:

Algorithm 2: MaEP Evolutionary Operations

Input:
- Population Pop
- Personal best and velocity of each individual

Output: Next generation's population Pop'

1 **begin**
2      $gBest$ = findBestIndividual(Pop);
3   **foreach** $p \in Pop$ **do**
4   Calculate the acceleration $c_i{}^t$;
5   Generate random r_1, r_2 ;
6   Update the velocity and location of the individuals;
7   **end**
8 **end**

---

5 Numerical Results

In order to validate the efficiency and precision of the proposed algorithms, a series of experiments were conducted, encompassing diverse experimental scenarios, for the purpose of comparison. These experiments underwent comprehensive evaluations and analyses to provide thorough insights into the resulting data. The numerical computations were executed using Java on a computing system equipped with an Intel®

Xeon® CPU E5-2660 2.20GHz processor, featuring 16 logical cores (comprising 8 physical cores), and 16 GB of RAM. The operating environment for these experiments was Ubuntu 18.04.5 LTS.

5.1 Parameters Settings

We conducted simulations encompassing a total of five distinct topologies, each aligned with varying numbers of sensor nodes within the region of interest. These simulations were organized into five separate datasets.

For each topology, we generate ten random instances denoted as S_n_i, where n signifies the number of sensors in that particular instance ($n \in \{10, 20, 50, 100, 200\}$), and i denotes the instance index ($i \in \overline{1, 10}$). The sensor nodes within these datasets are uniformly and randomly deployed across the sensor field denoted as Ω. The dimensions of the sensor field are specified as $W = 500$ and $H = 100$. The source point is defined as $B(0, y_B)$, and the destination point is labeled as $D(100, y_D)$. The values of y_B and y_D are drawn from $\mathcal{U}(0, W)$, signifying that they are sampled uniformly from the interval $[0, W]$. The maximum length of a feasible path is drawn from $\mathcal{U}(d(B, D), 2d(B, D))$. The intruder's velocity, denoted as V_I, is assigned a value of 5. The value of Δt to approximately compute the exposure of the solution path is set as 0.1.

Table 1. The parameters for MaEP-PSO.

Parameter	Value
Number of generations	200
The population size	5000
Parameters c_1, c_2, ω	$c_1 = 0.5$, $c_2 = 2$, $\omega = 0.3$
Parameter m	50000

5.2 Experimental Result

In order to establish the accuracy and reliability of both our proposed model and algorithm, a comprehensive series of experiments has been conducted. Table 1 succinctly presents the optimal parameters meticulously determined for our MaEP-PSO algorithm, as ascertained through a rigorous array of experimental trials. Given the inherent non-deterministic nature of our proposed algorithm MaEP-PSO, it was executed 30 times on each instance, and the results are reported based on the calculated averages.

As discussed in the literature review, the BCCP problem has been the subject of investigation in prior research, often framed as the Maximal Support Path and typically addressed using Delaunay triangulation methodologies. To ensure an equitable and unbiased evaluation, adjustments were made to facilitate direct comparison between our proposed algorithm and the Adjusted Best-Point Heuristic (ABPH) methods, as outlined in [14]. Additionally, comparisons were drawn with the Minimum Spanning Trees (MST) algorithm, as delineated in [6].

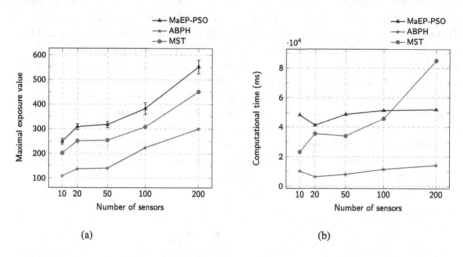

(a)   (b)

Fig. 4. Comparison between our proposed MaEP-PSO with the previous literature's approaches, i.e. ABPH [14] and MST [6]: (a) with respect to exposure value; (b) with respect to computational time (ms). The results are reported on average.

The results from the experiment depicted in Fig. 4 reveal the following findings:

- Regarding the quality of the solutions, Fig. 4a illustrates the maximal exposure values acquired by three algorithms while varying the number of sensors from 10 to 200. An observation of the results indicates that MaEP-PSO consistently outperforms both ABPH and MST in terms of maximal exposure values. This observation strongly suggests that our proposed algorithm is superior in terms of solution quality. This outcome aligns with expectations as the MaEP-PSO algorithm employs a diverse and intricate set of operators, contributing to its enhanced performance.
- Concerning computational time, Fig. 4b presents a graphical representation of the computation times for each algorithm. Evidently, the ABPH algorithm exhibits the shortest running times across all instances. However, it is notable that MaEP-PSO necessitates more time for computation than MST in the case of small-scale

instances, where the number of sensors varies from 10 to 100. Conversely, for large-scale instances, where the number of sensors exceeds 100, MST requires a longer computation time compared to MaEP-PSO.

Table 2 provides a comprehensive overview of essential metrics, including the best maximal exposure values, the average maximal exposure value, standard deviation, and running time, derived from 30 iterations of our proposed MaEP algorithm. Upon careful examination, it becomes apparent that there exists a proportional relationship between the number of deployed sensors in the region of interest and both the average maximal exposure value and the running time, as well as the best maximal exposure value. This observation signifies that an increased number of sensors in the deployment area yields larger maximal exposure values. Such results align with theoretical expectations, as a higher exposure value corresponds to a more efficient sensor network deployment, indicative of enhanced coverage quality. Furthermore, the data presented in Table 2, along with the graphical representation in Fig. 4a, unequivocally indicate that the standard deviation associated with the MaEP algorithm is exceptionally low, approaching zero. Figure 5 reveals that the algorithm converges to a solution consistently after approximately 130 to 150 generations across all data instances. These empirical findings provide substantial and persuasive evidence substantiating the stability and convergence attributes of our proposed algorithm.

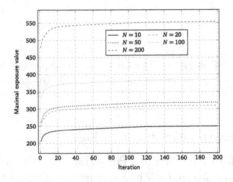

Fig. 5. The convergence of the MaEP-PSO algorithm is evident across experimental data topologies. The results are reported on average.

Table 2. The maximal exposure value, The average exposure, The standard deviation, and the average running time on datasets in each dataset for 30 running Time.

Instance	Best exposure value	Average exposure value	Standard deviation (%)	Average running time
S_10_1	316.39	300.86	4.66	46568
S_10_2	305.24	298.99	5.57	43209
S_10_3	384.50	359.22	5.32	46852
S_10_4	285.46	272.79	4.76	44364
S_10_5	201.26	192.82	4.59	47374
S_10_6	295.86	284.62	5.05	46130
S_10_7	203.79	193.26	4.64	43501
S_10_8	196.45	187.78	3.79	49264
S_10_9	209.95	200.59	5.12	43737
S_10_10	191.79	186.90	3.42	46585
S_20_1	366.11	349.07	4.92	46146
S_20_2	304.20	291.24	4.00	43701
S_20_3	378.90	355.10	3.13	43260
S_20_4	369.59	353.54	4.45	47111
S_20_5	387.41	363.33	4.79	43477
S_20_6	212.13	197.54	5.95	53313
S_20_7	306.63	292.31	5.25	49915
S_20_8	289.69	279.44	4.81	50524
S_20_9	404.93	378.83	4.19	41125
S_20_10	289.87	277.08	4.16	45879
S_50_1	379.22	357.57	4.81	48658
S_50_2	368.45	354.56	4.55	48102
S_50_3	293.13	282.55	4.58	48565
S_50_4	289.05	279.77	3.70	49716
S_50_5	343.41	323.09	3.96	49115
S_50_6	298.68	288.63	3.79	44396
S_50_7	277.62	262.76	5.89	52338
S_50_8	287.34	272.10	4.94	44960
S_50_9	385.50	368.61	5.72	46907
S_50_10	292.04	278.34	5.64	42423
S_100_1	362.71	341.43	5.46	47426
S_100_2	493.31	470.93	4.92	45690
S_100_3	376.08	352.15	5.01	49400
S_100_4	298.55	283.18	4.53	53878
S_100_5	391.20	367.89	5.39	51399
S_100_6	475.09	458.63	4.99	52734
S_100_7	502.40	480.59	2.54	46403
S_100_8	385.09	370.62	5.46	51011
S_100_9	330.54	310.68	5.51	50197
S_100_10	379.24	361.00	4.53	51696
S_200_1	592.80	572.61	3.47	44462
S_200_2	495.87	476.68	3.35	52430
S_200_3	611.08	574.93	5.23	50527
S_200_4	678.30	636.89	5.63	47632
S_200_5	469.88	446.41	4.50	50312
S_200_6	564.80	526.66	6.64	47886
S_200_7	501.13	476.31	5.06	49094
S_200_8	670.14	635.80	5.20	52754
S_200_9	585.64	565.25	4.98	49187
S_200_10	584.55	553.87	4.69	47305

6   Conclusions

In conclusion, this paper has presented a highly efficient method called MaEP-PSO to address the challenging maximal exposure path problem of finding the best coverage path in WASNs. The quest for an optimal coverage path in sensor networks is a crucial endeavor with wide-ranging applications, from environmental monitoring to surveillance and beyond. By leveraging the inherent characteristics of PSO, we have achieved a balance between exploration and exploitation, allowing our algorithm to efficiently search for near-optimal coverage paths. Through extensive experimentation and evaluation, we have showcased the superiority of our PSO-based method in delivering high-quality solutions for the best coverage path problem. It not only enhances network performance but also contributes to energy efficiency, a critical factor in the context of wireless sensor networks. As the demand for robust and energy-efficient sensor networks continues to grow, the presented approach offers a promising avenue for researchers and practitioners to address real-world challenges effectively. In summary, our work underscores the potential of PSO as a valuable tool in the toolkit of optimization techniques for improving the operational efficiency and effectiveness of homogeneous WASNs. Future research can further refine and extend these principles to accommodate the evolving requirements of emerging applications in the field.

References

1. Binh, H.T.T., Binh, N.T.M., Hoang, N.H., Tu, P.A.: Heuristic algorithm for finding maximal breach path in wireless sensor network with omnidirectional sensors. In: 2016 IEEE Region 10 Humanitarian Technology Conference (R10-HTC), pp. 1–6. IEEE (2016)
2. Binh, H.T.T., Binh, N.T.M., Ngoc, N.H., Ly, D.T.H., Nghia, N.D.: Efficient approximation approaches to minimal exposure path problem in probabilistic coverage model for wireless sensor networks. Appl. Soft Comput. **76**, 726–743 (2019)
3. Binh, N.T.M., Binh, H.T.T., Ngoc, N.H., Anh, M.D.Q., Phuong, N.K.: Maximizing lifetime of heterogeneous wireless turnable camera sensor networks ensuring strong barrier coverage. J. Comput. Sci. Cybern. **37**(1), 57–70 (2021)
4. Binh, N.T.M., Hoang Long, D., Ngoc, N., Thanh Binh, H.T., Phuong, N.K.: Investigate evolutionary strategies for black-box attacks to deepfake forensic systems. In: Proceedings of the 11th International Symposium on Information and Communication Technology, pp. 126–133 (2022)
5. Binh, N.T.M., Ngoc, N.H., Binh, H.T.T., Van, N.K., Yu, S.: A family system based evolutionary algorithm for obstacle-evasion minimal exposure path problem in internet of things. Expert Syst. Appl. **200**, 116943 (2022)
6. Lee, C., Shin, D., Bae, S.W., Choi, S.: Best and worst-case coverage problems for arbitrary paths in wireless sensor networks. Ad Hoc Netw. **11**(6), 1699–1714 (2013)
7. Majid, M., et al.: Applications of wireless sensor networks and internet of things frameworks in the industry revolution 4.0: a systematic literature review. Sensors **22**(6), 2087 (2022)
8. Megerian, S., Koushanfar, F., Potkonjak, M., Srivastava, M.B.: Worst and best-case coverage in sensor networks. IEEE Trans. Mob. Comput. **4**(1), 84–92 (2005)
9. My, B.N.T., Thanh, B.H.T., Yu, S., et al.: Efficient meta-heuristic approaches in solving minimal exposure path problem for heterogeneous wireless multimedia sensor networks in internet of things. Appl. Intell. **50**(6), 1889–1907 (2020)

10. Nguyen, T.M.B., Thang, C.M., Nguyen, D.N., Huynh, T.T.B.: Genetic algorithm for solving minimal exposure path in mobile sensor networks. In: 2017 IEEE Symposium Series on Computational Intelligence (SSCI), pp. 1–8. IEEE (2017)

11. Osamy, W., Khedr, A.M., Salim, A., Al Ali, A.I., El-Sawy, A.A.: Coverage, deployment and localization challenges in wireless sensor networks based on artificial intelligence techniques: a review. IEEE Access **10**, 30232–30257 (2022)

12. Paul, S.P., Vetrithangam, D.: A comprehensive analysis on issues and challenges of wireless sensor network communication in commercial applications. In: 2022 International Conference on Computing, Communication, and Intelligent Systems (ICCCIS), pp. 377–382. IEEE (2022)

13. Thi My Binh, N., et al.: An elite hybrid particle swarm optimization for solving minimal exposure path problem in mobile wireless sensor networks. Sensors **20**(9), 2586 (2020)

14. Veltri, G., Huang, Q., Qu, G., Potkonjak, M.: Minimal and maximal exposure path algorithms for wireless embedded sensor networks. In: Proceedings of the 1st International Conference on Embedded Networked Sensor Systems, pp. 40–50 (2003)

15. Wang, B.: Coverage Control in Sensor Networks. Springer, Berlin (2010)

Performance of Uplink Ultra Dense Network with Antenna Selection

Trung Ninh Bui[1] , Sinh Cong Lam[1]([✉]) , Duc Tan Tran[2] ,
and Nguyen Thi Dieu Linh[1,2,3]

[1] Faculty of Electronics and Telecommunications, VNU University of Engineering
and Technology, Hanoi, Vietnam
{ninhbt,congls}@vnu.edu.vn
[2] Faculty of Electrical and Electronic Engineering, Phenikaa University,
Ha Dong, Vietnam
[3] Faculty of Electronics Engineering Technology, Hanoi University of Industry,
Hanoi, Vietnam

Abstract. Ultra Dense Network is promising as the potential topology
of the 5G and Beyond network systems where various advanced techniques are being developed to improve the user performance. In this
paper, the antenna selection technique is studied in terms of uplink coverage probability analysis. With assumption that the wireless transmission condition is under the effects of Nakagami-m as the fast fading and
Stretched Path Loss Model (SPLM) as the slow fading, the paper derives
the uplink coverage probability of the user in the Spatial Poisson Point
Process network layout. Through the analytical results and Monte Carlo
simulation, the paper illustrates that an increase in the number of antennas at the user can moderately reduce the its coverage probability.

Keywords: 5G · ultra dense network · antenna selection · Poisson
point process

1 Introduction

Utilization of multi-antenna at both users and BSs is a potential technique to
provide a high Quality of Service in the Ultra Dense network where BSs (Base
Stations) are distributed with a very high density. In this technique, the users
may use more than one antennas to convey its message to the serving BS. At
the BSs, several copies of the transmitted messages are received but only the
messages are carried by the strongest signal is processed. Conventionally, a higher
number of antennas results in a better desired signal at the BS.

Research on antenna selection technique has been studied in the literature
such as [6–9]. In [6], the multi-antenna is studied to assist the short packet
communication in the IoT network. The analytical results proved that the packet
loss can be improved by increasing the number of antennas. The network with
limited - feedback and interference have been studied in [7,9] for device-to-device

N. Thi Dieu Linh et al. (Eds.): ADHOCNETS 2023, LNICST 558, pp. 196–204, 2024.
https://doi.org/10.1007/978-3-031-55993-8_15

network and moving interfers. In both cases, it was shown that the network performance in terms of outage probability and ergodic data capacity increases with the number of antennas. The benefits of utilizing multi-antenna were also presented in Reference [8] where the antennas are distributed as a Spatial Poisson Point Process (PPP). Therefore, it is clear that the utilization of multi-antenna, particularly antenna selection technique, is a possible solution to improve the 5G and Beyond cellular networks.

Although these papers illustrated the significant benefits of the antenna selection technique, main characteristics of the wireless transmission have not been well-captured. Particularly, these works either ignores the slow fading, or utilizes the regular path loss model, which is not well-captured the characteristics of millimeter wave transmission, as the slow fading, or model the fast fading as the Rayleigh random variable. This paper employs the Stretched Path Loss model (SPLM) and Nakagami-m as the slow fading and fast fading, respectively. While SPLM was recently developed as the most suitable to capture the complicated transmission phenomenon of millimeter wave, the Nakagami-m is considered the general case of fast fading. Thus, it can be said that the analysis of system model in this paper can reflect the practical network performance.

2   System Model

In this paper, an uplink millimeter wave cellular network where both the active users and the BSs are distributed according to independent Spatial Poisson Point Processes with a density of $\lambda^{(u)}$ $(user/m^2)$ and λ (BS/m^2), is studied. In an ultra dense network, the BSs are usually distributed at a very high of density. According to the authors in [2], the density of BSs may be upto $1 - 10$ stations in every m^2. Meanwhile, the number of users dynamically change by time. Therefore, some BSs do not have any associated user and turn into the idle mode to reduce the power consumption as well as intercell interference. As proved in the literature [3], the density of active BSs, which have at least an user, is

$$\overline{\lambda} = \lambda \left[1 - \frac{1}{\left(1 + \frac{\lambda^{(u)}}{q\lambda} \right)^q} \right] \tag{1}$$

where q is obtained from empirical activities, particularly $q = 3.5$.

To analyze the uplink network performance, both slow fading and fast fading are considered in this paper. To capture the slow fading, the Stretched Path Loss model (SPLM), which was recently developed to estimate the path loss in the ultra dense network with complicated transmission environments [4], is utilized. Particularly, the path loss over a distance of r (m) in the linear unit is computed by

$$L(r) = \exp\left(-\alpha r^\beta\right) \tag{2}$$

where β and α are empirical values which represent the density of obstacles and their signal resistance properties, respectively. In addition, the instantaneous value of fast fading is assumed to have a Nakagami-m distribution. Thus, the channel power is an normalized Gamma random variable $G(m, 1/m)$ with a cumulative density function of

$$F = \frac{\gamma(m, mx)}{\Gamma(m)} \qquad (3)$$

where $\gamma(.,.)$ and $\Gamma(m)$ are the lower incomplete and complete Gamma functions.

To enhance the network performance, the users and BSs are usually equipped with multi-antennas. It is assumed that each user simultaneously uses N to transmit the signal to its serving BS, i.e. the nearest BS. Thus, each BS receives N copies of the desired signal from its associated user at distance r, where the power of the signal from k^{th} antenna is

$$S_k = Pg_k L(r) \qquad (4)$$

where P is the transmission power of the user; g_k and $L(r_k)$ are respectively the instantaneous power gain and the path loss.

With assumption that all antennas of the user transmit on the same subband, all N signals suffer the same intercell interference that originated from the user at adjacent cells. Since each user transmits on N antennas at the same time, the total intercell interference at the BS is given by

$$I = \sum_{n=1}^{N} \sum_{h \in \theta} Pg_{n,h} L(r_h) = \sum_{h \in \theta} PL(r_h) \sum_{n=1}^{N} g_{n,h} \qquad (5)$$

where θ is the set of interfering users. Since each user is only served by an unique BS, the density of interfering users is determined in Eq. 1. Since $g_{n,h}$ is the normalized Gamma random variable $G(m, 1/m)$, $g_h = \sum_{n=1}^{N} g_{n,h}$ is a Gamma random variable $G(Nm, 1/m)$.

Consequently, the uplink SINR that the BS receives from the kth antenna of the user is

$$SINR_k = \frac{S_k}{I} \qquad (6)$$

where the Gaussian noise power σ^2.

To reduce the processing complexity, the BS only process the signal with the highest quality. In other words, the received SINR at the BS is

$$SINR = \max_{1 \le k \le N} SINR_k = \frac{PL(r)}{I} \max_{1 \le k \le N} g_k \qquad (7)$$

Let $g = \max_{1 \le k \le N} g_k$, the cumulative density function of g is determined as the following step

$$F_G(g) = P(G < g) = P\left(\max_{1 \le k \le N} g_k < g \right) \qquad (8)$$

Since g_k $(1 \leq k \leq N)$ are random variables,

$$F_G(g) = \prod_{1 \leq k \leq N} P(g_k < T) = \left[\frac{\gamma(m, mx)}{\Gamma(m)}\right]^N \tag{9}$$

According to the result in Reference [5], the cumulative density function $F_G(g)$ is approximated by

$$F_G(g) = [1 - \exp(-\tau g)]^{mN}$$
$$= \sum_{u=0}^{mN}(-1)^u \mathbf{C}_{mN}^k \exp(-\tau u g) \tag{10}$$

where $\tau = \frac{m}{[\Gamma(m+1)]^{1/m}}$ and $\mathbf{C}_n^k = \frac{n!}{k!(n-k)!}$.

3   Coverage Probability

In this section, we derive the coverage probability expression of the user in the network with multi-antenna selection technique. Theoretically, the uplink coverage probability is defined by

$$\mathcal{P}(T) = \mathbf{P}(SINR > T) \tag{11}$$

where T is the minimum required SINR of the BS to successfully decode the received signal from the user.

Theorem 1. *The uplink coverage probability of the user in the system - enabled transmit antenna selection technique under the affects of Nakagami-m and general path loss model $L(r)$ is given by*

$$\mathcal{P}(T) = \sum_{u=1}^{mN}(-1)^{u+1}\mathbf{E}\left[\prod_{k=0}^{mN-1}\exp\left(-\pi\lambda\int_0^\infty \frac{\frac{\tau u T}{m}\frac{L(r_h)}{L(r)}r_h dr_h}{\left(1 + \frac{\tau u T}{m}\frac{L(r_h)}{L(r)}\right)^{k+1}}\right)\right] \tag{12}$$

Proof. Substituting the formulation of $SINR$ in Eq. 7 into the coverage probability definition in Eq. 11, we obtain

$$\mathcal{P}(T) = \mathbf{P}\left(\frac{PL(r)}{I}g > T\right)$$
$$= \mathbf{P}\left(g > T\frac{I}{PL(r)}\right) \tag{13}$$

Utilizing the approximated form of $F_G(g)$ in Eq. 10, we get

$$\mathcal{P}(T) = 1 - \sum_{u=0}^{mN}(-1)^u \exp\left(-\tau u T\frac{I}{PL(r)}\right) \tag{14}$$

Substituting the definition of I in Eq. 5 with notice that $g_h = \sum_{n=1}^{N} g_{n,h}$, the coverage probability is given by

$$P(T) = 1 - \sum_{u=0}^{mN} (-1)^u \mathbf{E} \left[\prod_{h \in \theta} \exp\left(-\tau u T \frac{L(r_h)}{L(r)} g_h \right) \right] \quad (15)$$

where $\overline{\gamma} = \frac{P}{\sigma^2}$.

Since g_h is the Gamma random variable with a shape of Nm and a scale of $1/m$, its MGF is $M(s) = (1 + s/m)^{-Nm}$. Hence,

$$P(T) = 1 - \sum_{u=0}^{mN} (-1)^u \mathbf{E} \left[\prod_{h \in \theta} \frac{1}{\left(1 + \frac{\tau u T}{m} \frac{L(r_h)}{L(r)}\right)^{Nm}} \right] \quad (16)$$

Utilizing the probability of the Moment Generating Function with recalling that the distance from user to its interfering users and to serving BS are independent random Variables, we obtain

$$P(T) = 1 - \sum_{u=0}^{mN} (-1)^u \mathbf{E} \left[\exp\left(-2\pi\lambda \int_0^\infty 1 - \frac{1}{\left(1 + \frac{\tau u T}{m} \frac{L(r_h)}{L(r)}\right)^{Nm}} r_h dr_h \right) \right]$$

$$= 1 - \sum_{u=0}^{mN} (-1)^u \mathbf{E} \left[\prod_{k=0}^{mN-1} \exp\left(-2\pi\lambda \int_0^\infty \frac{\frac{\tau u T}{m} \frac{L(r_h)}{L(r)} r_h dr_h}{\left(1 + \frac{\tau u T}{m} \frac{L(r_h)}{L(r)}\right)^{k+1}} \right) \right]$$

The Theorem is proved.

Lemma 1. *The closed-form expression of coverage probability of the user in the system with antenna selection under the Nakagami-m and regular path loss model* $L(r) = r^{-\alpha}$ *is given by*

$$P(T) = \sum_{u=1}^{mN} (-1)^{u+1} \frac{1}{1 + \sum_{k=0}^{mN-1} \left[\frac{\tau u T}{m}\right]^{2-\alpha} \mathbf{B}(\alpha - 2, k - 2 + \alpha)} \quad (17)$$

Proof. Substituting $L(r) = r^{-\alpha}$ into Eq. 12, we obtain

$$P(T) = \sum_{u=1}^{mN} (-1)^u \mathbf{E} \left[\prod_{k=0}^{mN-1} \exp\left(-2\pi\lambda \int_0^\infty \frac{\frac{\tau u T}{m} \frac{r_h^{-\alpha}}{r^{-\alpha}} r_h dr_h}{\left(1 + \frac{\tau u T}{m} \frac{L(r_h)}{L(r)}\right)^{k+1}} \right) \right]$$

Employing a change of variable $y = r/r_h$, then

$$P(T) = \sum_{u=1}^{mN} (-1)^u \mathbf{E} \left[\prod_{k=0}^{mN-1} \exp\left(-\pi\lambda r^2 \int_0^\infty \frac{\frac{\tau u T}{m} y^{\alpha-3} dy}{\left(1 + \frac{\tau u T}{m} y^\alpha\right)^{k+1}} \right) \right]$$

Utilizing the result in Reference [1, p.315] with $\mu = a-2$, $\beta = \frac{\tau u T}{m}$ and $v = k+1$, the coverage probability is given by

$$\mathcal{P}(T) = \sum_{u=1}^{mN}(-1)^u \mathbf{E}\left[\prod_{u=0}^{mN-1} \exp\left(-\pi\lambda r^2 \left[\frac{\tau u T}{m}\right]^{2-\alpha} \mathbf{B}(\alpha - 2, k - 2 + \alpha)\right)\right]$$

where $\mathbf{B}(.,.)$ is the Beta function.

Evaluating the expectation with respect to the random variable r whose PDF is $2\pi\lambda \exp\left(-\pi\lambda r^2\right)$, then

$$\mathcal{P}(T) = \sum_{u=1}^{mN}(-1)^u$$

$$\int_0^\infty \exp\left(-\pi\lambda r^2 \left[1 + \sum_{k=0}^{mN-1}\left[\frac{\tau u T}{m}\right]^{2-\alpha} \mathbf{B}(\alpha - 2, k - 2 + \alpha)\right]\right) d(\pi\lambda r^2)$$

$$= \sum_{u=1}^{mN}(-1)^u \frac{1}{1 + \sum_{k=0}^{mN-1}\left[\frac{\tau u T}{m}\right]^{2-\alpha} \mathbf{B}(\alpha - 2, k - 2 + \alpha)} \tag{18}$$

The theorem is proved.

4   Simulation and Analysis

4.1   Verification of Theoretical Analysis

This section utilizes Monte Carlo to verify the analytical result in Theorem 1 in the case of SPLM. Particularly, the SPLM parameters are selected at $\alpha = 0.5$ and $\beta = 0.5$; Nakagami-m with $m = 2$; the density of active BSs is $\lambda = 500/1e6\ (BS/km^2)$. The uplink user coverage probability is plotted with different values of SINR threshold T. As seen from Fig. 1, the Monte Carlo simulation curves visually match the theoretical ones, which illustrates the accuracy of the analytical approach and results.

Since the SINR threshold is the minimum value of uplink SINR that the BS requires to successfully detect the signal from the user, a larger value of SINR means a stronger requirement of the BS on uplink SINR quality. In other words, the probability of successful signal detection of the BS reduces as SINR threshold increases. Therefore, the uplink user coverage probability has a fast decline trend as SINR threshold increases as illustrated in Fig. 1. For example, when SINR threshold T increases from $T = -18$ dB to $T = -12$ dB, the coverage probability reduces approximately 25% in the case of $m = 1, N = 1$. This fast decline trend can be seen from Eq. 12 where the coverage probability likely exponentially reduce with SINR threshold T.

5   Coverage Probability Vs Number of Antennas

Figure 2 examines the effects of number of antennas that the user uses to convey the signal to its serving BS. While most of works in the literature proved that

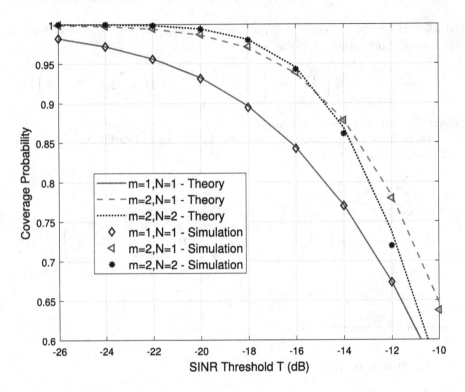

Fig. 1. Coverage Probability vs SINR threshold T (dB)

the utilization of antenna selection technique can improve the user performance, Fig. 2 illustrates the user coverage probability reduces as the number of antennas increases.

Particularly, when the number of antennas N increases from 4 to 10, the uplink coverage probability reduces by 53.6% from 0.41 to 0.19. This decline trend can be explained as follows: When the number of antennas at the user increases, the BSs has more change to receive the signal with the highest quality. However, due to the policy of the antenna selection, the user only receives the best signal from the transmitted antenna. Furthermore, a higher number of antennas also causes a worse wireless condition, particularly a higher intercell interference. When the benefit of a higher antenna utilization can not overcome the intercell interference, the coverage probability of the user decline. Thus, to improving the performance of the multi-antenna ultra dense network, the following critical problems need to be studied

– *Interference Mitigation* This is one of the most popular techniques to improve the uplink SINR of the user. In the previous cellular system, the interference coordination technique is the recommended solution to reduce the intercell interference. Thus, the combination of this technique and multi-antenna one should be studied.

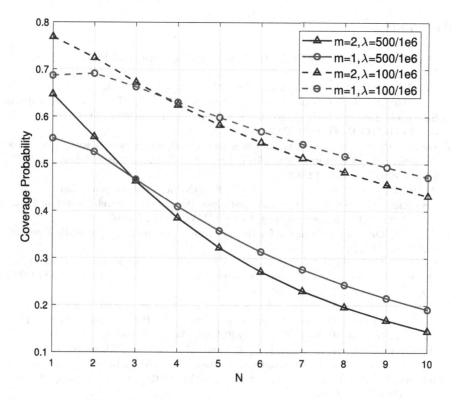

Fig. 2. Coverage probability vs number of antennas

– *Desired signal power improvement* Due to the deployment of the antenna selection technique, the user only receives and processes the signal from the best antenna. To improve the quality of the desired signal, the more effective technique such as Maximum Ratio Combining may be used to combine the signal from different antennas, so that the desired signal power can significantly improve. Hence, the feasibility of Maximum Ratio Combining in the ultra dense network with multi-antenna technique should be examined.

6   Conclusion

In this paper, the performance of ultra dense networks that utilize the antenna selection is evaluated under conditions of Nakagami-m fading. In this system, the user utilizes more than one antennas to convey the messages to its serving BSs, while the BSs compares the signal power from different antennas and select the strongest signal to perform further process. The uplink coverage probability of the user is derived in the case of SPLM and in closed-form when the path loss follows the regular model. While most of the related works showed that the user perform with increases with the number of antennas, the analytical results in this paper show that due to the rapid increase of intercell interference, the coverage probability reduces with the number of antennas.

References

1. Gradshteyn, I.S., Ryzhik, I.M.: Table of Integrals, Series, and Products Academic Press (2007)
2. Chafii, M., Bariah, L., Muhaidat, S., Debbah, M.: Twelve scientific challenges for 6G: rethinking the foundations of communications theory. In: IEEE Communications Surveys & Tutorials, vol. 25, no. 2, pp. 868–904. Secondquarter (2023). https://doi.org/10.1109/COMST.2023.3243918
3. Lee, S., Huang, K.: Coverage and economy of cellular networks with many base stations. IEEE Commun. Lett. **16**(7), 1038–1040 (2012). https://doi.org/10.1109/LCOMM.2012.042512.120426
4. AlAmmouri, A., Andrews, J.G., Baccelli, F.: SINR and throughput of dense cellular networks with stretched exponential path loss. IEEE Trans. Wirel. Commun. **17**(2), 1147–1160 (2018). https://doi.org/10.1109/TWC.2017.2776905
5. Alzer, H.: On some inequalities for the incomplete gamma function. Math. Comput. **66**(218), 771–778 (1997)
6. Chen, D., Li, J., Hu, J., Zhang, X., Zhang, S.: Multi-antenna jammer-assisted secure short packet communications in IoT networks. Future Internet **15**(10), 320 (2023). https://doi.org/10.3390/fi15100320
7. Krauss, R., Peron, G., Brante, G., Souza, R.D.: Area energy efficiency of antenna selection in limited feedback device-to-device networks. IEEE Wirel. Commun. Lett. **8**(3), 949–952 (2019). https://doi.org/10.1109/LWC.2019.2901475
8. AbdelNabi, A.A., Al-Qahtani, F.S., Shaqfeh, M., Ikki, S.S., Alnuweiri, H.M.: Performance analysis of MIMO multi-hop system with TAS/MRC in Poisson field of interferers. IEEE Trans. Commun. **64**(2), 525–540 (2016). https://doi.org/10.1109/TCOMM.2015.2496291
9. Do, D.-T., Nguyen, T.-L., Lee, B.M.: Transmit antenna selection schemes for NOMA with randomly moving interferers in interference-limited environment. Electronics **9**(1), 36 (2020). https://doi.org/10.3390/electronics9010036

Author Index

© ICST Institute for Computer Sciences, Social Informatics and Telecommunications Engineering 2024
Published by Springer Nature Switzerland AG 2024. All Rights Reserved
N. Thi Dieu Linh et al. (Eds.): ADHOCNETS 2023, LNICST 558, p. 205, 2024.
https://doi.org/10.1007/978-3-031-55993-8

Printed in the United States
by Baker & Taylor Publisher Services